THE GREEN LANTERN CHRONICLES

VOLUME ONE

ALL STORIES WRITTEN BY JOHN BROOME, AND ALL COVER AND INTERIOR ART
PENCILLED BY GIL KANE AND INKED BY JOE GIELLA, UNLESS OTHERWISE NOTED.

Dan DiDio SENIOR VP-EXECUTIVE EDITOR ✩ Julius Schwartz EDITOR-ORIGINAL SERIES ✩ Bob Joy EDITOR-COLLECTED EDITION
Robbin Brosterman SENIOR ART DIRECTOR ✩ Paul Levitz PRESIDENT & PUBLISHER ✩ Georg Brewer VP-DESIGN & DC DIRECT CREATIVE
Richard Bruning SENIOR VP-CREATIVE DIRECTOR ✩ Patrick Caldon EXECUTIVE VP-FINANCE & OPERATIONS ✩ Chris Caramalis VP-FINANCE
John Cunningham VP-MARKETING ✩ Terri Cunningham VP-MANAGING EDITOR ✩ Amy Genkins SENIOR VP-BUSINESS & LEGAL AFFAIRS
Alison Gill VP-MANUFACTURING ✩ David Hyde VP-PUBLICITY ✩ Hank Kanalz VP-GENERAL MANAGER, WILDSTORM
Jim Lee EDITORIAL DIRECTOR-WILDSTORM ✩ Gregory Noveck SENIOR VP-CREATIVE AFFAIRS ✩ Sue Pohja VP-BOOK TRADE SALES
Steve Rotterdam SENIOR VP-SALES & MARKETING ✩ Cheryl Rubin SENIOR VP-BRAND MANAGEMENT
Alysse Soll VP-ADVERTISING & CUSTOM PUBLISHING ✩ Jeff Trojan VP-BUSINESS DEVELOPMENT, DC DIRECT ✩ Bob Wayne VP-SALES

DC Comics, 1700 Broadway, New York, NY 10019
A Warner Bros. Entertainment Company
Printed in Canada. First Printing.
ISBN: 978-1-4012-2163-8
Cover art by Gil Kane and Joe Giella

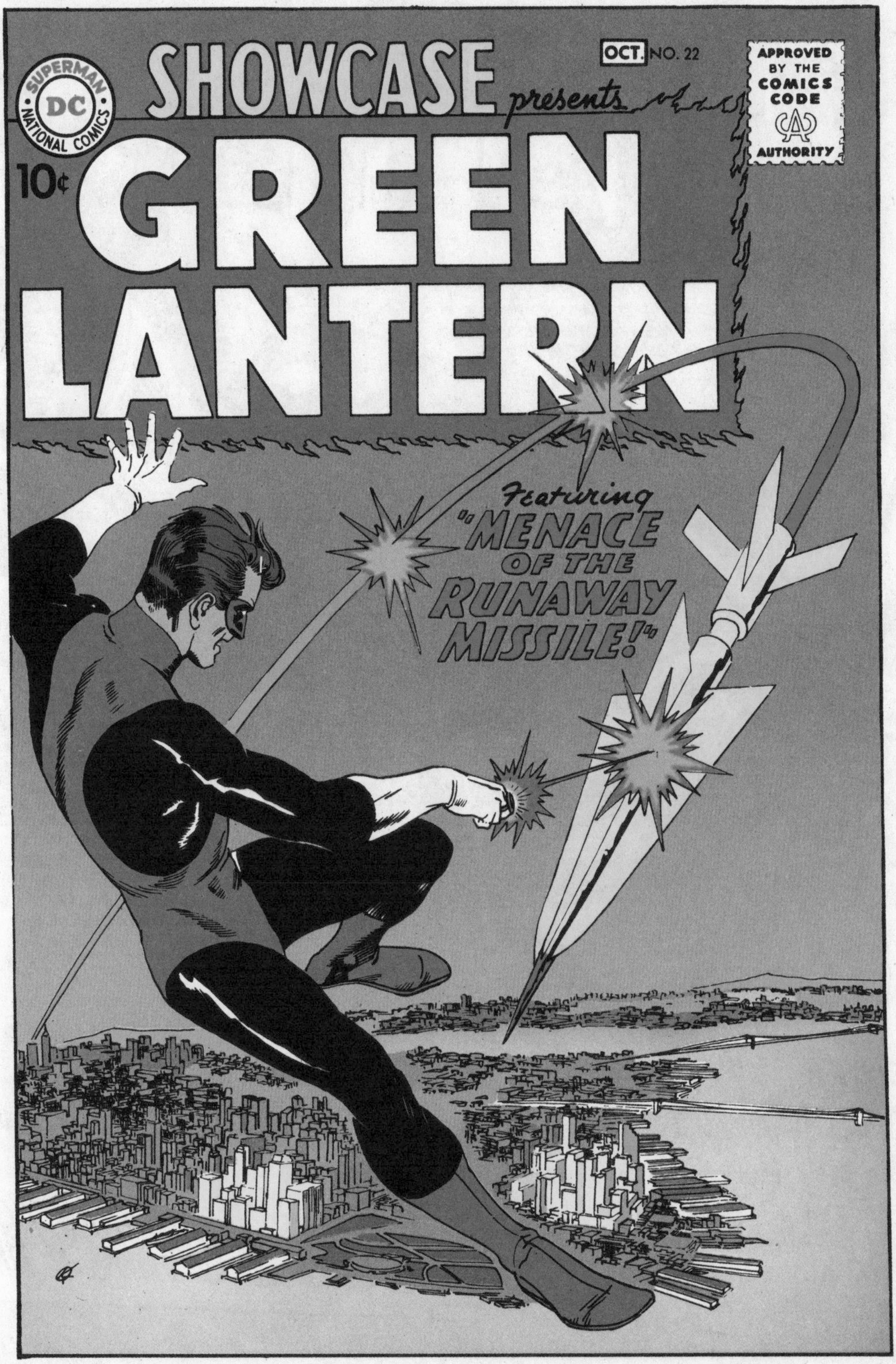
SHOWCASE
OCT. NO. 22
APPROVED BY THE COMICS CODE AUTHORITY
SUPERMAN DC NATIONAL COMICS
10¢
presents
GREEN LANTERN
Featuring "MENACE OF THE RUNAWAY MISSILE!"

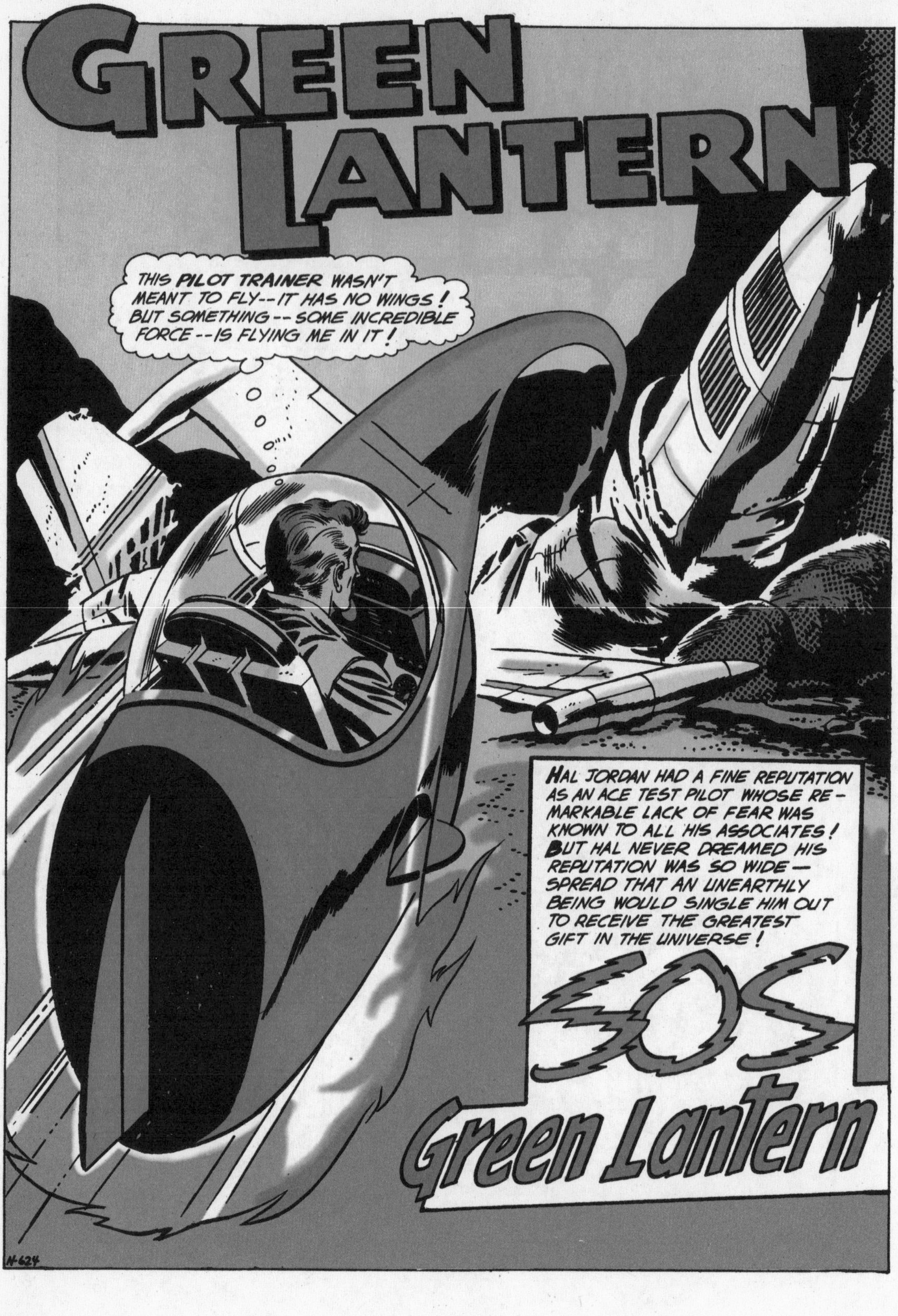
GREEN LANTERN
THIS PILOT TRAINER WASN'T MEANT TO FLY--IT HAS NO WINGS! BUT SOMETHING--SOME INCREDIBLE FORCE--IS FLYING ME IN IT!
HAL JORDAN HAD A FINE REPUTATION AS AN ACE TEST PILOT WHOSE REMARKABLE LACK OF FEAR WAS KNOWN TO ALL HIS ASSOCIATES! BUT HAL NEVER DREAMED HIS REPUTATION WAS SO WIDESPREAD THAT AN UNEARTHLY BEING WOULD SINGLE HIM OUT TO RECEIVE THE GREATEST GIFT IN THE UNIVERSE!
SOS Green Lantern
N-624

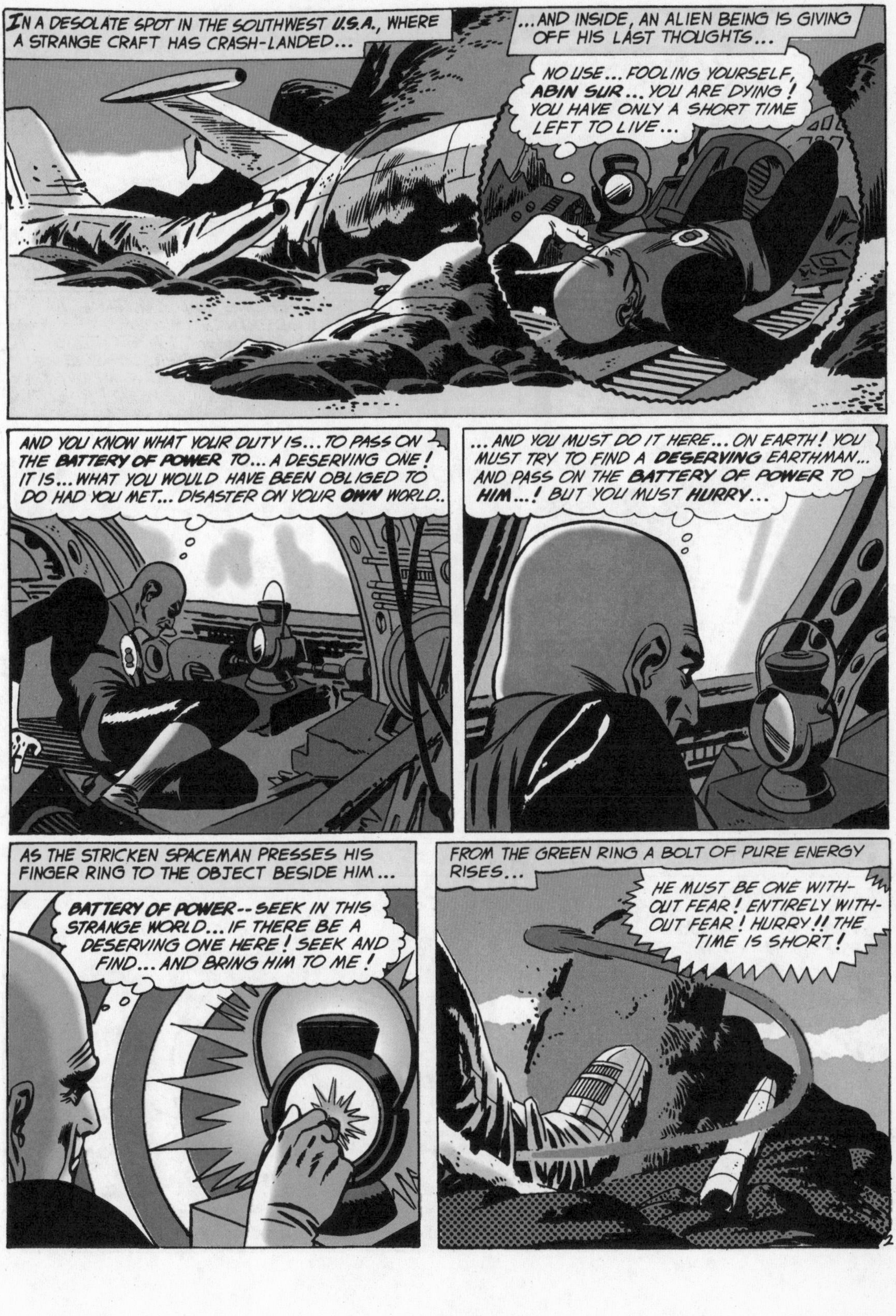

IN A DESOLATE SPOT IN THE SOUTHWEST U.S.A., WHERE A STRANGE CRAFT HAS CRASH-LANDED...
...AND INSIDE, AN ALIEN BEING IS GIVING OFF HIS LAST THOUGHTS...
NO USE... FOOLING YOURSELF, ABIN SUR... YOU ARE DYING! YOU HAVE ONLY A SHORT TIME LEFT TO LIVE...
AND YOU KNOW WHAT YOUR DUTY IS... TO PASS ON THE BATTERY OF POWER TO... A DESERVING ONE! IT IS... WHAT YOU WOULD HAVE BEEN OBLIGED TO DO HAD YOU MET... DISASTER ON YOUR OWN WORLD..
...AND YOU MUST DO IT HERE... ON EARTH! YOU MUST TRY TO FIND A DESERVING EARTHMAN... AND PASS ON THE BATTERY OF POWER TO HIM...! BUT YOU MUST HURRY...
AS THE STRICKEN SPACEMAN PRESSES HIS FINGER RING TO THE OBJECT BESIDE HIM...
BATTERY OF POWER-- SEEK IN THIS STRANGE WORLD... IF THERE BE A DESERVING ONE HERE! SEEK AND FIND... AND BRING HIM TO ME!
FROM THE GREEN RING A BOLT OF PURE ENERGY RISES...
HE MUST BE ONE WITH-OUT FEAR! ENTIRELY WITH-OUT FEAR! HURRY!! THE TIME IS SHORT!
2

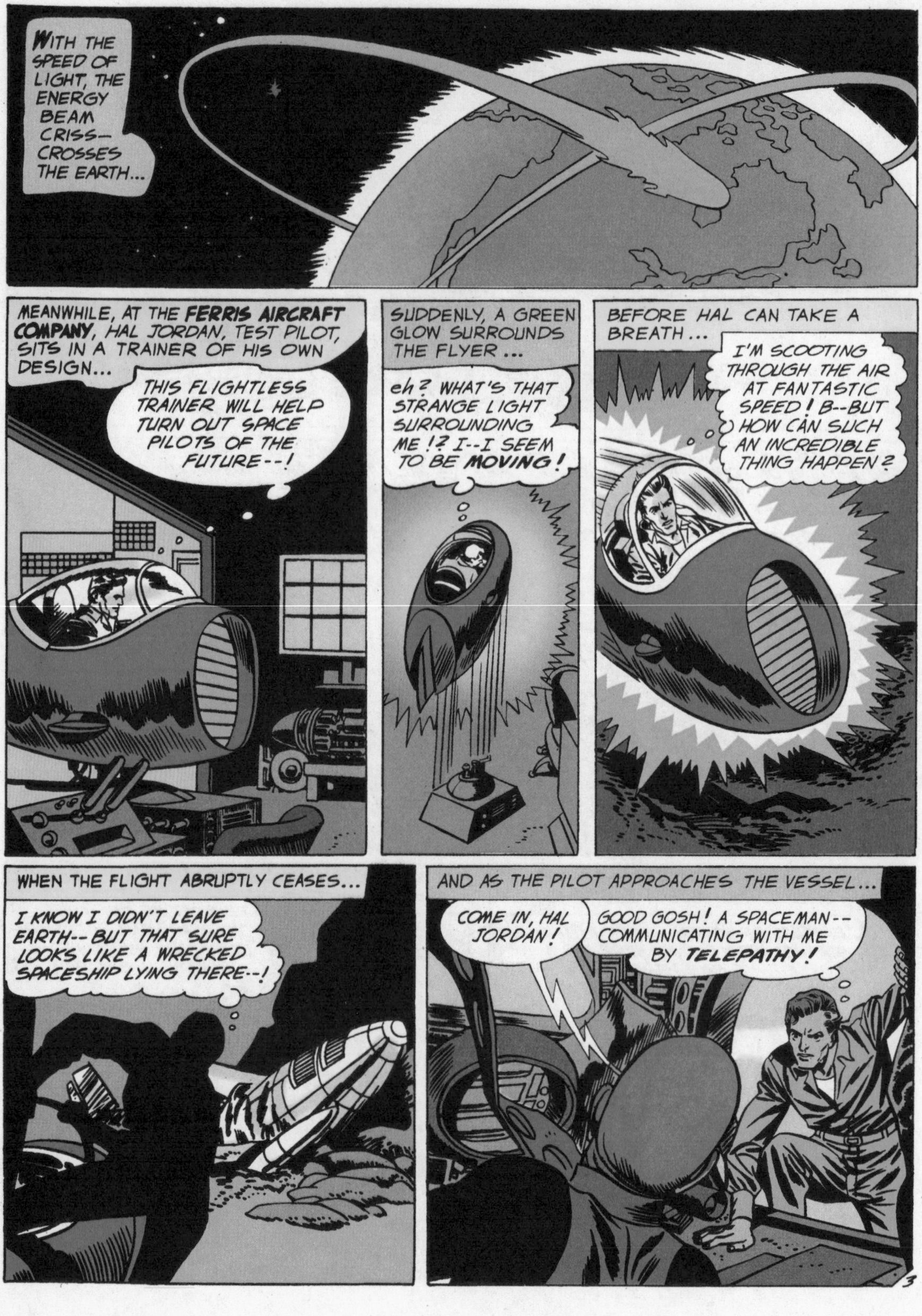
WITH THE SPEED OF LIGHT, THE ENERGY BEAM CRISS-CROSSES THE EARTH...
MEANWHILE, AT THE FERRIS AIRCRAFT COMPANY, HAL JORDAN, TEST PILOT, SITS IN A TRAINER OF HIS OWN DESIGN...
THIS FLIGHTLESS TRAINER WILL HELP TURN OUT SPACE PILOTS OF THE FUTURE--!
SUDDENLY, A GREEN GLOW SURROUNDS THE FLYER...
eh? WHAT'S THAT STRANGE LIGHT SURROUNDING ME!? I--I SEEM TO BE MOVING!
BEFORE HAL CAN TAKE A BREATH...
I'M SCOOTING THROUGH THE AIR AT FANTASTIC SPEED! B--BUT HOW CAN SUCH AN INCREDIBLE THING HAPPEN?
WHEN THE FLIGHT ABRUPTLY CEASES...
I KNOW I DIDN'T LEAVE EARTH-- BUT THAT SURE LOOKS LIKE A WRECKED SPACESHIP LYING THERE--!
AND AS THE PILOT APPROACHES THE VESSEL...
COME IN, HAL JORDAN!
GOOD GOSH! A SPACEMAN-- COMMUNICATING WITH ME BY TELEPATHY!
3

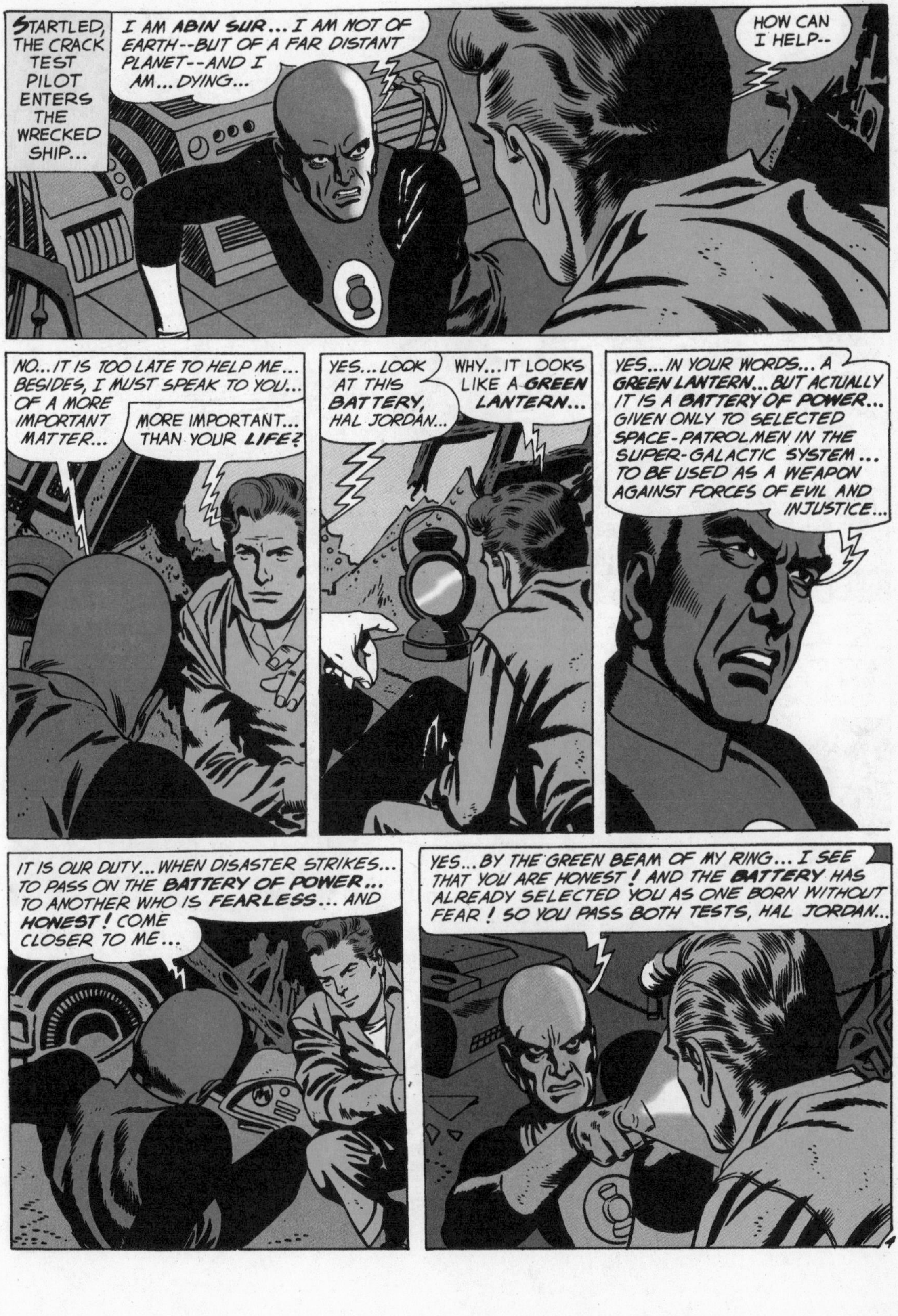
STARTLED, THE CRACK TEST PILOT ENTERS THE WRECKED SHIP...
I AM ABIN SUR... I AM NOT OF EARTH--BUT OF A FAR DISTANT PLANET--AND I AM... DYING...
HOW CAN I HELP--
NO... IT IS TOO LATE TO HELP ME... BESIDES, I MUST SPEAK TO YOU... OF A MORE IMPORTANT MATTER...
MORE IMPORTANT... THAN YOUR LIFE?
YES... LOOK AT THIS BATTERY, HAL JORDAN...
WHY... IT LOOKS LIKE A GREEN LANTERN...
YES... IN YOUR WORDS... A GREEN LANTERN... BUT ACTUALLY IT IS A BATTERY OF POWER... GIVEN ONLY TO SELECTED SPACE-PATROLMEN IN THE SUPER-GALACTIC SYSTEM... TO BE USED AS A WEAPON AGAINST FORCES OF EVIL AND INJUSTICE...
IT IS OUR DUTY... WHEN DISASTER STRIKES... TO PASS ON THE BATTERY OF POWER... TO ANOTHER WHO IS FEARLESS... AND HONEST! COME CLOSER TO ME...
YES... BY THE GREEN BEAM OF MY RING... I SEE THAT YOU ARE HONEST! AND THE BATTERY HAS ALREADY SELECTED YOU AS ONE BORN WITHOUT FEAR! SO YOU PASS BOTH TESTS, HAL JORDAN...
4

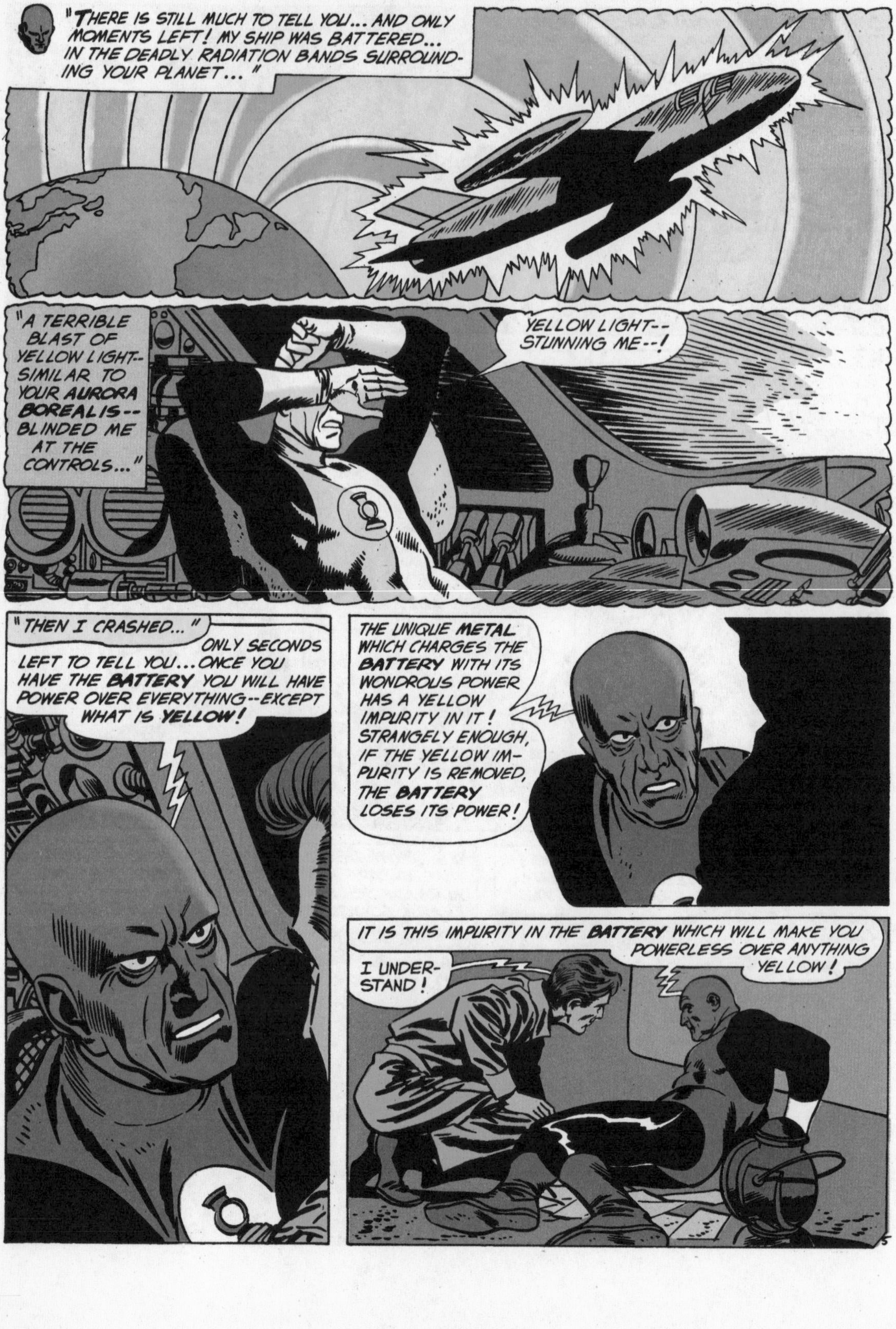
"THERE IS STILL MUCH TO TELL YOU... AND ONLY MOMENTS LEFT! MY SHIP WAS BATTERED... IN THE DEADLY RADIATION BANDS SURROUNDING YOUR PLANET..."
"A TERRIBLE BLAST OF YELLOW LIGHT-- SIMILAR TO YOUR AURORA BOREALIS-- BLINDED ME AT THE CONTROLS..."
YELLOW LIGHT-- STUNNING ME--!
"THEN I CRASHED..."
ONLY SECONDS LEFT TO TELL YOU... ONCE YOU HAVE THE BATTERY YOU WILL HAVE POWER OVER EVERYTHING--EXCEPT WHAT IS YELLOW!
THE UNIQUE METAL WHICH CHARGES THE BATTERY WITH ITS WONDROUS POWER HAS A YELLOW IMPURITY IN IT! STRANGELY ENOUGH, IF THE YELLOW IMPURITY IS REMOVED, THE BATTERY LOSES ITS POWER!
IT IS THIS IMPURITY IN THE BATTERY WHICH WILL MAKE YOU POWERLESS OVER ANYTHING YELLOW!
I UNDERSTAND!
5

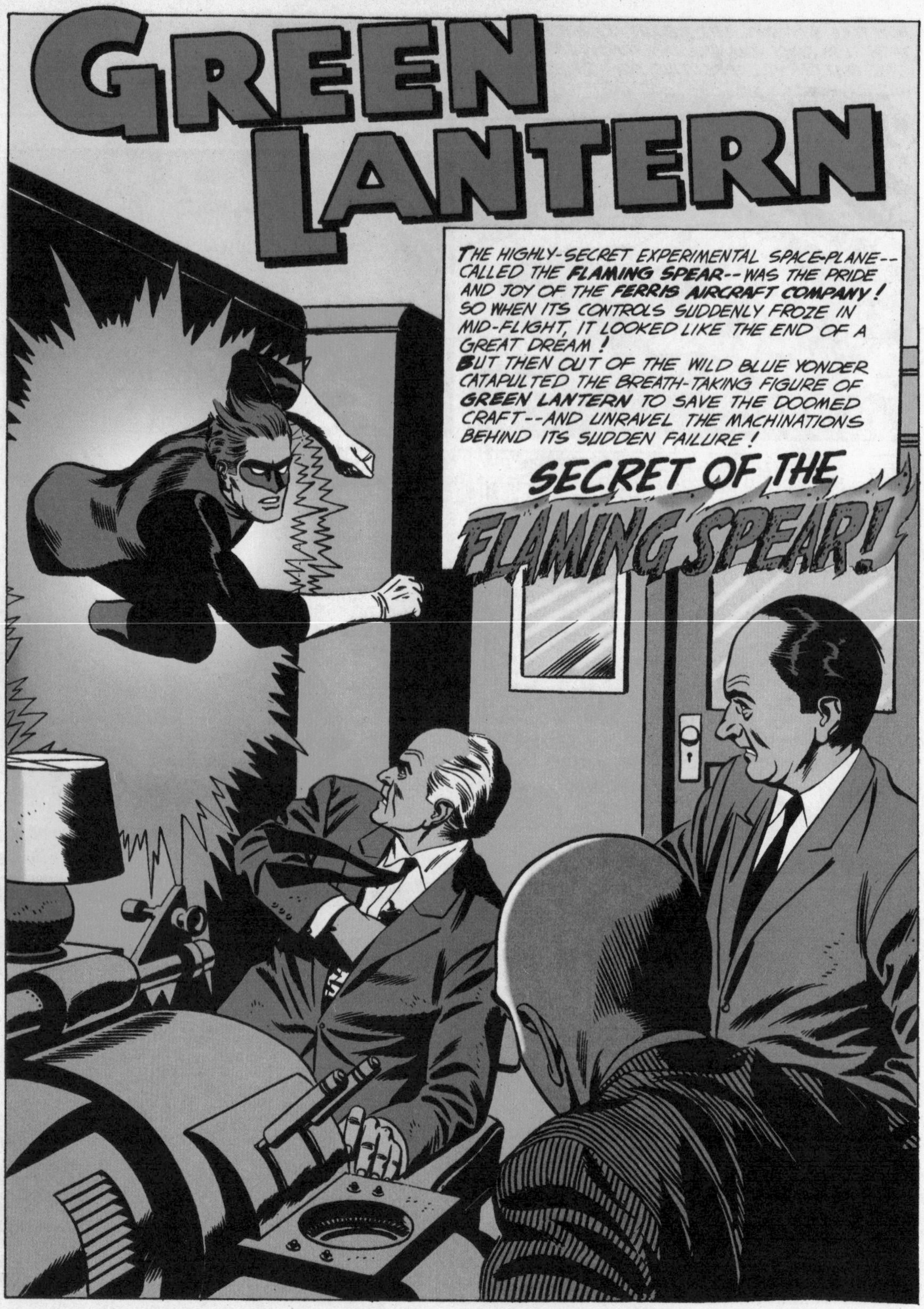
GREEN LANTERN
THE HIGHLY-SECRET EXPERIMENTAL SPACE-PLANE--CALLED THE FLAMING SPEAR--WAS THE PRIDE AND JOY OF THE FERRIS AIRCRAFT COMPANY! SO WHEN ITS CONTROLS SUDDENLY FROZE IN MID-FLIGHT, IT LOOKED LIKE THE END OF A GREAT DREAM!
BUT THEN OUT OF THE WILD BLUE YONDER CATAPULTED THE BREATH-TAKING FIGURE OF GREEN LANTERN TO SAVE THE DOOMED CRAFT--AND UNRAVEL THE MACHINATIONS BEHIND ITS SUDDEN FAILURE!
SECRET OF THE FLAMING SPEAR!

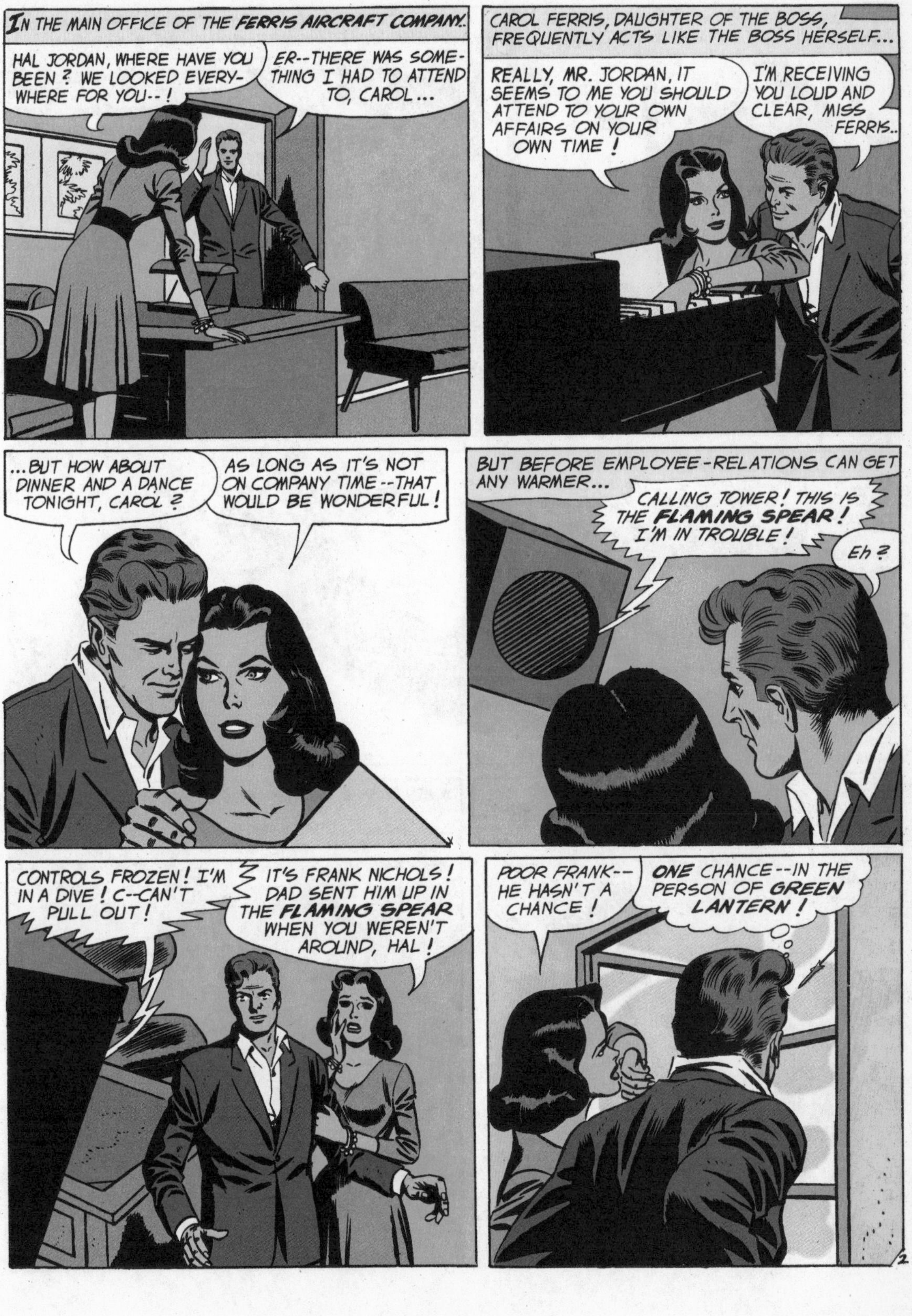
IN THE MAIN OFFICE OF THE FERRIS AIRCRAFT COMPANY.
HAL JORDAN, WHERE HAVE YOU BEEN? WE LOOKED EVERYWHERE FOR YOU--!
ER--THERE WAS SOMETHING I HAD TO ATTEND TO, CAROL...
CAROL FERRIS, DAUGHTER OF THE BOSS, FREQUENTLY ACTS LIKE THE BOSS HERSELF...
REALLY, MR. JORDAN, IT SEEMS TO ME YOU SHOULD ATTEND TO YOUR OWN AFFAIRS ON YOUR OWN TIME!
I'M RECEIVING YOU LOUD AND CLEAR, MISS FERRIS..
...BUT HOW ABOUT DINNER AND A DANCE TONIGHT, CAROL?
AS LONG AS IT'S NOT ON COMPANY TIME--THAT WOULD BE WONDERFUL!
BUT BEFORE EMPLOYEE-RELATIONS CAN GET ANY WARMER...
CALLING TOWER! THIS IS THE FLAMING SPEAR! I'M IN TROUBLE!
Eh?
CONTROLS FROZEN! I'M IN A DIVE! C--CAN'T PULL OUT!
IT'S FRANK NICHOLS! DAD SENT HIM UP IN THE FLAMING SPEAR WHEN YOU WEREN'T AROUND, HAL!
POOR FRANK--HE HASN'T A CHANCE!
ONE CHANCE--IN THE PERSON OF GREEN LANTERN!
2

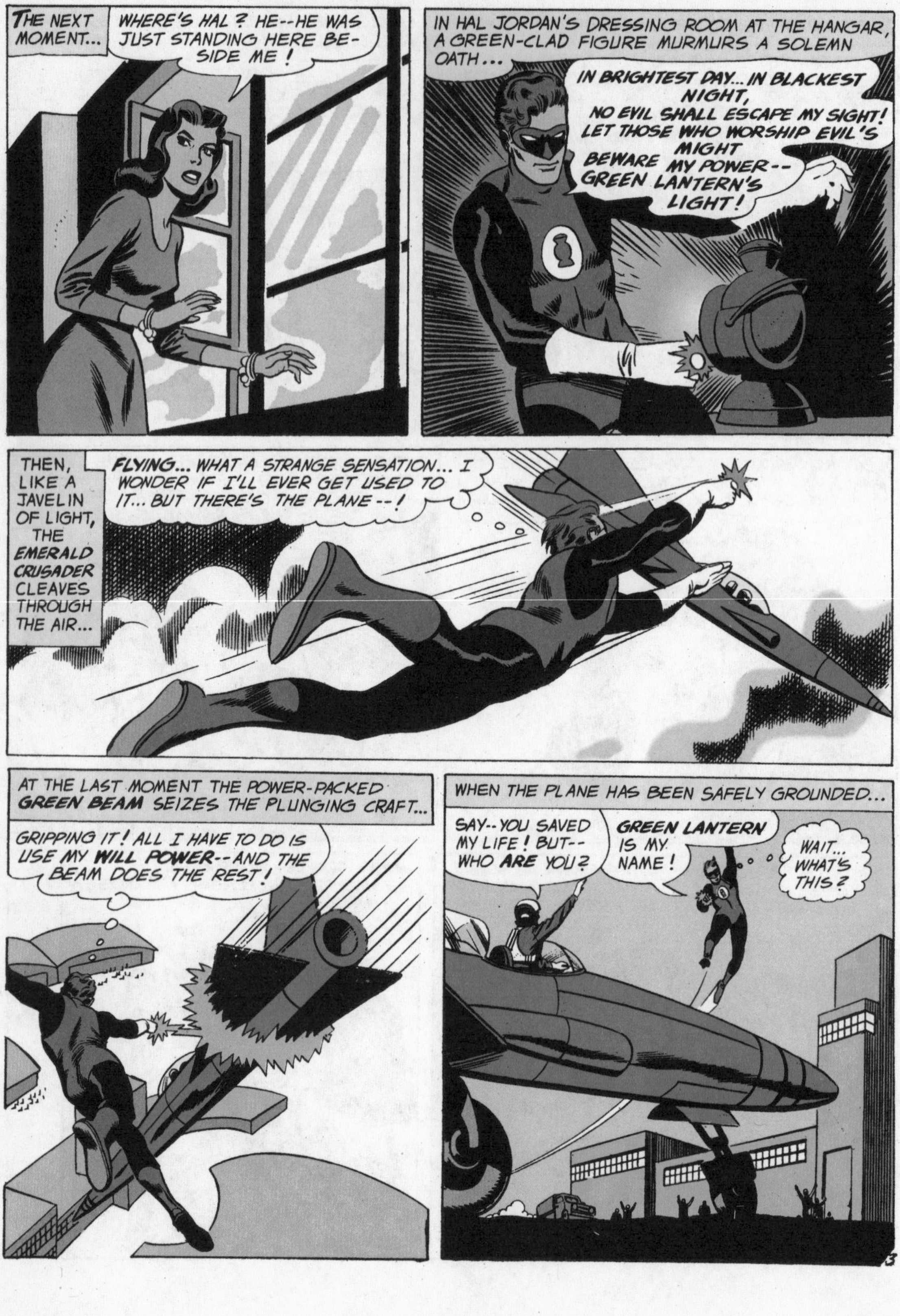

THE NEXT MOMENT...
WHERE'S HAL? HE--HE WAS JUST STANDING HERE BESIDE ME!
IN HAL JORDAN'S DRESSING ROOM AT THE HANGAR, A GREEN-CLAD FIGURE MURMURS A SOLEMN OATH...
IN BRIGHTEST DAY... IN BLACKEST NIGHT, NO EVIL SHALL ESCAPE MY SIGHT! LET THOSE WHO WORSHIP EVIL'S MIGHT BEWARE MY POWER-- GREEN LANTERN'S LIGHT!
THEN, LIKE A JAVELIN OF LIGHT, THE EMERALD CRUSADER CLEAVES THROUGH THE AIR...
FLYING... WHAT A STRANGE SENSATION... I WONDER IF I'LL EVER GET USED TO IT... BUT THERE'S THE PLANE--!
AT THE LAST MOMENT THE POWER-PACKED GREEN BEAM SEIZES THE PLUNGING CRAFT...
GRIPPING IT! ALL I HAVE TO DO IS USE MY WILL POWER--AND THE BEAM DOES THE REST!
WHEN THE PLANE HAS BEEN SAFELY GROUNDED...
SAY--YOU SAVED MY LIFE! BUT--WHO ARE YOU?
GREEN LANTERN IS MY NAME!
WAIT... WHAT'S THIS?
3

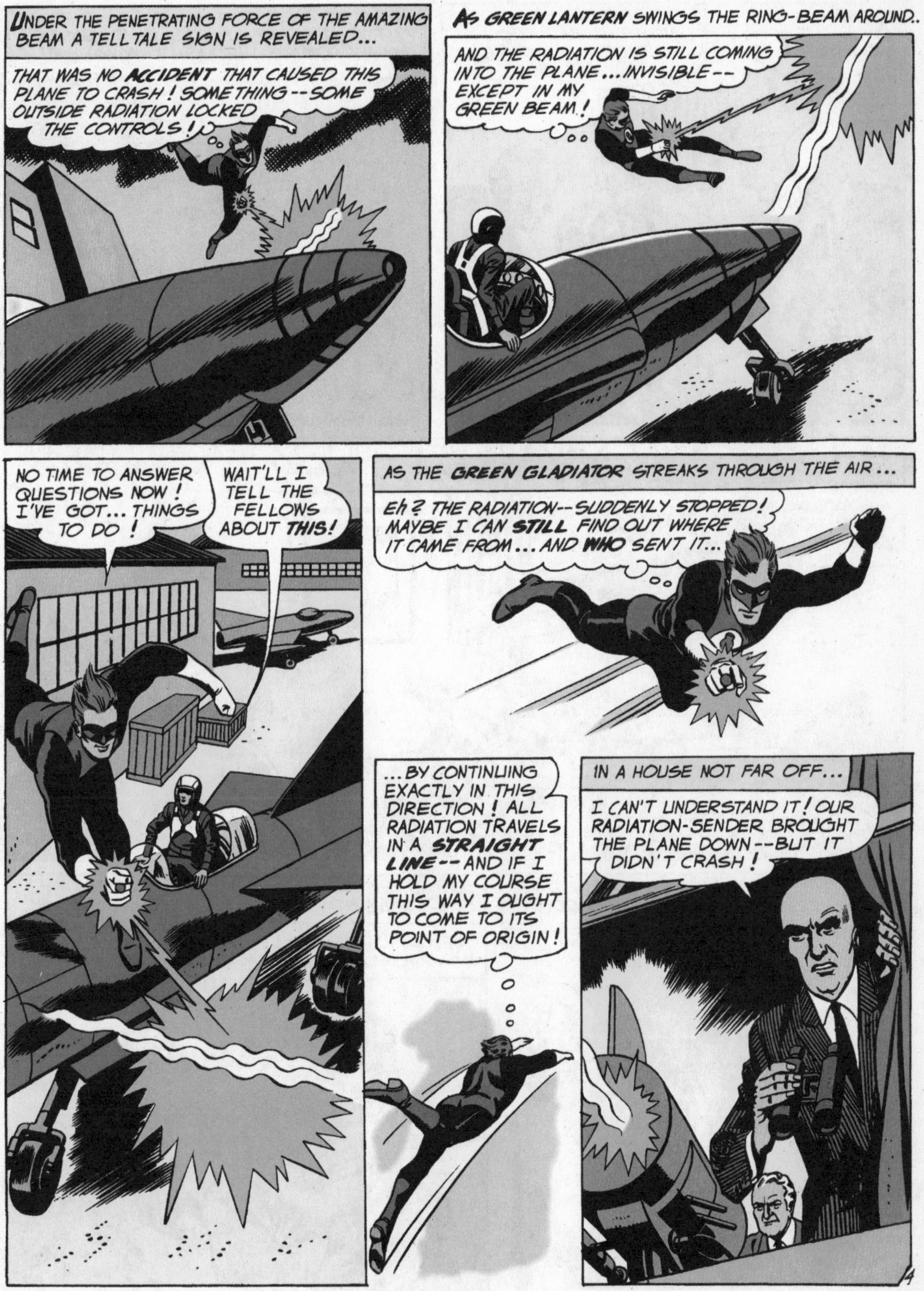
UNDER THE PENETRATING FORCE OF THE AMAZING BEAM A TELLTALE SIGN IS REVEALED...
THAT WAS NO ACCIDENT THAT CAUSED THIS PLANE TO CRASH! SOMETHING--SOME OUTSIDE RADIATION LOCKED THE CONTROLS!
AS GREEN LANTERN SWINGS THE RING-BEAM AROUND..
AND THE RADIATION IS STILL COMING INTO THE PLANE...INVISIBLE--EXCEPT IN MY GREEN BEAM!
NO TIME TO ANSWER QUESTIONS NOW! I'VE GOT... THINGS TO DO!
WAIT'LL I TELL THE FELLOWS ABOUT THIS!
AS THE GREEN GLADIATOR STREAKS THROUGH THE AIR...
Eh? THE RADIATION--SUDDENLY STOPPED! MAYBE I CAN STILL FIND OUT WHERE IT CAME FROM...AND WHO SENT IT...
...BY CONTINUING EXACTLY IN THIS DIRECTION! ALL RADIATION TRAVELS IN A STRAIGHT LINE--AND IF I HOLD MY COURSE THIS WAY I OUGHT TO COME TO ITS POINT OF ORIGIN!
IN A HOUSE NOT FAR OFF...
I CAN'T UNDERSTAND IT! OUR RADIATION-SENDER BROUGHT THE PLANE DOWN--BUT IT DIDN'T CRASH!
4

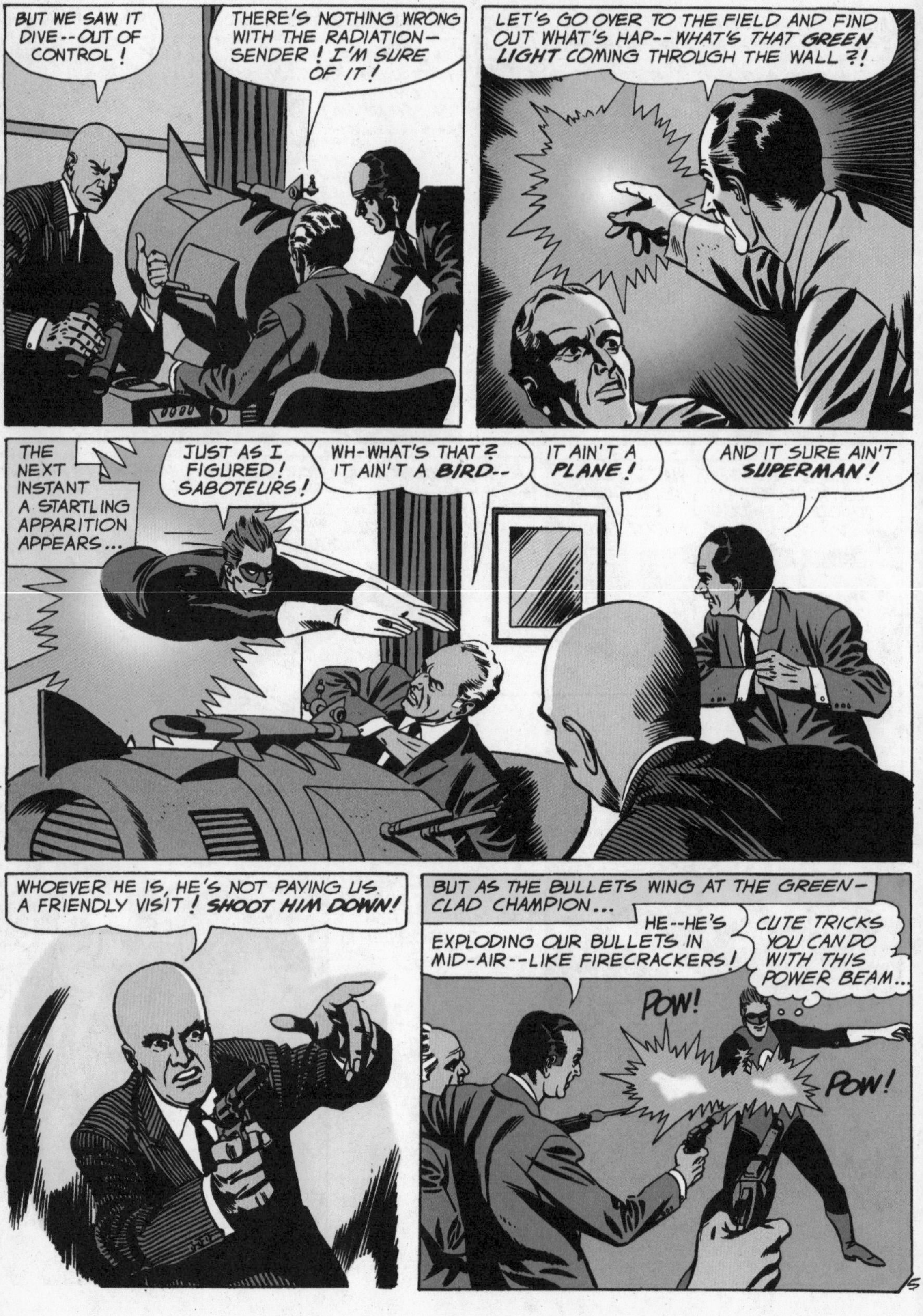
BUT WE SAW IT DIVE--OUT OF CONTROL!
THERE'S NOTHING WRONG WITH THE RADIATION-SENDER! I'M SURE OF IT!
LET'S GO OVER TO THE FIELD AND FIND OUT WHAT'S HAP--WHAT'S THAT GREEN LIGHT COMING THROUGH THE WALL?!
THE NEXT INSTANT A STARTLING APPARITION APPEARS...
JUST AS I FIGURED! SABOTEURS!
WH-WHAT'S THAT? IT AIN'T A BIRD--
IT AIN'T A PLANE!
AND IT SURE AIN'T SUPERMAN!
WHOEVER HE IS, HE'S NOT PAYING US A FRIENDLY VISIT! SHOOT HIM DOWN!
BUT AS THE BULLETS WING AT THE GREEN-CLAD CHAMPION...
HE--HE'S EXPLODING OUR BULLETS IN MID-AIR--LIKE FIRECRACKERS!
CUTE TRICKS YOU CAN DO WITH THIS POWER BEAM...
POW!
POW!
15

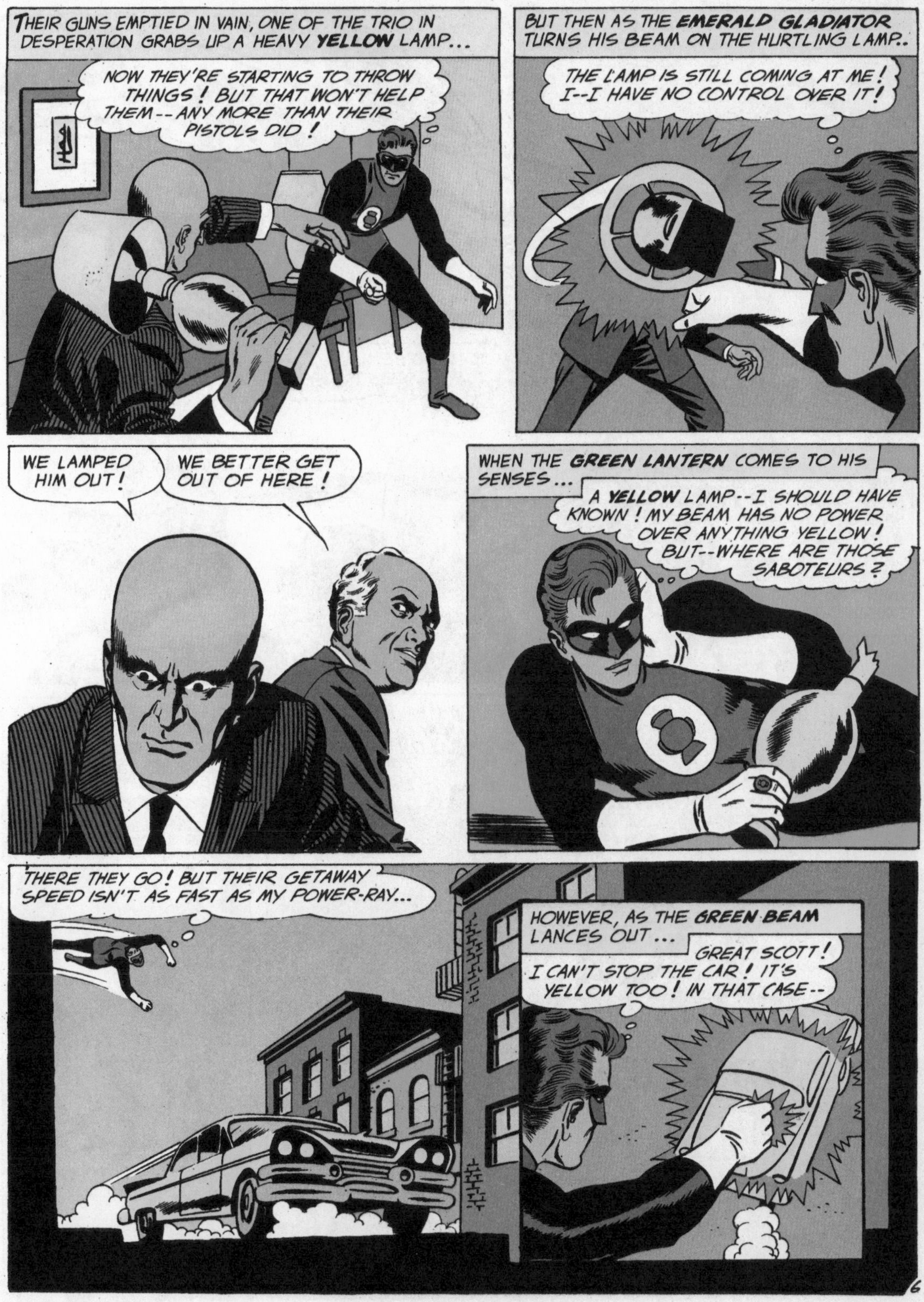
THEIR GUNS EMPTIED IN VAIN, ONE OF THE TRIO IN DESPERATION GRABS UP A HEAVY YELLOW LAMP...
NOW THEY'RE STARTING TO THROW THINGS! BUT THAT WON'T HELP THEM--ANY MORE THAN THEIR PISTOLS DID!
BUT THEN AS THE EMERALD GLADIATOR TURNS HIS BEAM ON THE HURTLING LAMP..
THE LAMP IS STILL COMING AT ME! I--I HAVE NO CONTROL OVER IT!
WE LAMPED HIM OUT!
WE BETTER GET OUT OF HERE!
WHEN THE GREEN LANTERN COMES TO HIS SENSES...
A YELLOW LAMP--I SHOULD HAVE KNOWN! MY BEAM HAS NO POWER OVER ANYTHING YELLOW! BUT--WHERE ARE THOSE SABOTEURS?
THERE THEY GO! BUT THEIR GETAWAY SPEED ISN'T AS FAST AS MY POWER-RAY...
HOWEVER, AS THE GREEN BEAM LANCES OUT...
GREAT SCOTT! I CAN'T STOP THE CAR! IT'S YELLOW TOO! IN THAT CASE--
6

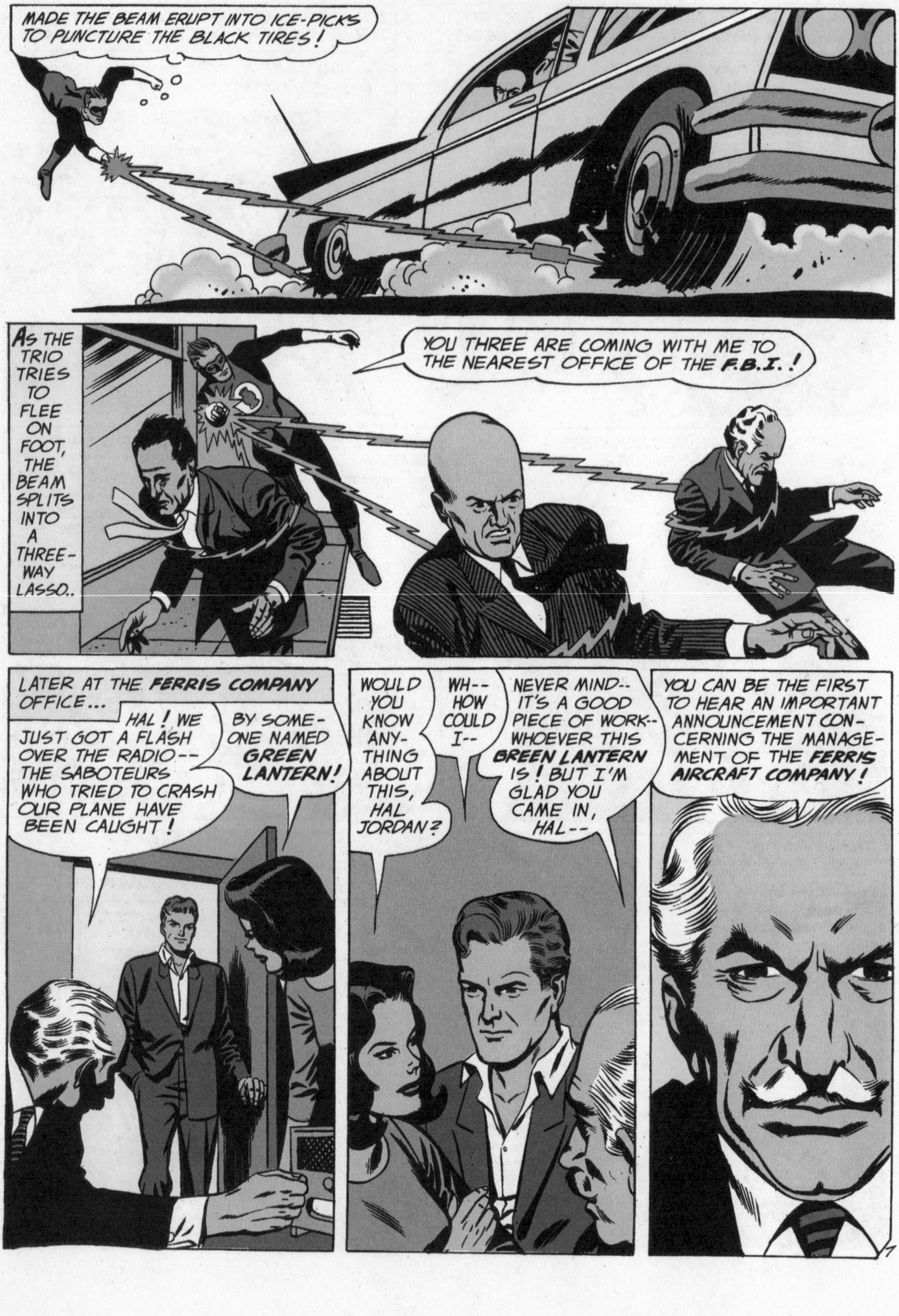
MADE THE BEAM ERUPT INTO ICE-PICKS TO PUNCTURE THE BLACK TIRES!
AS THE TRIO TRIES TO FLEE ON FOOT, THE BEAM SPLITS INTO A THREE-WAY LASSO..
YOU THREE ARE COMING WITH ME TO THE NEAREST OFFICE OF THE F.B.I.!
LATER AT THE FERRIS COMPANY OFFICE...
HAL! WE JUST GOT A FLASH OVER THE RADIO-- THE SABOTEURS WHO TRIED TO CRASH OUR PLANE HAVE BEEN CAUGHT!
BY SOME-ONE NAMED GREEN LANTERN!
WOULD YOU KNOW ANY-THING ABOUT THIS, HAL JORDAN?
WH-- HOW COULD I--
NEVER MIND-- IT'S A GOOD PIECE OF WORK-- WHOEVER THIS GREEN LANTERN IS! BUT I'M GLAD YOU CAME IN, HAL--
YOU CAN BE THE FIRST TO HEAR AN IMPORTANT ANNOUNCEMENT CON-CERNING THE MANAGE-MENT OF THE FERRIS AIRCRAFT COMPANY!
7

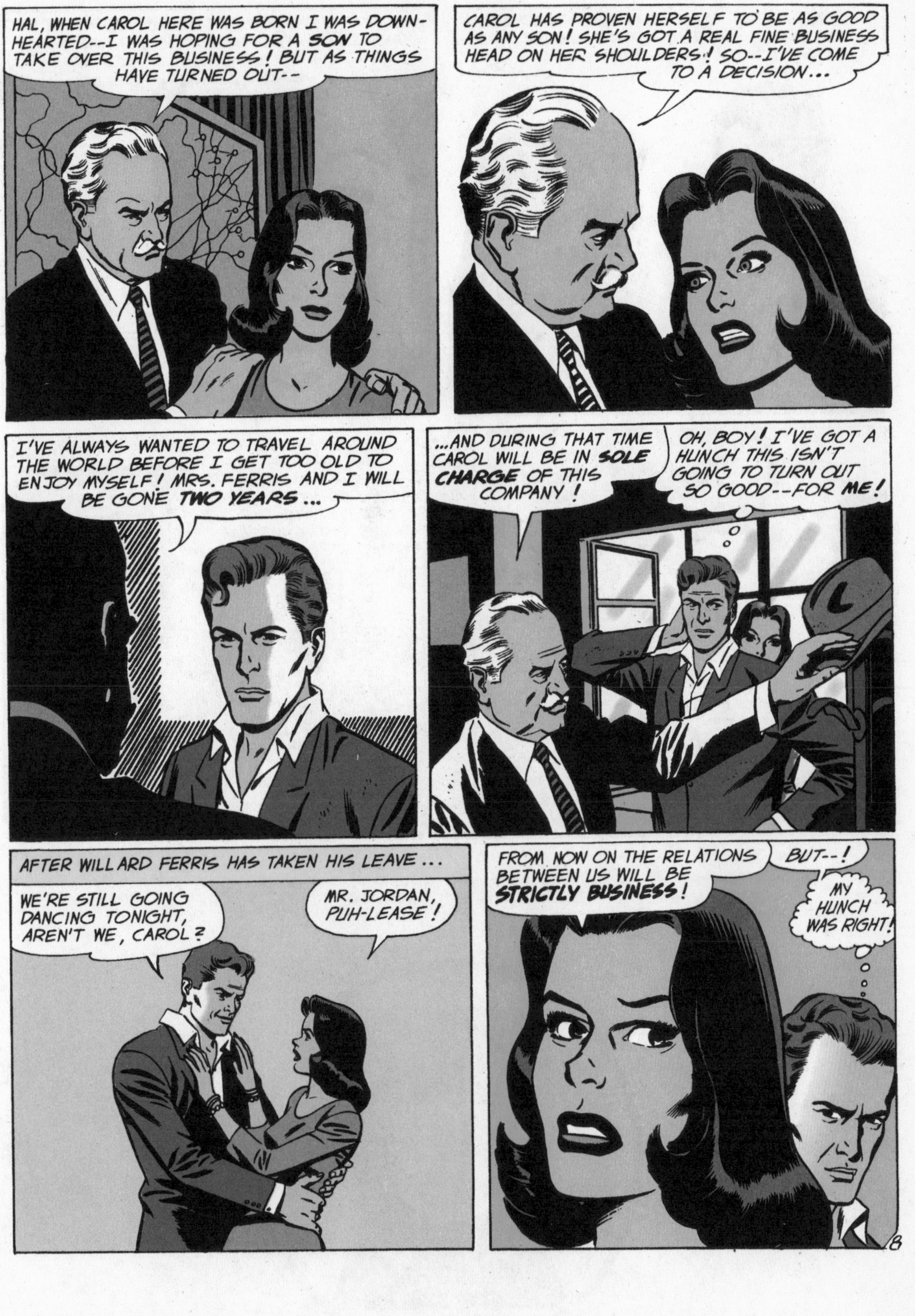
HAL, WHEN CAROL HERE WAS BORN I WAS DOWN-HEARTED--I WAS HOPING FOR A SON TO TAKE OVER THIS BUSINESS! BUT AS THINGS HAVE TURNED OUT--
CAROL HAS PROVEN HERSELF TO BE AS GOOD AS ANY SON! SHE'S GOT A REAL FINE BUSINESS HEAD ON HER SHOULDERS! SO--I'VE COME TO A DECISION...
I'VE ALWAYS WANTED TO TRAVEL AROUND THE WORLD BEFORE I GET TOO OLD TO ENJOY MYSELF! MRS. FERRIS AND I WILL BE GONE TWO YEARS...
...AND DURING THAT TIME CAROL WILL BE IN SOLE CHARGE OF THIS COMPANY!
OH, BOY! I'VE GOT A HUNCH THIS ISN'T GOING TO TURN OUT SO GOOD--FOR ME!
AFTER WILLARD FERRIS HAS TAKEN HIS LEAVE...
WE'RE STILL GOING DANCING TONIGHT, AREN'T WE, CAROL?
MR. JORDAN, PUH-LEASE!
FROM NOW ON THE RELATIONS BETWEEN US WILL BE STRICTLY BUSINESS!
BUT--!
MY HUNCH WAS RIGHT!
8

NO HARM IN MIXING BUSINESS WITH PLEASURE--
YOU HEARD WHAT DAD SAID! I'VE GOT TO SATISFY HIS FAITH IN ME--
AND THAT MEANS THAT DURING THE NEXT TWO YEARS I'LL HAVE ABSOLUTELY NO TIME FOR ROMANCE! I'M YOUR BOSS, MR. JORDAN-- AND THAT'S ORDERS!
Whew!
TWO YEARS!?
LATER, A CRESTFALLEN PILOT MOONS OVER HIS FATE...
(sigh) MY POWER RING CAN DO ANYTHING FOR ME EXCEPT GET ME THE ONE THING IN THE WORLD I WANT MOST--CAROL!
The End
9

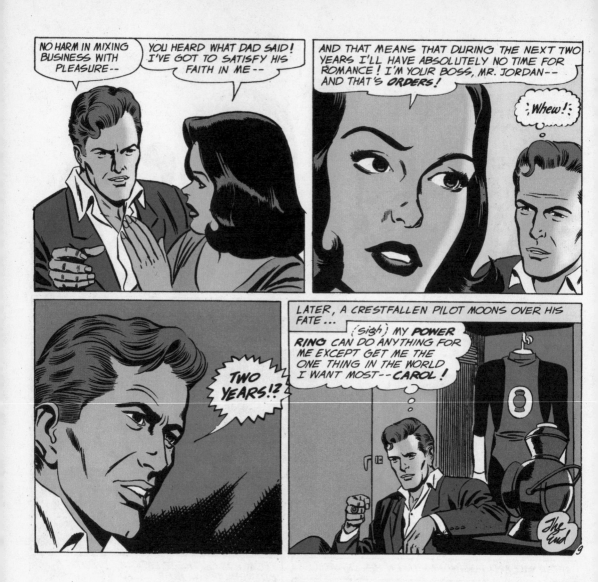

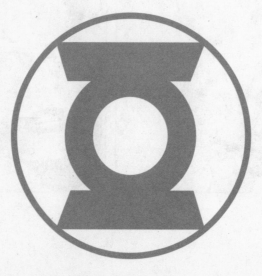

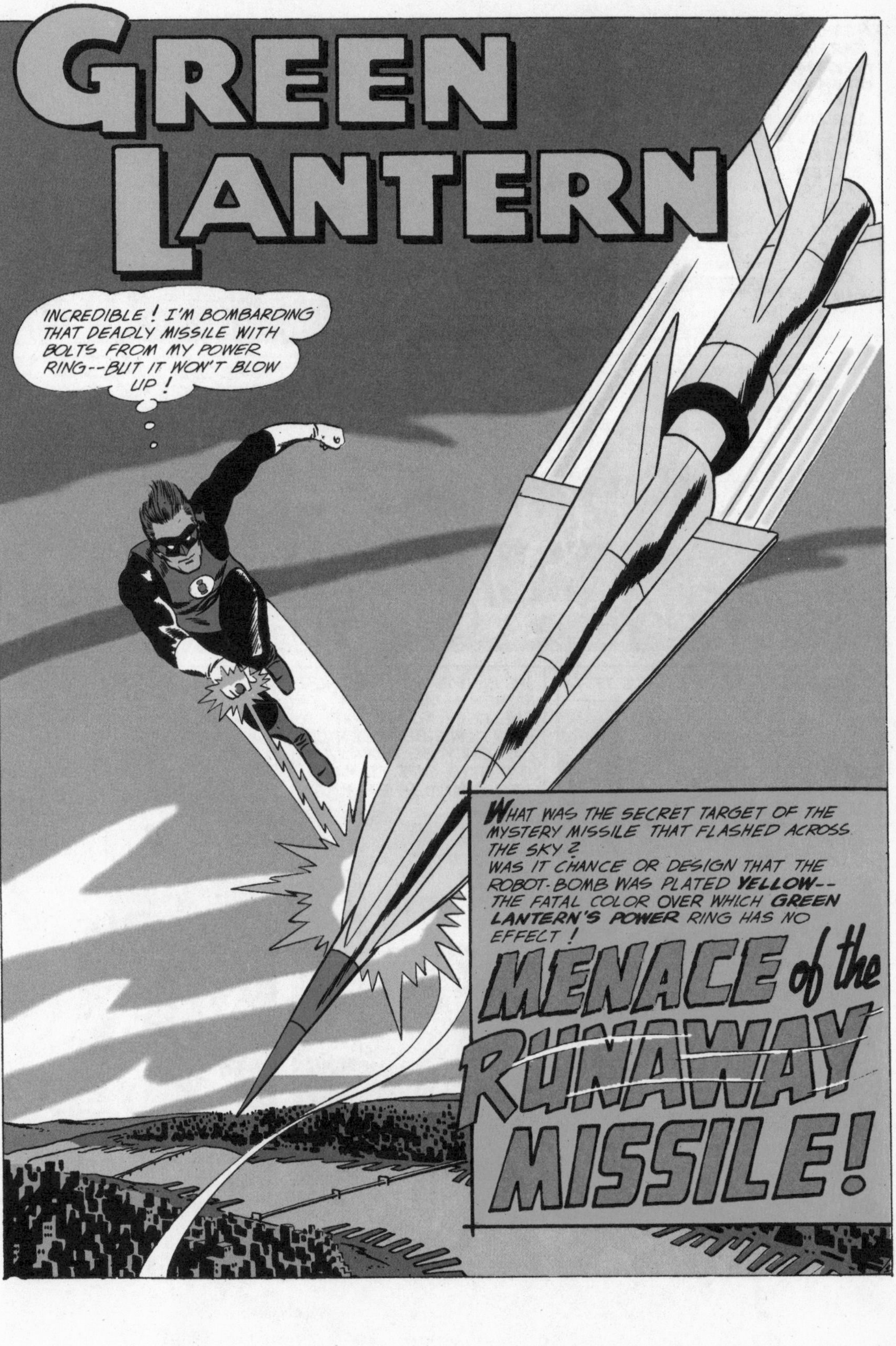
GREEN LANTERN
INCREDIBLE! I'M BOMBARDING THAT DEADLY MISSILE WITH BOLTS FROM MY POWER RING--BUT IT WON'T BLOW UP!
WHAT WAS THE SECRET TARGET OF THE MYSTERY MISSILE THAT FLASHED ACROSS THE SKY? WAS IT CHANCE OR DESIGN THAT THE ROBOT-BOMB WAS PLATED YELLOW-- THE FATAL COLOR OVER WHICH GREEN LANTERN'S POWER RING HAS NO EFFECT!
MENACE of the RUNAWAY MISSILE!

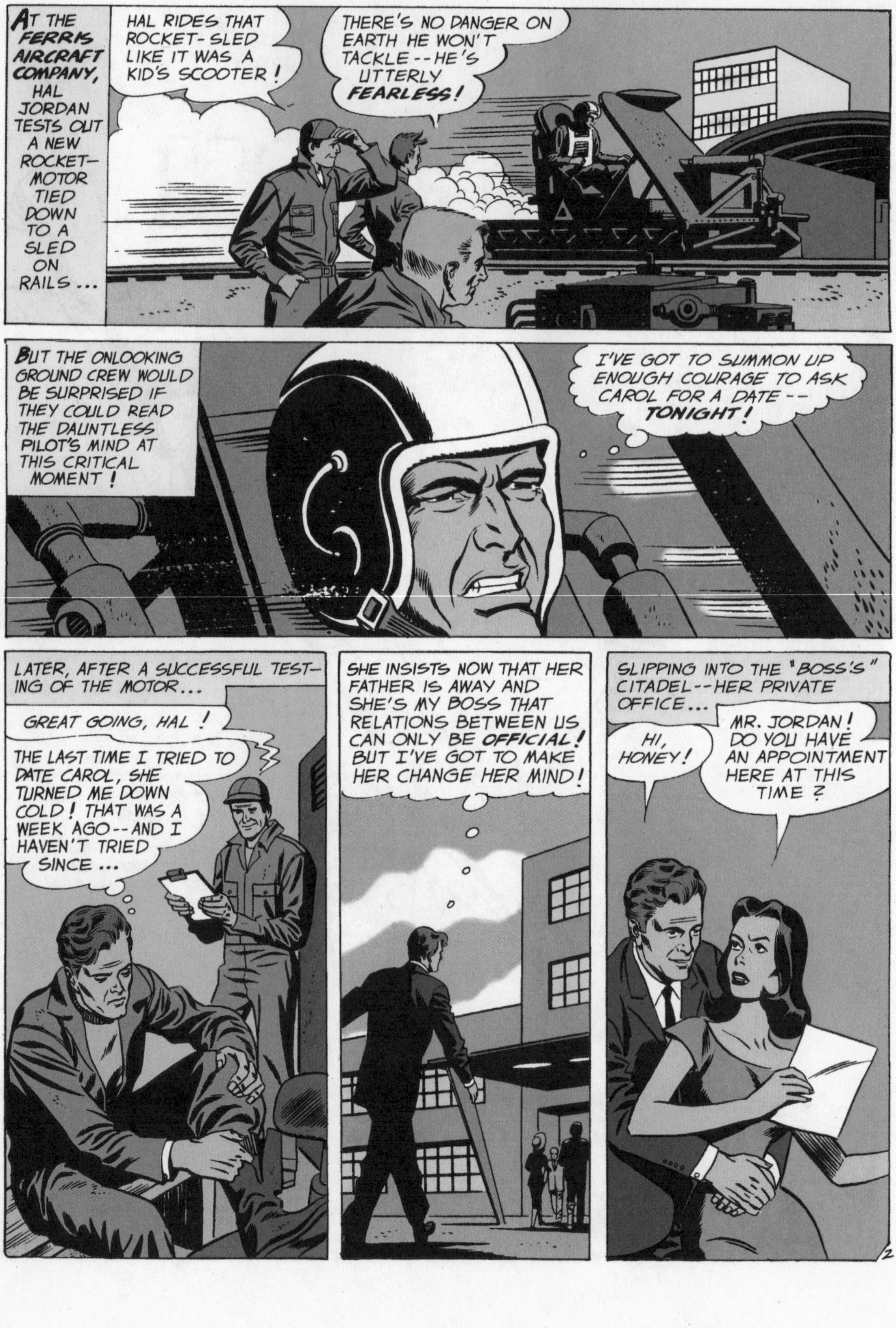
AT THE FERRIS AIRCRAFT COMPANY, HAL JORDAN TESTS OUT A NEW ROCKET-MOTOR TIED DOWN TO A SLED ON RAILS...
HAL RIDES THAT ROCKET-SLED LIKE IT WAS A KID'S SCOOTER!
THERE'S NO DANGER ON EARTH HE WON'T TACKLE--HE'S UTTERLY FEARLESS!
BUT THE ONLOOKING GROUND CREW WOULD BE SURPRISED IF THEY COULD READ THE DAUNTLESS PILOT'S MIND AT THIS CRITICAL MOMENT!
I'VE GOT TO SUMMON UP ENOUGH COURAGE TO ASK CAROL FOR A DATE--TONIGHT!
LATER, AFTER A SUCCESSFUL TESTING OF THE MOTOR...
GREAT GOING, HAL!
THE LAST TIME I TRIED TO DATE CAROL, SHE TURNED ME DOWN COLD! THAT WAS A WEEK AGO--AND I HAVEN'T TRIED SINCE...
SHE INSISTS NOW THAT HER FATHER IS AWAY AND SHE'S MY BOSS THAT RELATIONS BETWEEN US CAN ONLY BE OFFICIAL! BUT I'VE GOT TO MAKE HER CHANGE HER MIND!
SLIPPING INTO THE "BOSS'S" CITADEL--HER PRIVATE OFFICE...
HI, HONEY!
MR. JORDAN! DO YOU HAVE AN APPOINTMENT HERE AT THIS TIME?
2

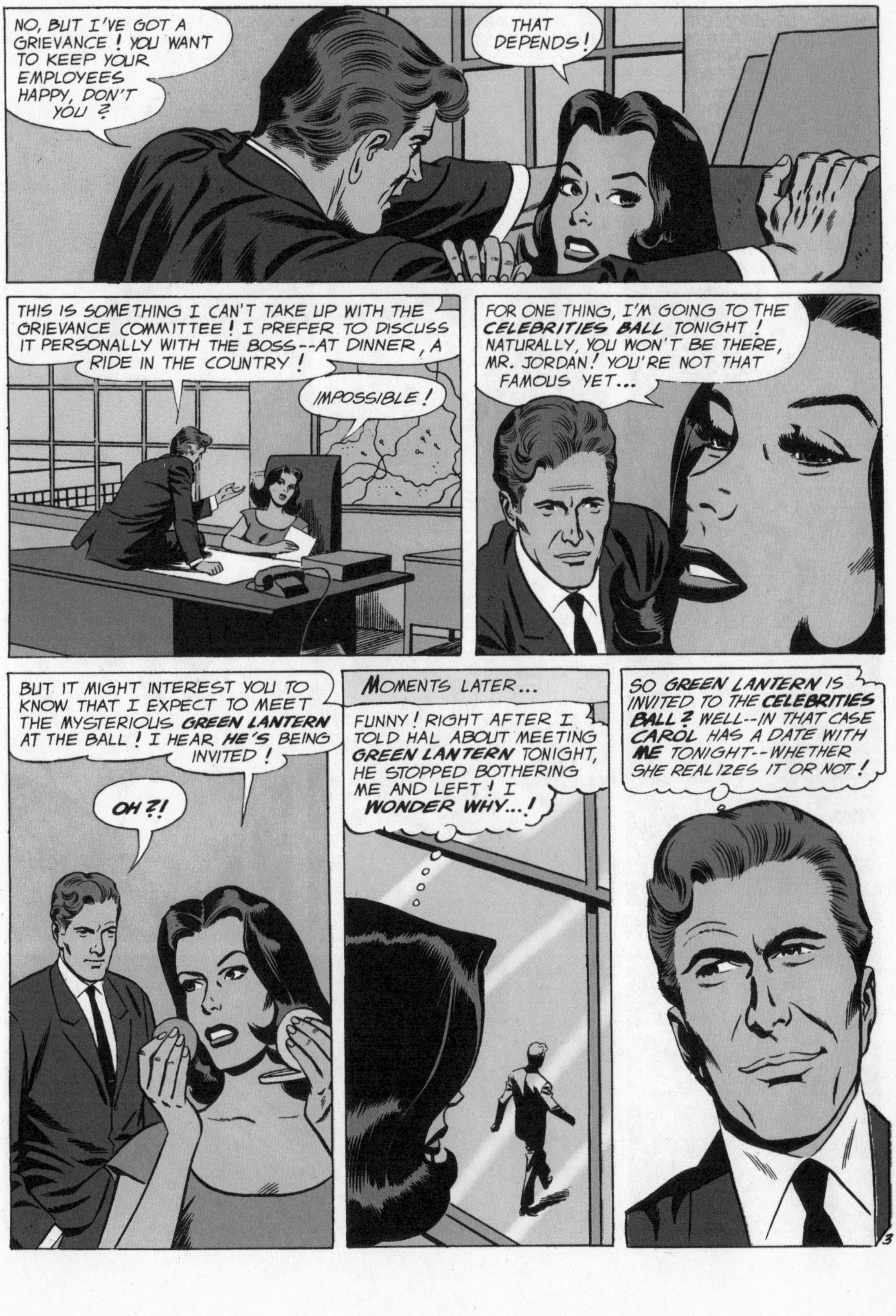
NO, BUT I'VE GOT A GRIEVANCE! YOU WAN'T TO KEEP YOUR EMPLOYEES HAPPY, DON'T YOU?
THAT DEPENDS!
THIS IS SOMETHING I CAN'T TAKE UP WITH THE GRIEVANCE COMMITTEE! I PREFER TO DISCUSS IT PERSONALLY WITH THE BOSS--AT DINNER, A RIDE IN THE COUNTRY!
IMPOSSIBLE!
FOR ONE THING, I'M GOING TO THE CELEBRITIES BALL TONIGHT! NATURALLY, YOU WON'T BE THERE, MR. JORDAN! YOU'RE NOT THAT FAMOUS YET...
BUT IT MIGHT INTEREST YOU TO KNOW THAT I EXPECT TO MEET THE MYSTERIOUS GREEN LANTERN AT THE BALL! I HEAR HE'S BEING INVITED!
OH?!
MOMENTS LATER...
FUNNY! RIGHT AFTER I TOLD HAL ABOUT MEETING GREEN LANTERN TONIGHT, HE STOPPED BOTHERING ME AND LEFT! I WONDER WHY...!
SO GREEN LANTERN IS INVITED TO THE CELEBRITIES BALL? WELL--IN THAT CASE CAROL HAS A DATE WITH ME TONIGHT--WHETHER SHE REALIZES IT OR NOT!
3

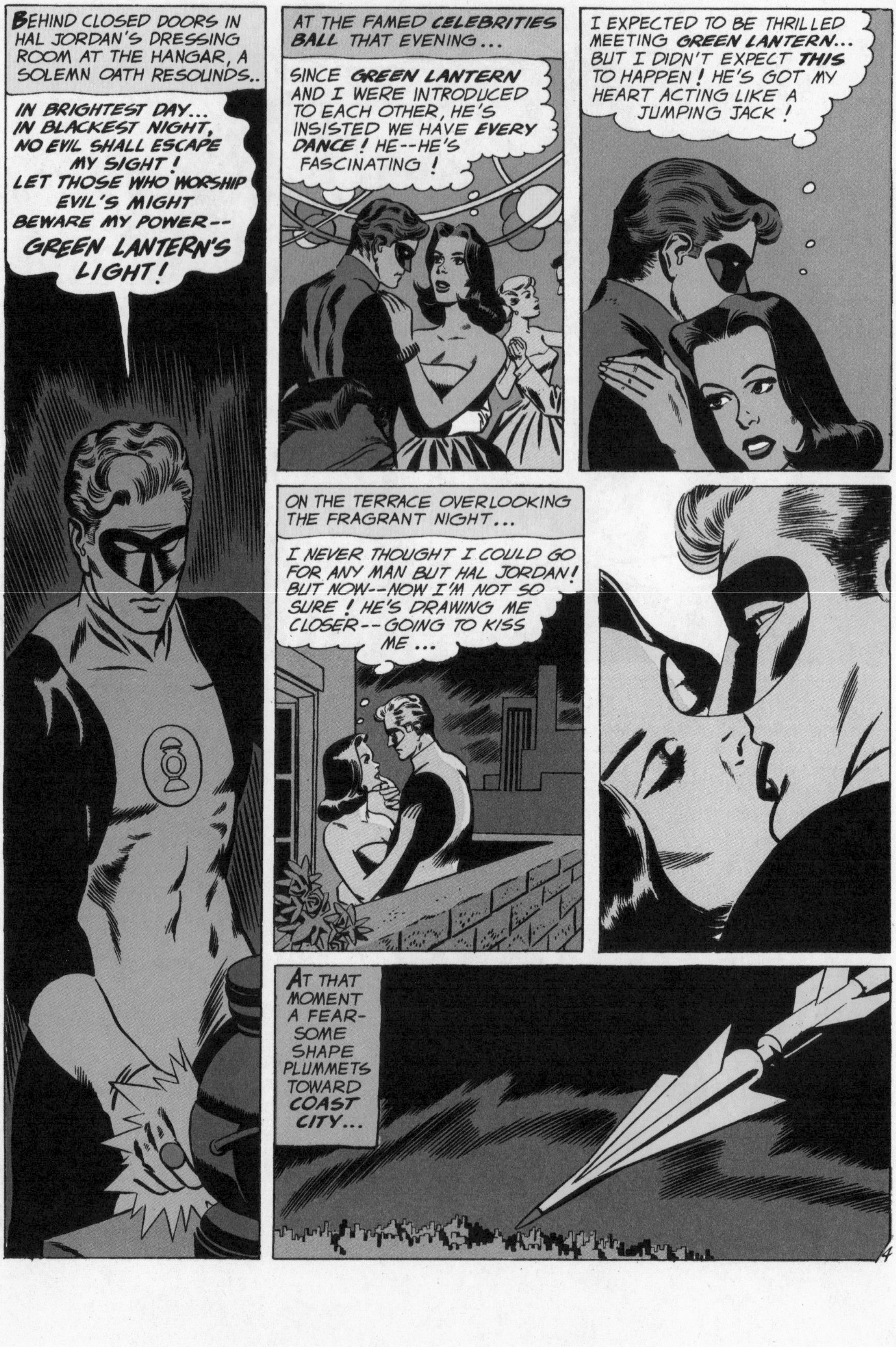
BEHIND CLOSED DOORS IN HAL JORDAN'S DRESSING ROOM AT THE HANGAR, A SOLEMN OATH RESOUNDS..
IN BRIGHTEST DAY... IN BLACKEST NIGHT, NO EVIL SHALL ESCAPE MY SIGHT! LET THOSE WHO WORSHIP EVIL'S MIGHT BEWARE MY POWER-- GREEN LANTERN'S LIGHT!
AT THE FAMED CELEBRITIES BALL THAT EVENING...
SINCE GREEN LANTERN AND I WERE INTRODUCED TO EACH OTHER, HE'S INSISTED WE HAVE EVERY DANCE! HE--HE'S FASCINATING!
I EXPECTED TO BE THRILLED MEETING GREEN LANTERN... BUT I DIDN'T EXPECT THIS TO HAPPEN! HE'S GOT MY HEART ACTING LIKE A JUMPING JACK!
ON THE TERRACE OVERLOOKING THE FRAGRANT NIGHT...
I NEVER THOUGHT I COULD GO FOR ANY MAN BUT HAL JORDAN! BUT NOW--NOW I'M NOT SO SURE! HE'S DRAWING ME CLOSER--GOING TO KISS ME...
AT THAT MOMENT A FEARSOME SHAPE PLUMMETS TOWARD COAST CITY...
4

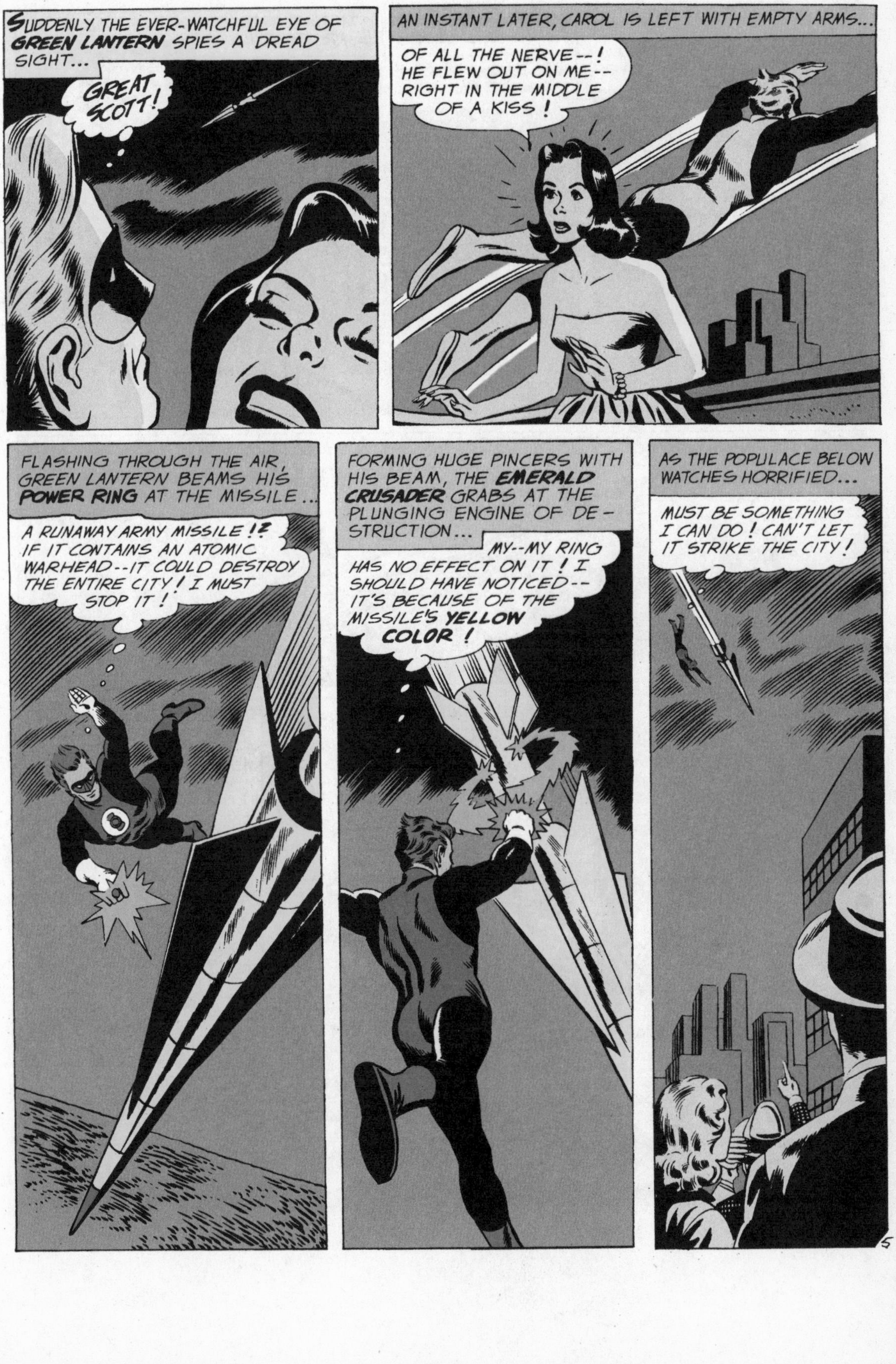
SUDDENLY THE EVER-WATCHFUL EYE OF GREEN LANTERN SPIES A DREAD SIGHT...
GREAT SCOTT!
AN INSTANT LATER, CAROL IS LEFT WITH EMPTY ARMS...
OF ALL THE NERVE--! HE FLEW OUT ON ME-- RIGHT IN THE MIDDLE OF A KISS!
FLASHING THROUGH THE AIR, GREEN LANTERN BEAMS HIS POWER RING AT THE MISSILE...
A RUNAWAY ARMY MISSILE!? IF IT CONTAINS AN ATOMIC WARHEAD--IT COULD DESTROY THE ENTIRE CITY! I MUST STOP IT!
FORMING HUGE PINCERS WITH HIS BEAM, THE EMERALD CRUSADER GRABS AT THE PLUNGING ENGINE OF DE-STRUCTION...
MY--MY RING HAS NO EFFECT ON IT! I SHOULD HAVE NOTICED-- IT'S BECAUSE OF THE MISSILE'S YELLOW COLOR!
AS THE POPULACE BELOW WATCHES HORRIFIED...
MUST BE SOMETHING I CAN DO! CAN'T LET IT STRIKE THE CITY!
5

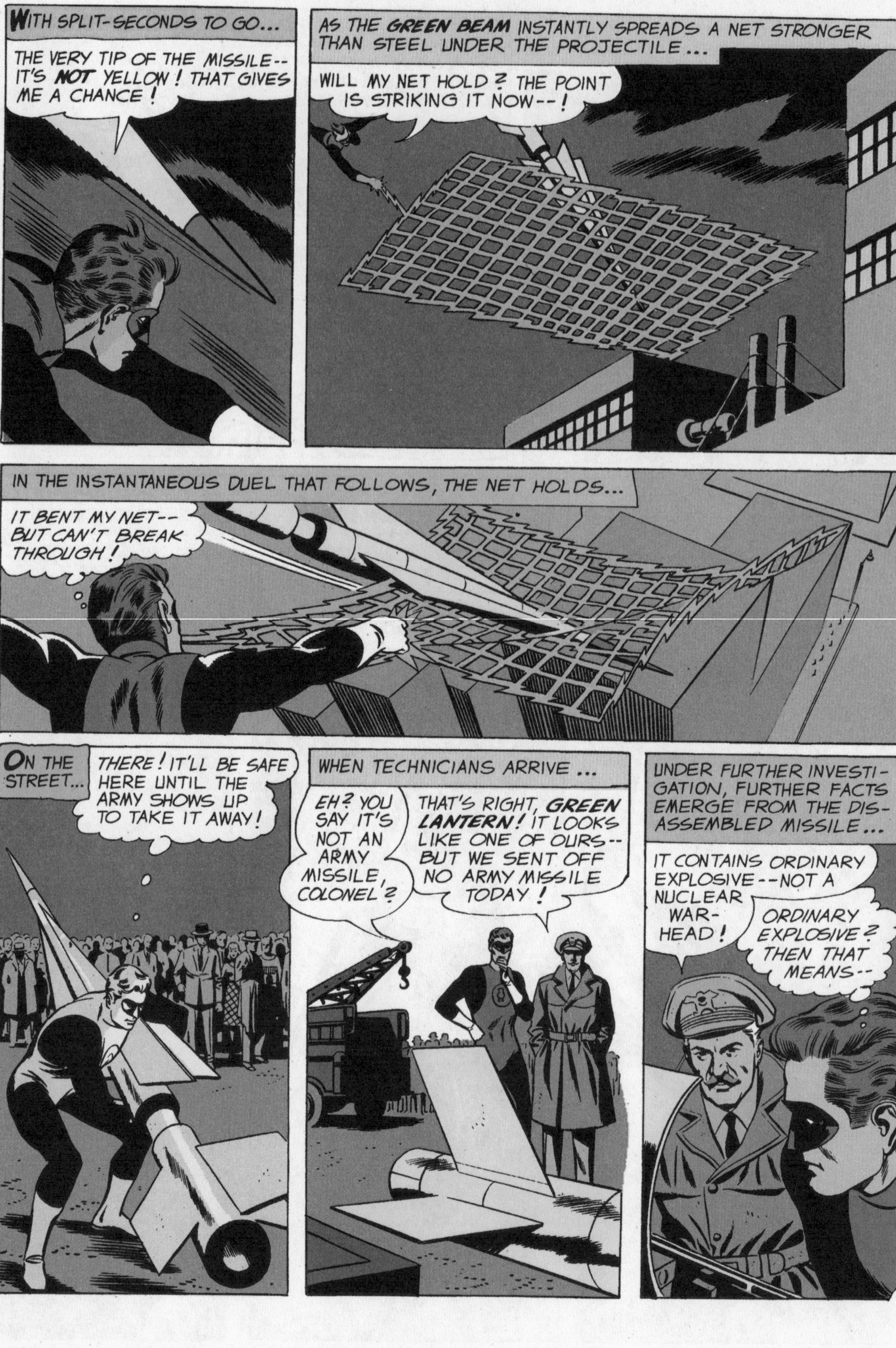

WITH SPLIT-SECONDS TO GO...
THE VERY TIP OF THE MISSILE--IT'S NOT YELLOW! THAT GIVES ME A CHANCE!
AS THE GREEN BEAM INSTANTLY SPREADS A NET STRONGER THAN STEEL UNDER THE PROJECTILE...
WILL MY NET HOLD? THE POINT IS STRIKING IT NOW--!
IN THE INSTANTANEOUS DUEL THAT FOLLOWS, THE NET HOLDS...
IT BENT MY NET--BUT CAN'T BREAK THROUGH!
ON THE STREET...
THERE! IT'LL BE SAFE HERE UNTIL THE ARMY SHOWS UP TO TAKE IT AWAY!
WHEN TECHNICIANS ARRIVE...
EH? YOU SAY IT'S NOT AN ARMY MISSILE, COLONEL?
THAT'S RIGHT, GREEN LANTERN! IT LOOKS LIKE ONE OF OURS--BUT WE SENT OFF NO ARMY MISSILE TODAY!
UNDER FURTHER INVESTIGATION, FURTHER FACTS EMERGE FROM THE DISASSEMBLED MISSILE...
IT CONTAINS ORDINARY EXPLOSIVE--NOT A NUCLEAR WAR-HEAD!
ORDINARY EXPLOSIVE? THEN THAT MEANS--
6

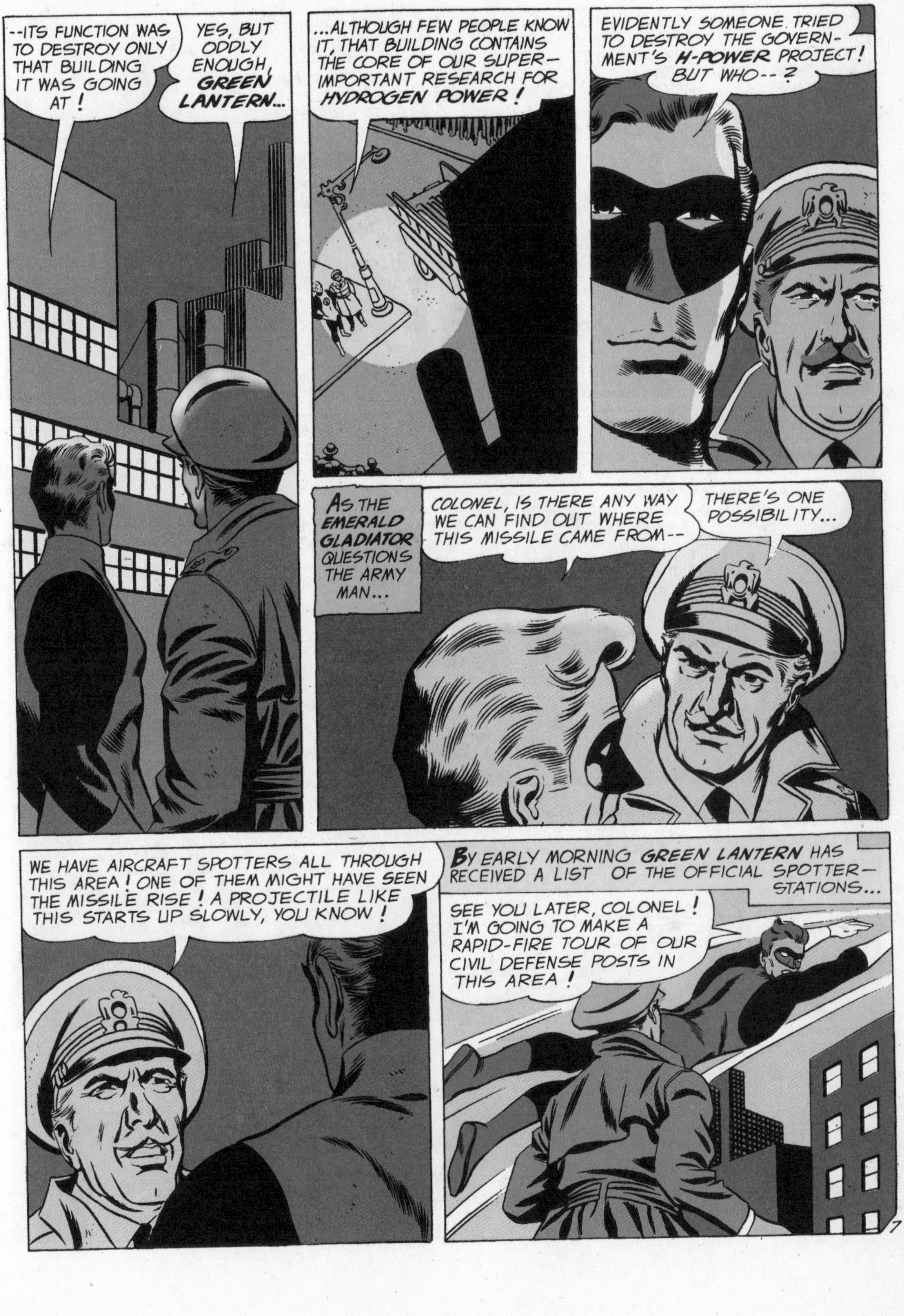
--ITS FUNCTION WAS TO DESTROY ONLY THAT BUILDING IT WAS GOING AT!
YES, BUT ODDLY ENOUGH, GREEN LANTERN...
...ALTHOUGH FEW PEOPLE KNOW IT, THAT BUILDING CONTAINS THE CORE OF OUR SUPER-IMPORTANT RESEARCH FOR HYDROGEN POWER!
EVIDENTLY SOMEONE TRIED TO DESTROY THE GOVERNMENT'S H-POWER PROJECT! BUT WHO--?
AS THE EMERALD GLADIATOR QUESTIONS THE ARMY MAN...
COLONEL, IS THERE ANY WAY WE CAN FIND OUT WHERE THIS MISSILE CAME FROM--
THERE'S ONE POSSIBILITY...
WE HAVE AIRCRAFT SPOTTERS ALL THROUGH THIS AREA! ONE OF THEM MIGHT HAVE SEEN THE MISSILE RISE! A PROJECTILE LIKE THIS STARTS UP SLOWLY, YOU KNOW!
BY EARLY MORNING GREEN LANTERN HAS RECEIVED A LIST OF THE OFFICIAL SPOTTER-STATIONS...
SEE YOU LATER, COLONEL! I'M GOING TO MAKE A RAPID-FIRE TOUR OF OUR CIVIL DEFENSE POSTS IN THIS AREA!
7

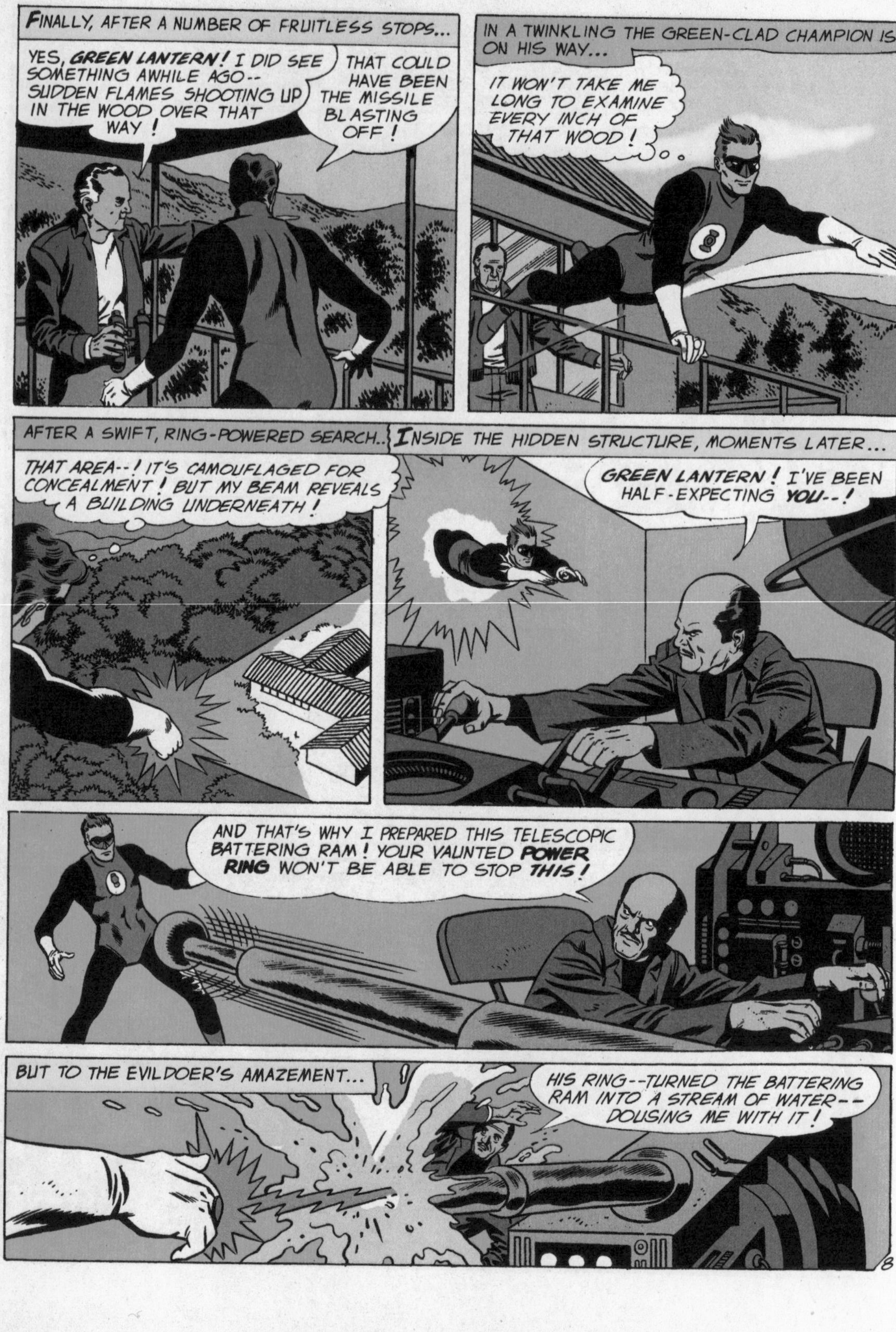
FINALLY, AFTER A NUMBER OF FRUITLESS STOPS...
YES, GREEN LANTERN! I DID SEE SOMETHING AWHILE AGO-- SUDDEN FLAMES SHOOTING UP IN THE WOOD OVER THAT WAY!
THAT COULD HAVE BEEN THE MISSILE BLASTING OFF!
IN A TWINKLING THE GREEN-CLAD CHAMPION IS ON HIS WAY...
IT WON'T TAKE ME LONG TO EXAMINE EVERY INCH OF THAT WOOD!
AFTER A SWIFT, RING-POWERED SEARCH...
THAT AREA--! IT'S CAMOUFLAGED FOR CONCEALMENT! BUT MY BEAM REVEALS A BUILDING UNDERNEATH!
INSIDE THE HIDDEN STRUCTURE, MOMENTS LATER...
GREEN LANTERN! I'VE BEEN HALF-EXPECTING YOU--!
AND THAT'S WHY I PREPARED THIS TELESCOPIC BATTERING RAM! YOUR VAUNTED POWER RING WON'T BE ABLE TO STOP THIS!
BUT TO THE EVILDOER'S AMAZEMENT...
HIS RING--TURNED THE BATTERING RAM INTO A STREAM OF WATER-- DOUSING ME WITH IT!
8

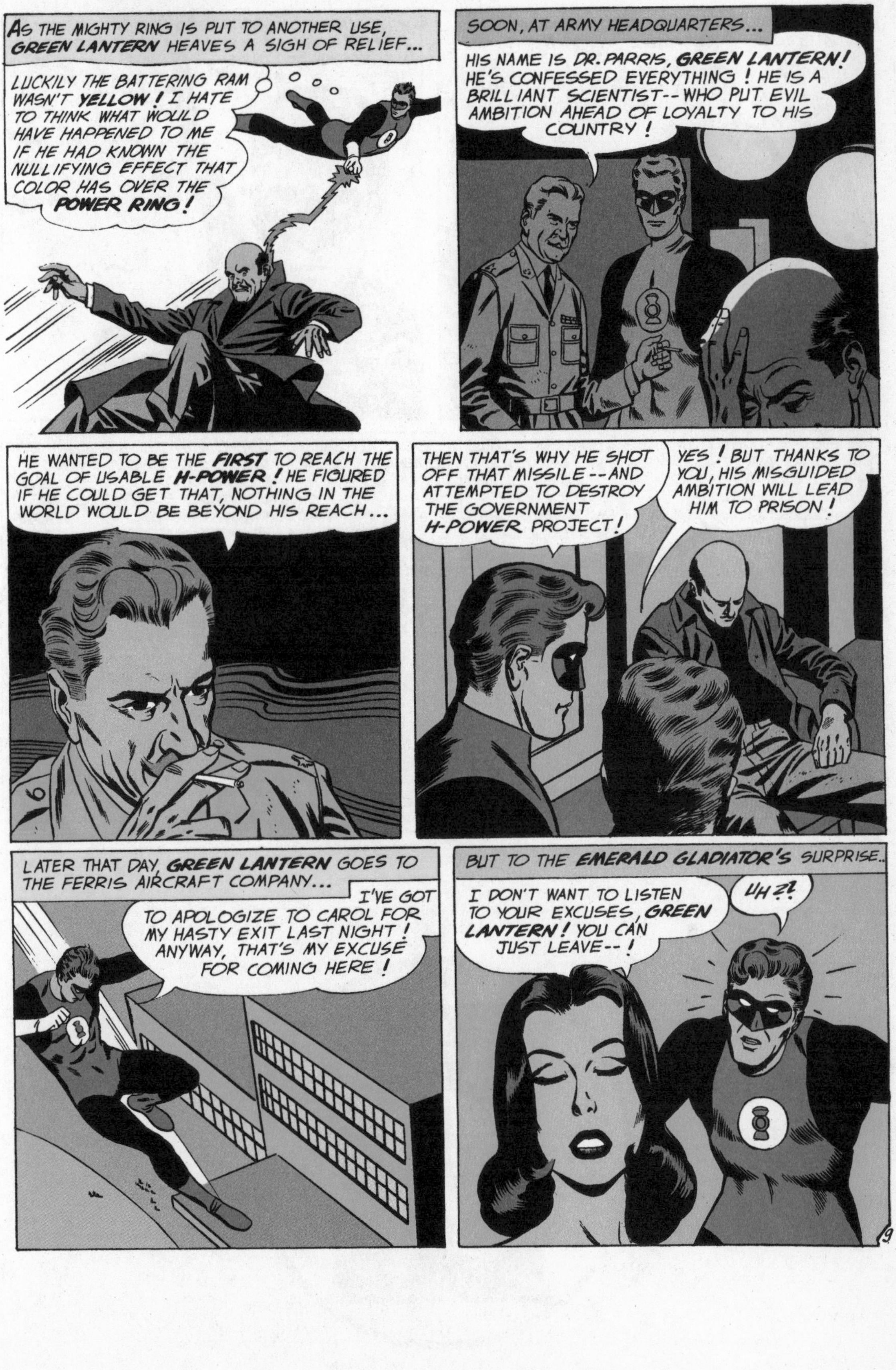
AS THE MIGHTY RING IS PUT TO ANOTHER USE, GREEN LANTERN HEAVES A SIGH OF RELIEF...
LUCKILY THE BATTERING RAM WASN'T YELLOW! I HATE TO THINK WHAT WOULD HAVE HAPPENED TO ME IF HE HAD KNOWN THE NULLIFYING EFFECT THAT COLOR HAS OVER THE POWER RING!
SOON, AT ARMY HEADQUARTERS...
HIS NAME IS DR. PARRIS, GREEN LANTERN! HE'S CONFESSED EVERYTHING! HE IS A BRILLIANT SCIENTIST-- WHO PUT EVIL AMBITION AHEAD OF LOYALTY TO HIS COUNTRY!
HE WANTED TO BE THE FIRST TO REACH THE GOAL OF USABLE H-POWER! HE FIGURED IF HE COULD GET THAT, NOTHING IN THE WORLD WOULD BE BEYOND HIS REACH...
THEN THAT'S WHY HE SHOT OFF THAT MISSILE--AND ATTEMPTED TO DESTROY THE GOVERNMENT H-POWER PROJECT!
YES! BUT THANKS TO YOU, HIS MISGUIDED AMBITION WILL LEAD HIM TO PRISON!
LATER THAT DAY, GREEN LANTERN GOES TO THE FERRIS AIRCRAFT COMPANY...
I'VE GOT TO APOLOGIZE TO CAROL FOR MY HASTY EXIT LAST NIGHT! ANYWAY, THAT'S MY EXCUSE FOR COMING HERE!
BUT TO THE EMERALD GLADIATOR'S SURPRISE..
I DON'T WANT TO LISTEN TO YOUR EXCUSES, GREEN LANTERN! YOU CAN JUST LEAVE--!
UH?!
9

BUT, CAROL -- MISS FERRIS -- WHAT HAVE I DONE ?
WHAT HAVE YOU DONE ? YOU -- YOU HEEL ! LAST NIGHT YOU KISSED ME --
YOU'RE NOT OBJECTING TO THAT ? THE WAY YOU KISSED ME, I COULD TELL --
IT'S THE WAY YOU KISSED ME THAT I'M REFERRING TO...
IF YOU HAD LOST YOURSELF IN THAT KISS... THE WAY I DID... YOUR EYES WOULD HAVE NATURALLY CLOSED...
BUT CAROL -- BE REASONABLE ! IF MY EYES HAD BEEN CLOSED, I WOULDN'T HAVE SEEN THAT MISSILE AND...
GOOD DAY, MR. GREEN LANTERN ! I AM BUSY !
WHEW! NOW I'M IN A DOUBLE DOGHOUSE AS FAR AS CAROL IS CONCERNED ! BOTH AS HAL JORDAN -- AND AS GREEN LANTERN ! HOW COULD THINGS GET WORSE ?
CAROL FERRIS PRIVATE
SLAM!
IN THE NEXT ISSUE OF SHOW-CASE, MORE THRILL-ING ADVEN-TURES WITH GREEN LANTERN!
The End
10

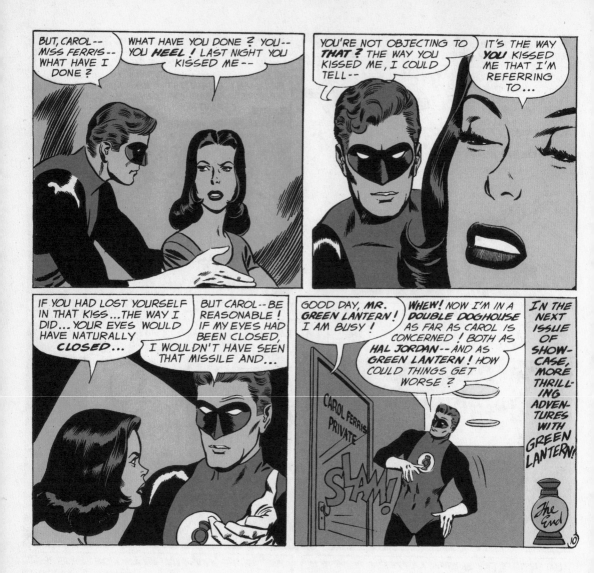

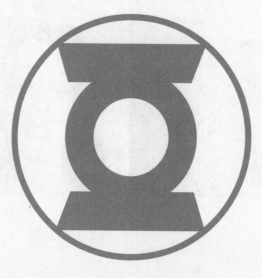

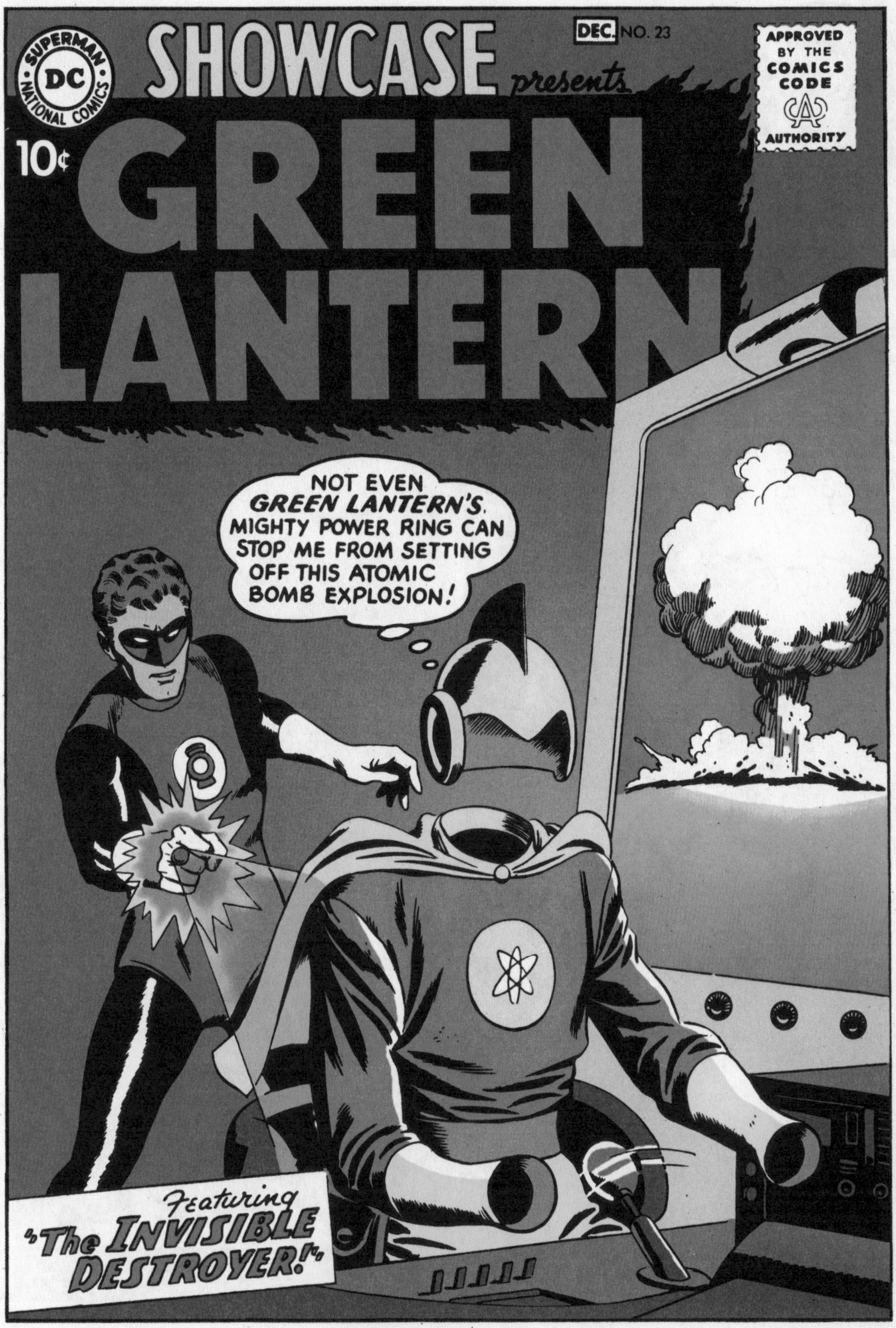
SUPERMAN DC NATIONAL COMICS
SHOWCASE presents
DEC. NO. 23
APPROVED BY THE COMICS CODE AUTHORITY
10¢
GREEN LANTERN
NOT EVEN GREEN LANTERN'S MIGHTY POWER RING CAN STOP ME FROM SETTING OFF THIS ATOMIC BOMB EXPLOSION!
Featuring "The INVISIBLE DESTROYER!"

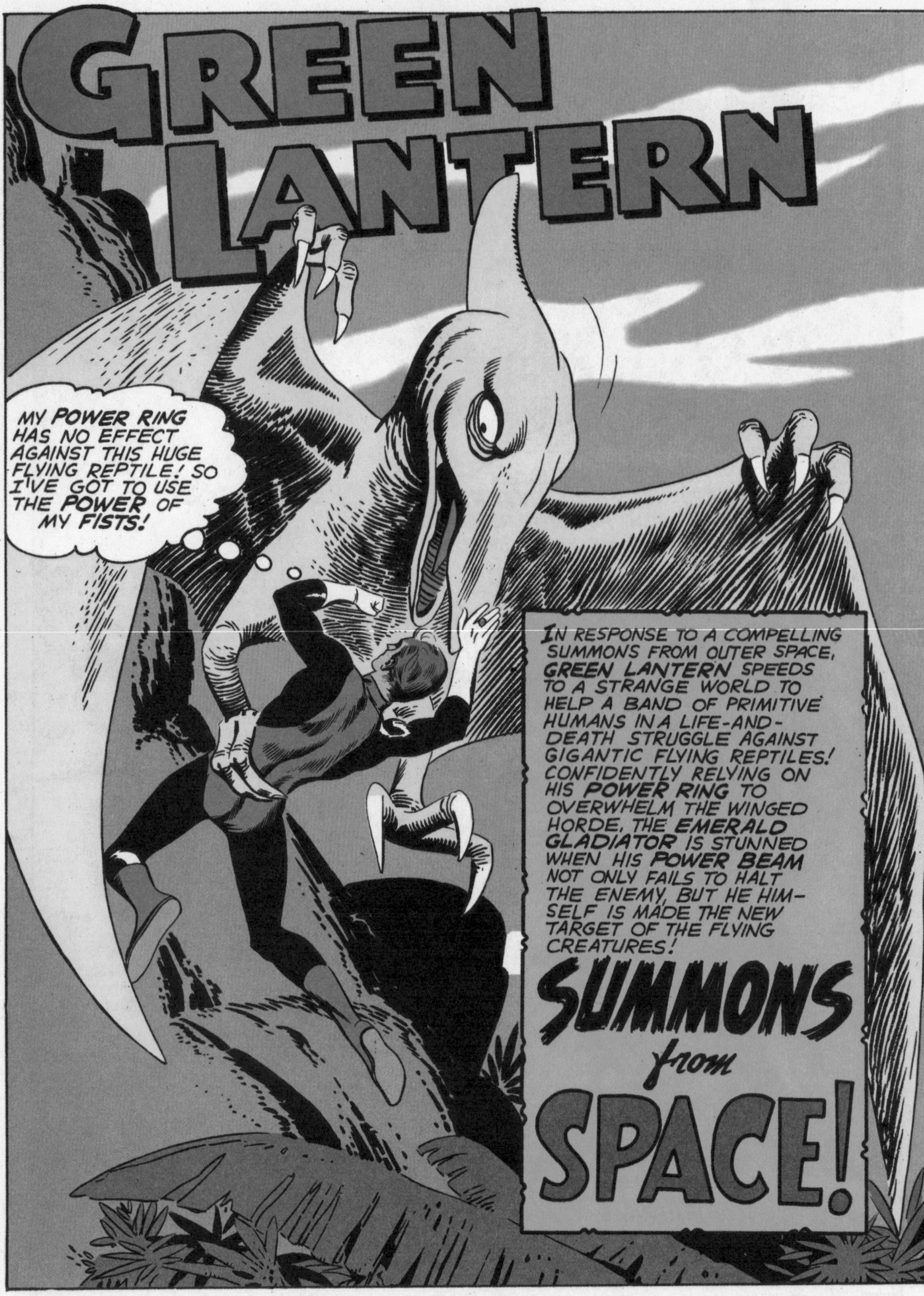
GREEN LANTERN
MY POWER RING HAS NO EFFECT AGAINST THIS HUGE FLYING REPTILE! SO I'VE GOT TO USE THE POWER OF MY FISTS!
IN RESPONSE TO A COMPELLING SUMMONS FROM OUTER SPACE, GREEN LANTERN SPEEDS TO A STRANGE WORLD TO HELP A BAND OF PRIMITIVE HUMANS IN A LIFE-AND-DEATH STRUGGLE AGAINST GIGANTIC FLYING REPTILES! CONFIDENTLY RELYING ON HIS POWER RING TO OVERWHELM THE WINGED HORDE, THE EMERALD GLADIATOR IS STUNNED WHEN HIS POWER BEAM NOT ONLY FAILS TO HALT THE ENEMY, BUT HE HIMSELF IS MADE THE NEW TARGET OF THE FLYING CREATURES!
SUMMONS from SPACE!

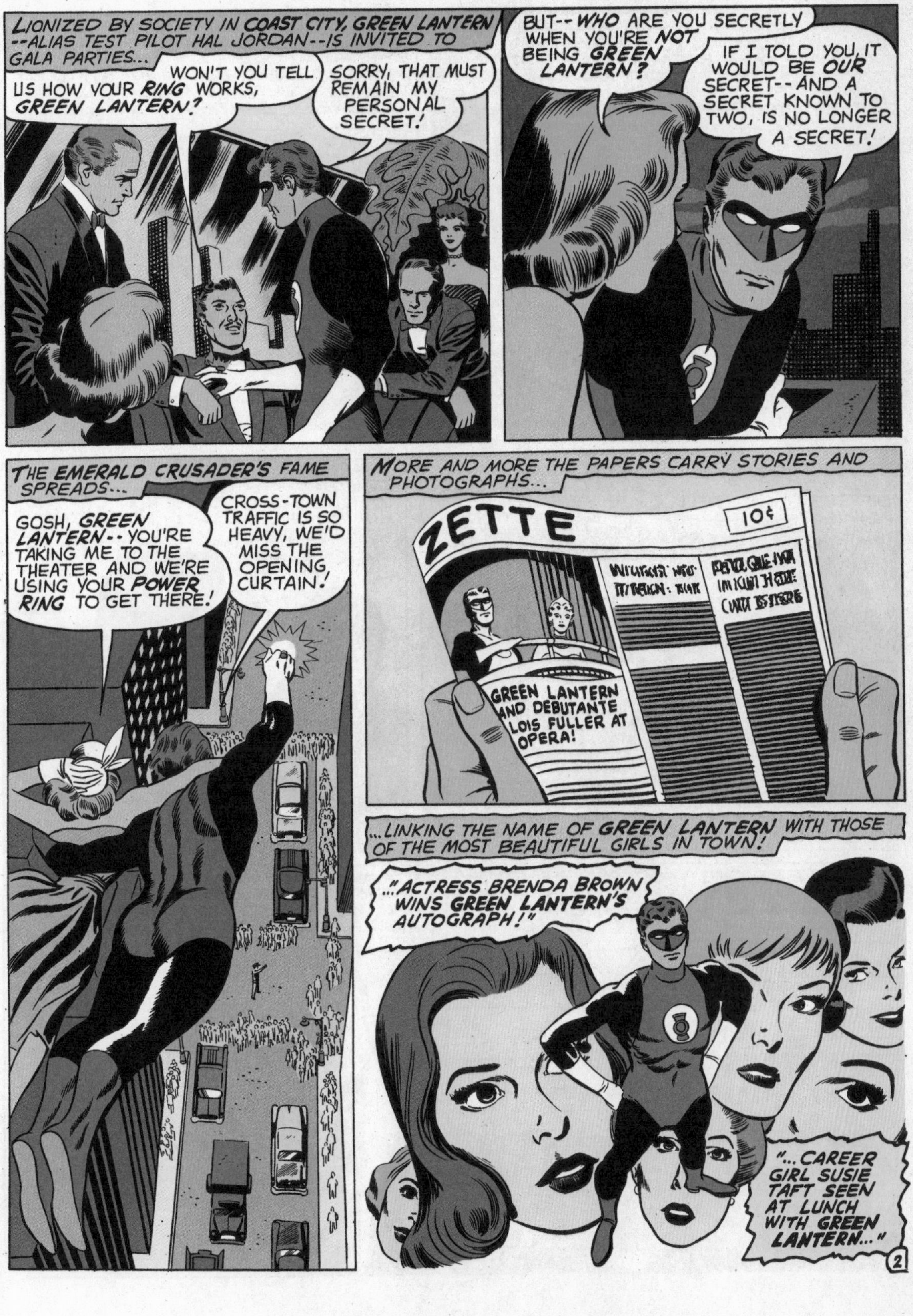
LIONIZED BY SOCIETY IN COAST CITY, GREEN LANTERN --ALIAS TEST PILOT HAL JORDAN--IS INVITED TO GALA PARTIES...
WON'T YOU TELL US HOW YOUR RING WORKS, GREEN LANTERN?
SORRY, THAT MUST REMAIN MY PERSONAL SECRET!
BUT--WHO ARE YOU SECRETLY WHEN YOU'RE NOT BEING GREEN LANTERN?
IF I TOLD YOU, IT WOULD BE OUR SECRET--AND A SECRET KNOWN TO TWO, IS NO LONGER A SECRET!
THE EMERALD CRUSADER'S FAME SPREADS...
GOSH, GREEN LANTERN--YOU'RE TAKING ME TO THE THEATER AND WE'RE USING YOUR POWER RING TO GET THERE!
CROSS-TOWN TRAFFIC IS SO HEAVY, WE'D MISS THE OPENING CURTAIN!
MORE AND MORE THE PAPERS CARRY STORIES AND PHOTOGRAPHS...
ZETTE
10¢
GREEN LANTERN AND DEBUTANTE LOIS FULLER AT OPERA!
...LINKING THE NAME OF GREEN LANTERN WITH THOSE OF THE MOST BEAUTIFUL GIRLS IN TOWN!
..."ACTRESS BRENDA BROWN WINS GREEN LANTERN'S AUTOGRAPH!"
"...CAREER GIRL SUSIE TAFT SEEN AT LUNCH WITH GREEN LANTERN..."
2

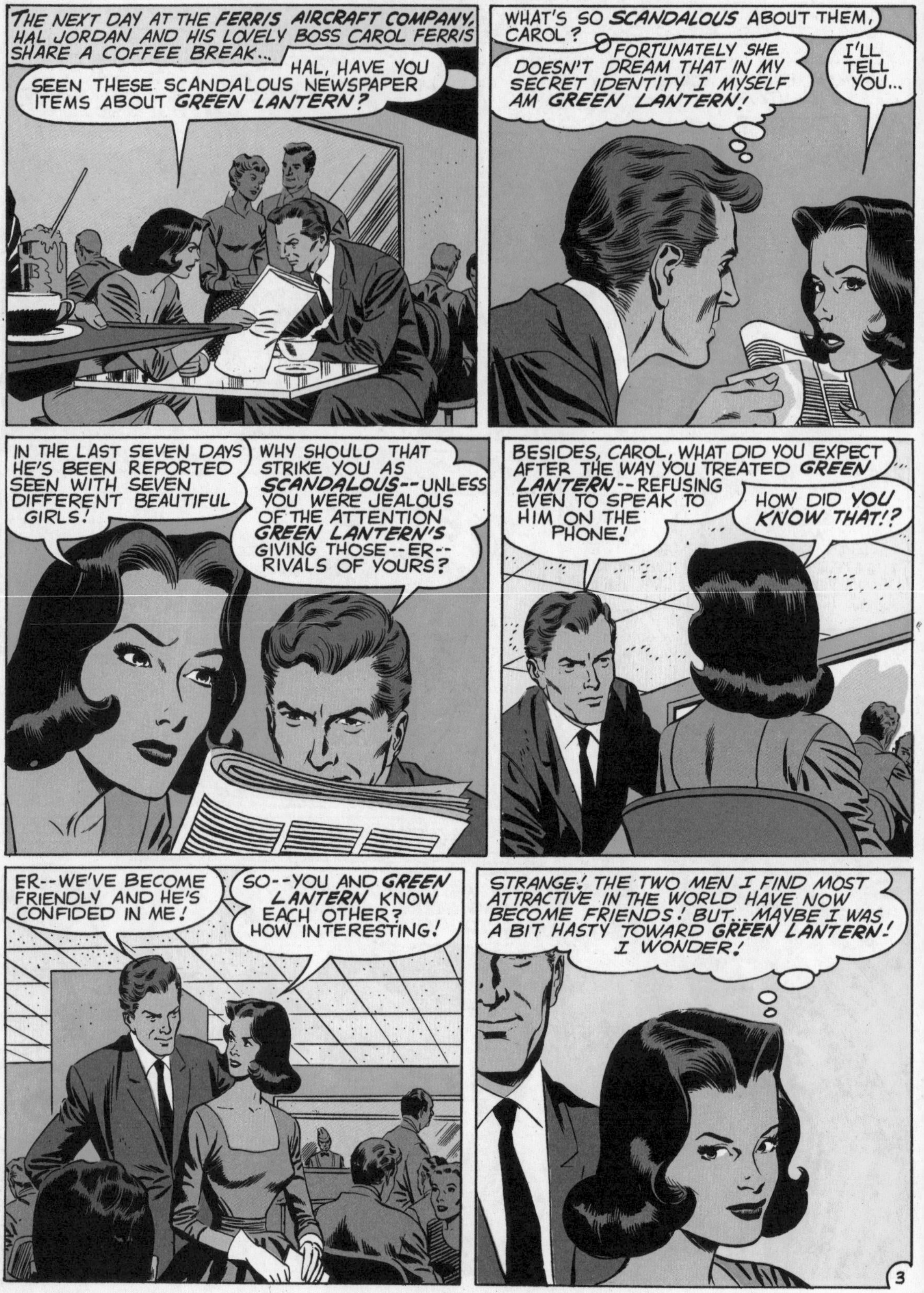
THE NEXT DAY AT THE FERRIS AIRCRAFT COMPANY, HAL JORDAN AND HIS LOVELY BOSS CAROL FERRIS SHARE A COFFEE BREAK...
HAL, HAVE YOU SEEN THESE SCANDALOUS NEWSPAPER ITEMS ABOUT GREEN LANTERN?
WHAT'S SO SCANDALOUS ABOUT THEM, CAROL?
FORTUNATELY SHE DOESN'T DREAM THAT IN MY SECRET IDENTITY I MYSELF AM GREEN LANTERN!
I'LL TELL YOU...
IN THE LAST SEVEN DAYS HE'S BEEN REPORTED SEEN WITH SEVEN DIFFERENT BEAUTIFUL GIRLS!
WHY SHOULD THAT STRIKE YOU AS SCANDALOUS--UNLESS YOU WERE JEALOUS OF THE ATTENTION GREEN LANTERN'S GIVING THOSE--ER--RIVALS OF YOURS?
BESIDES, CAROL, WHAT DID YOU EXPECT AFTER THE WAY YOU TREATED GREEN LANTERN--REFUSING EVEN TO SPEAK TO HIM ON THE PHONE!
HOW DID YOU KNOW THAT!?
ER--WE'VE BECOME FRIENDLY AND HE'S CONFIDED IN ME!
SO--YOU AND GREEN LANTERN KNOW EACH OTHER? HOW INTERESTING!
STRANGE! THE TWO MEN I FIND MOST ATTRACTIVE IN THE WORLD HAVE NOW BECOME FRIENDS! BUT... MAYBE I WAS A BIT HASTY TOWARD GREEN LANTERN! I WONDER!
3

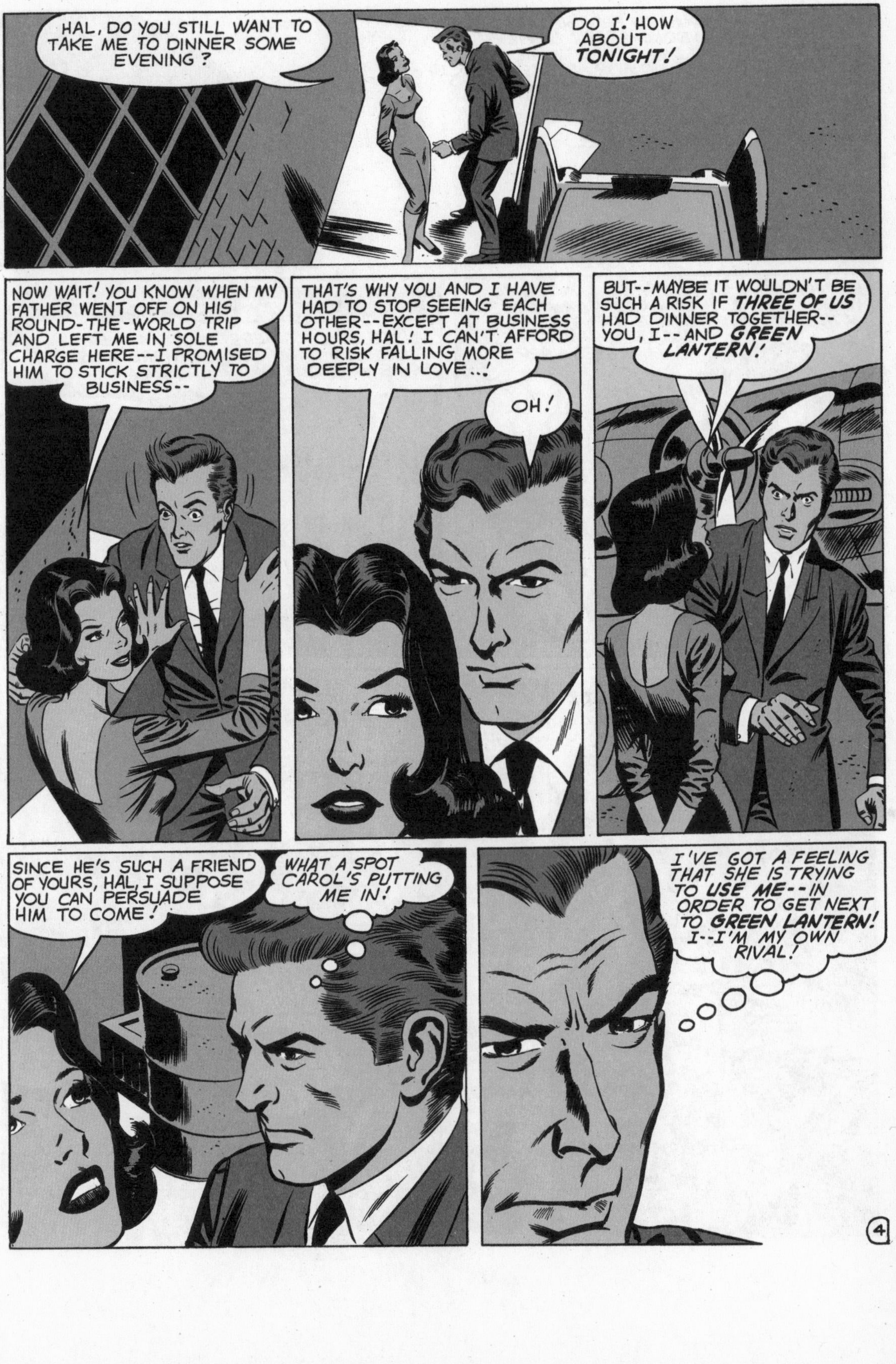
HAL, DO YOU STILL WANT TO TAKE ME TO DINNER SOME EVENING?
DO I! HOW ABOUT TONIGHT!
NOW WAIT! YOU KNOW WHEN MY FATHER WENT OFF ON HIS ROUND-THE-WORLD TRIP AND LEFT ME IN SOLE CHARGE HERE--I PROMISED HIM TO STICK STRICTLY TO BUSINESS--
THAT'S WHY YOU AND I HAVE HAD TO STOP SEEING EACH OTHER--EXCEPT AT BUSINESS HOURS, HAL! I CAN'T AFFORD TO RISK FALLING MORE DEEPLY IN LOVE..!
OH!
BUT--MAYBE IT WOULDN'T BE SUCH A RISK IF THREE OF US HAD DINNER TOGETHER--YOU, I--AND GREEN LANTERN!
SINCE HE'S SUCH A FRIEND OF YOURS, HAL, I SUPPOSE YOU CAN PERSUADE HIM TO COME!
WHAT A SPOT CAROL'S PUTTING ME IN!
I'VE GOT A FEELING THAT SHE IS TRYING TO USE ME--IN ORDER TO GET NEXT TO GREEN LANTERN! I--I'M MY OWN RIVAL!
4

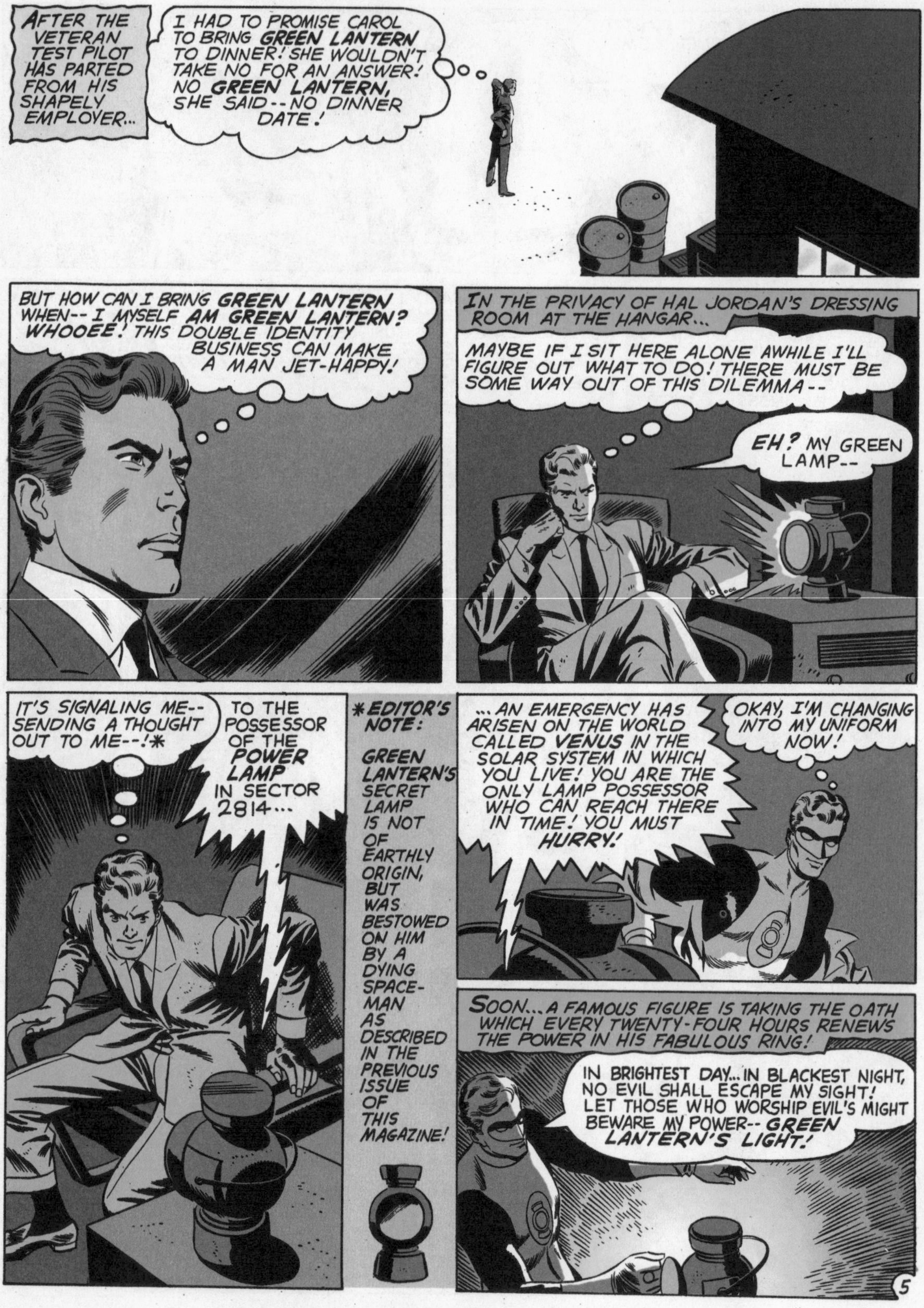
AFTER THE VETERAN TEST PILOT HAS PARTED FROM HIS SHAPELY EMPLOYER...
I HAD TO PROMISE CAROL TO BRING GREEN LANTERN TO DINNER! SHE WOULDN'T TAKE NO FOR AN ANSWER! NO GREEN LANTERN, SHE SAID--NO DINNER DATE!
BUT HOW CAN I BRING GREEN LANTERN WHEN-- I MYSELF AM GREEN LANTERN? WHOOEE! THIS DOUBLE IDENTITY BUSINESS CAN MAKE A MAN JET-HAPPY!
IN THE PRIVACY OF HAL JORDAN'S DRESSING ROOM AT THE HANGAR...
MAYBE IF I SIT HERE ALONE AWHILE I'LL FIGURE OUT WHAT TO DO! THERE MUST BE SOME WAY OUT OF THIS DILEMMA--
EH? MY GREEN LAMP--
IT'S SIGNALING ME--SENDING A THOUGHT OUT TO ME--!*
TO THE POSSESSOR OF THE POWER LAMP IN SECTOR 2814...
*EDITOR'S NOTE: GREEN LANTERN'S SECRET LAMP IS NOT OF EARTHLY ORIGIN, BUT WAS BESTOWED ON HIM BY A DYING SPACE-MAN AS DESCRIBED IN THE PREVIOUS ISSUE OF THIS MAGAZINE!
...AN EMERGENCY HAS ARISEN ON THE WORLD CALLED VENUS IN THE SOLAR SYSTEM IN WHICH YOU LIVE! YOU ARE THE ONLY LAMP POSSESSOR WHO CAN REACH THERE IN TIME! YOU MUST HURRY!
OKAY, I'M CHANGING INTO MY UNIFORM NOW!
SOON...A FAMOUS FIGURE IS TAKING THE OATH WHICH EVERY TWENTY-FOUR HOURS RENEWS THE POWER IN HIS FABULOUS RING!
IN BRIGHTEST DAY...IN BLACKEST NIGHT, NO EVIL SHALL ESCAPE MY SIGHT! LET THOSE WHO WORSHIP EVIL'S MIGHT BEWARE MY POWER-- GREEN LANTERN'S LIGHT!
5

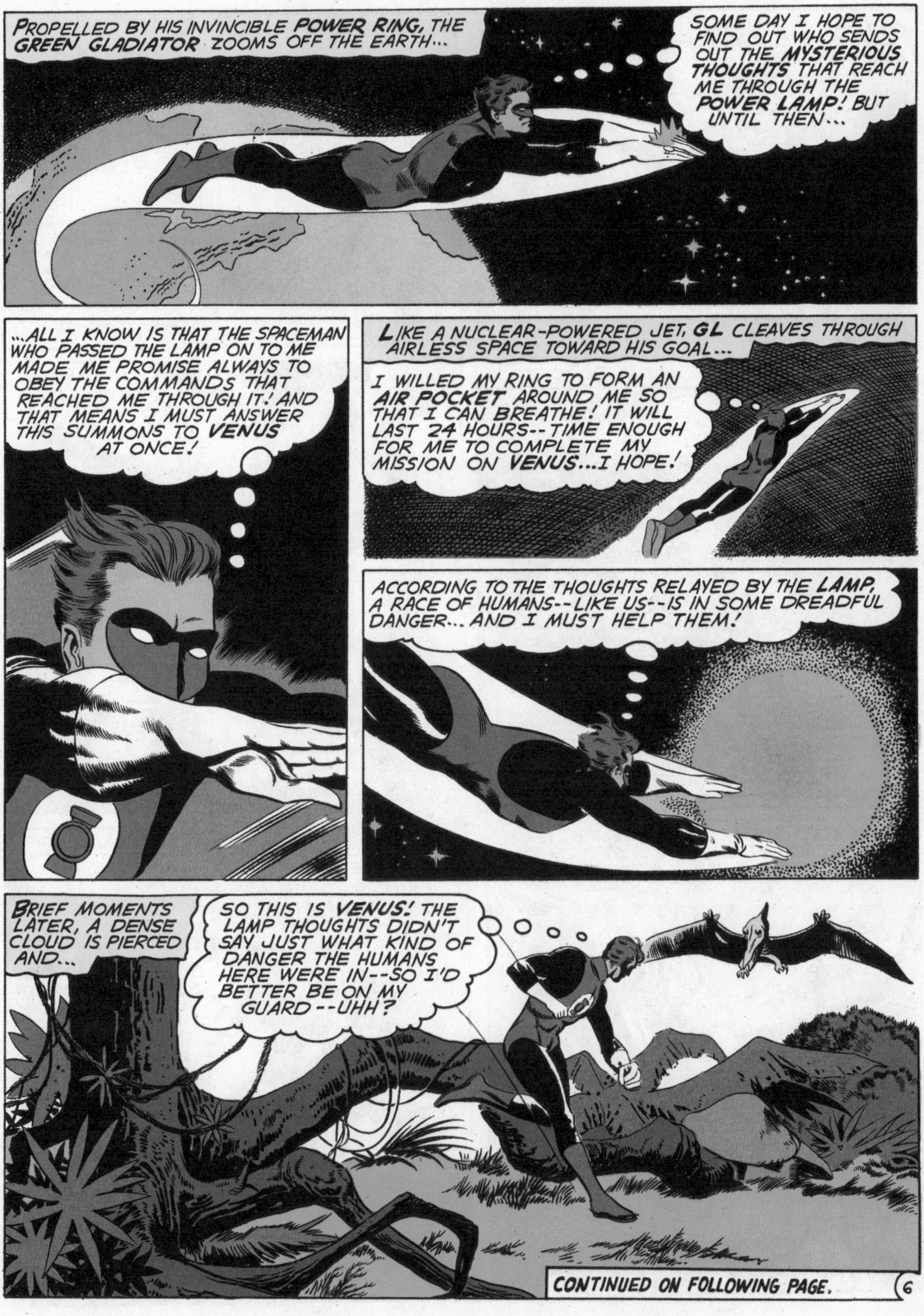
PROPELLED BY HIS INVINCIBLE POWER RING, THE GREEN GLADIATOR ZOOMS OFF THE EARTH...
SOME DAY I HOPE TO FIND OUT WHO SENDS OUT THE MYSTERIOUS THOUGHTS THAT REACH ME THROUGH THE POWER LAMP! BUT UNTIL THEN...
...ALL I KNOW IS THAT THE SPACEMAN WHO PASSED THE LAMP ON TO ME MADE ME PROMISE ALWAYS TO OBEY THE COMMANDS THAT REACHED ME THROUGH IT! AND THAT MEANS I MUST ANSWER THIS SUMMONS TO VENUS AT ONCE!
LIKE A NUCLEAR-POWERED JET, GL CLEAVES THROUGH AIRLESS SPACE TOWARD HIS GOAL...
I WILLED MY RING TO FORM AN AIR POCKET AROUND ME SO THAT I CAN BREATHE! IT WILL LAST 24 HOURS--TIME ENOUGH FOR ME TO COMPLETE MY MISSION ON VENUS...I HOPE!
ACCORDING TO THE THOUGHTS RELAYED BY THE LAMP, A RACE OF HUMANS--LIKE US--IS IN SOME DREADFUL DANGER... AND I MUST HELP THEM!
BRIEF MOMENTS LATER, A DENSE CLOUD IS PIERCED AND...
SO THIS IS VENUS! THE LAMP THOUGHTS DIDN'T SAY JUST WHAT KIND OF DANGER THE HUMANS HERE WERE IN--SO I'D BETTER BE ON MY GUARD--UHH?
CONTINUED ON FOLLOWING PAGE.
6

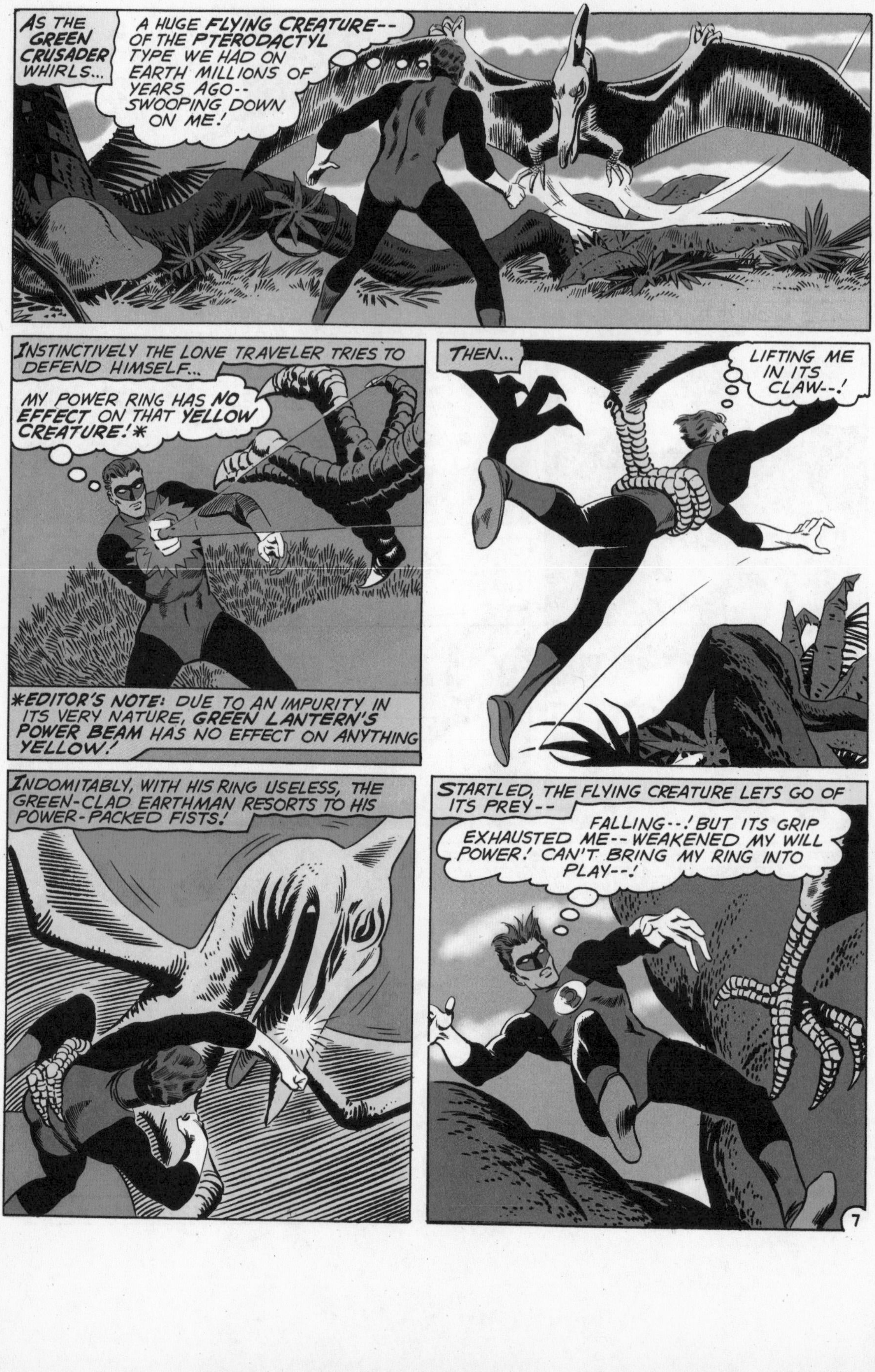
AS THE GREEN CRUSADER WHIRLS...
A HUGE FLYING CREATURE--OF THE PTERODACTYL TYPE WE HAD ON EARTH MILLIONS OF YEARS AGO--SWOOPING DOWN ON ME!
INSTINCTIVELY THE LONE TRAVELER TRIES TO DEFEND HIMSELF...
MY POWER RING HAS NO EFFECT ON THAT YELLOW CREATURE!*
*EDITOR'S NOTE: DUE TO AN IMPURITY IN ITS VERY NATURE, GREEN LANTERN'S POWER BEAM HAS NO EFFECT ON ANYTHING YELLOW!
THEN...
LIFTING ME IN ITS CLAW--!
INDOMITABLY, WITH HIS RING USELESS, THE GREEN-CLAD EARTHMAN RESORTS TO HIS POWER-PACKED FISTS!
STARTLED, THE FLYING CREATURE LETS GO OF ITS PREY--
FALLING--! BUT ITS GRIP EXHAUSTED ME--WEAKENED MY WILL POWER! CAN'T BRING MY RING INTO PLAY--!
7

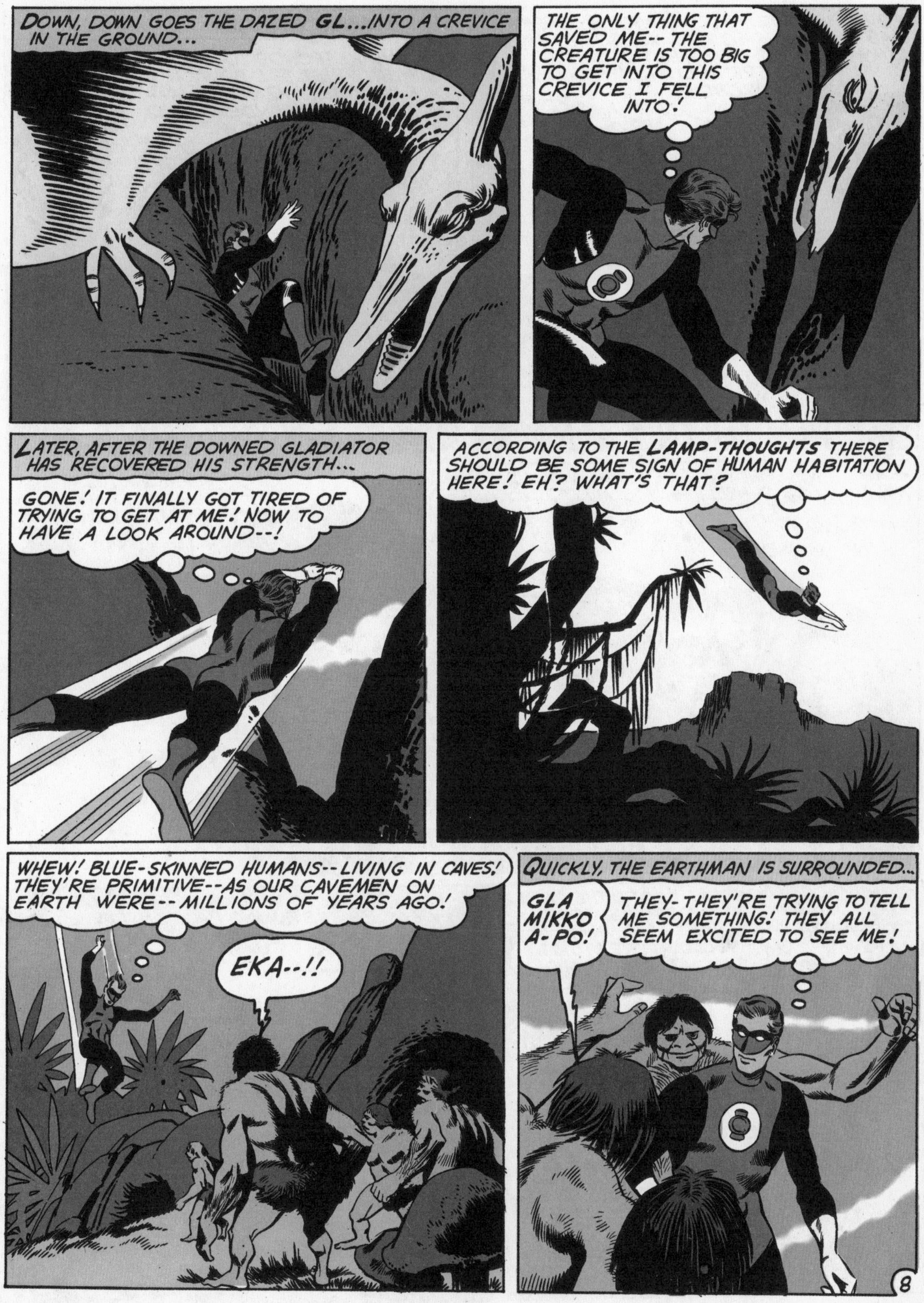
DOWN, DOWN GOES THE DAZED GL...INTO A CREVICE IN THE GROUND...
THE ONLY THING THAT SAVED ME-- THE CREATURE IS TOO BIG TO GET INTO THIS CREVICE I FELL INTO!
LATER, AFTER THE DOWNED GLADIATOR HAS RECOVERED HIS STRENGTH...
GONE! IT FINALLY GOT TIRED OF TRYING TO GET AT ME! NOW TO HAVE A LOOK AROUND--!
ACCORDING TO THE LAMP-THOUGHTS THERE SHOULD BE SOME SIGN OF HUMAN HABITATION HERE! EH? WHAT'S THAT?
WHEW! BLUE-SKINNED HUMANS--LIVING IN CAVES! THEY'RE PRIMITIVE--AS OUR CAVEMEN ON EARTH WERE--MILLIONS OF YEARS AGO!
EKA--!!
QUICKLY, THE EARTHMAN IS SURROUNDED...
GLA MIKKO A-PO!
THEY-THEY'RE TRYING TO TELL ME SOMETHING! THEY ALL SEEM EXCITED TO SEE ME!
8

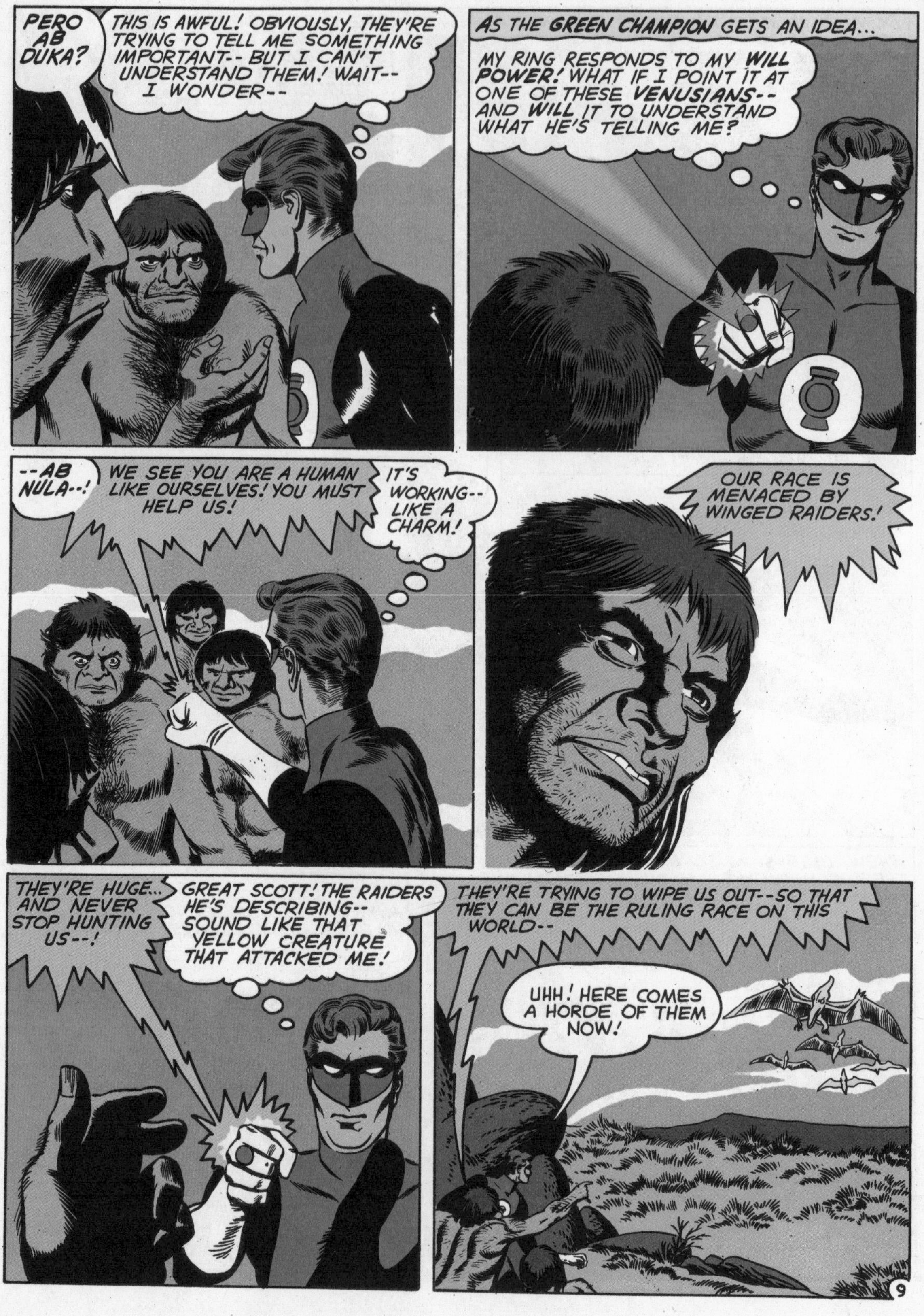
PERO AB DUKA?
THIS IS AWFUL! OBVIOUSLY, THEY'RE TRYING TO TELL ME SOMETHING IMPORTANT-- BUT I CAN'T UNDERSTAND THEM! WAIT-- I WONDER--
AS THE GREEN CHAMPION GETS AN IDEA...
MY RING RESPONDS TO MY WILL POWER! WHAT IF I POINT IT AT ONE OF THESE VENUSIANS-- AND WILL IT TO UNDERSTAND WHAT HE'S TELLING ME?
--AB NULA--!
WE SEE YOU ARE A HUMAN LIKE OURSELVES! YOU MUST HELP US!
IT'S WORKING-- LIKE A CHARM!
OUR RACE IS MENACED BY WINGED RAIDERS!
THEY'RE HUGE... AND NEVER STOP HUNTING US--!
GREAT SCOTT! THE RAIDERS HE'S DESCRIBING-- SOUND LIKE THAT YELLOW CREATURE THAT ATTACKED ME!
THEY'RE TRYING TO WIPE US OUT--SO THAT THEY CAN BE THE RULING RACE ON THIS WORLD--
UHH! HERE COMES A HORDE OF THEM NOW!
9

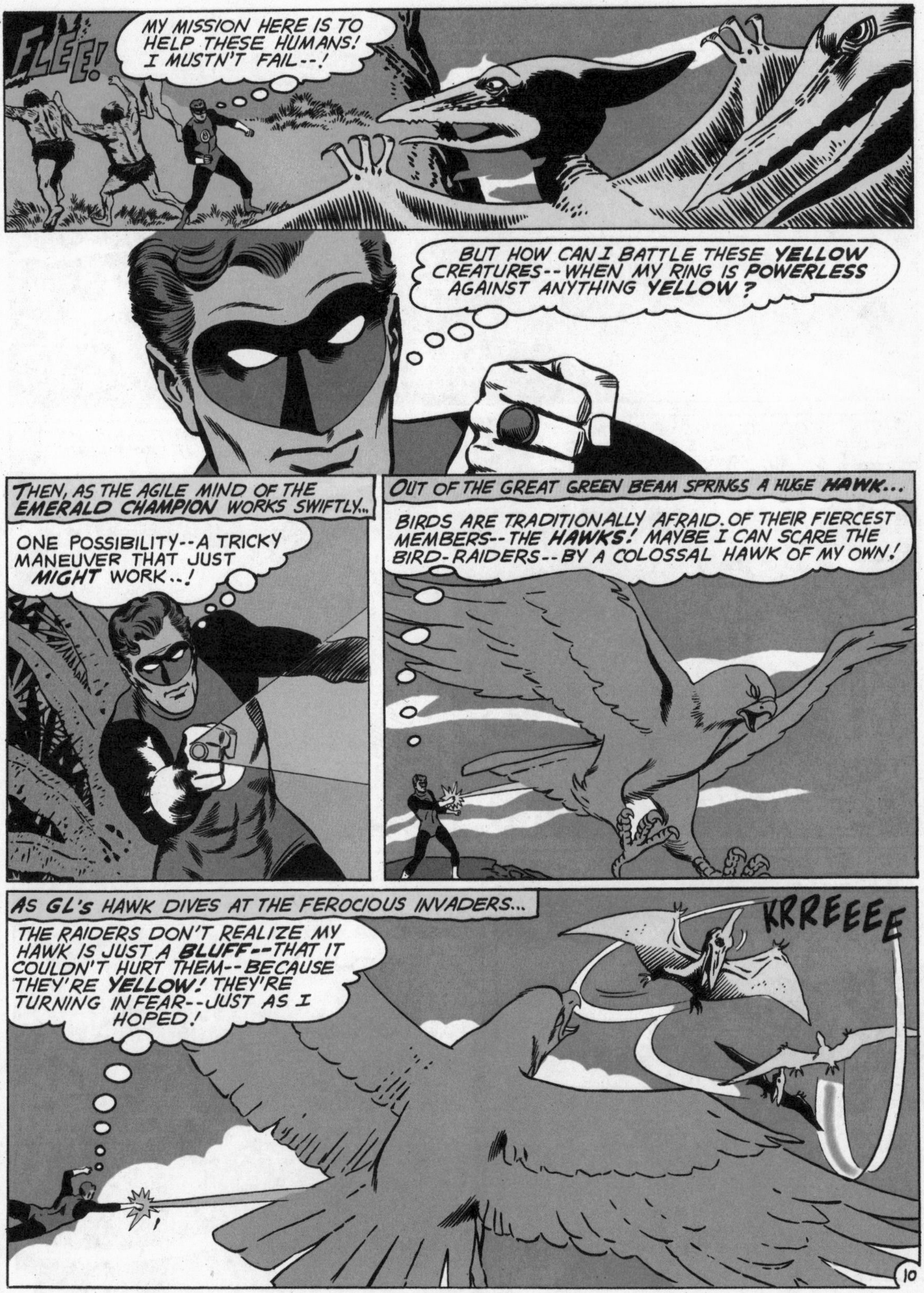
FLEEE!
MY MISSION HERE IS TO HELP THESE HUMANS! I MUSTN'T FAIL--!
BUT HOW CAN I BATTLE THESE YELLOW CREATURES--WHEN MY RING IS POWERLESS AGAINST ANYTHING YELLOW?
THEN, AS THE AGILE MIND OF THE EMERALD CHAMPION WORKS SWIFTLY...
ONE POSSIBILITY--A TRICKY MANEUVER THAT JUST MIGHT WORK..!
OUT OF THE GREAT GREEN BEAM SPRINGS A HUGE HAWK...
BIRDS ARE TRADITIONALLY AFRAID OF THEIR FIERCEST MEMBERS--THE HAWKS! MAYBE I CAN SCARE THE BIRD-RAIDERS--BY A COLOSSAL HAWK OF MY OWN!
AS GL's HAWK DIVES AT THE FEROCIOUS INVADERS...
THE RAIDERS DON'T REALIZE MY HAWK IS JUST A BLUFF--THAT IT COULDN'T HURT THEM--BECAUSE THEY'RE YELLOW! THEY'RE TURNING IN FEAR--JUST AS I HOPED!
KRREEEEE
10

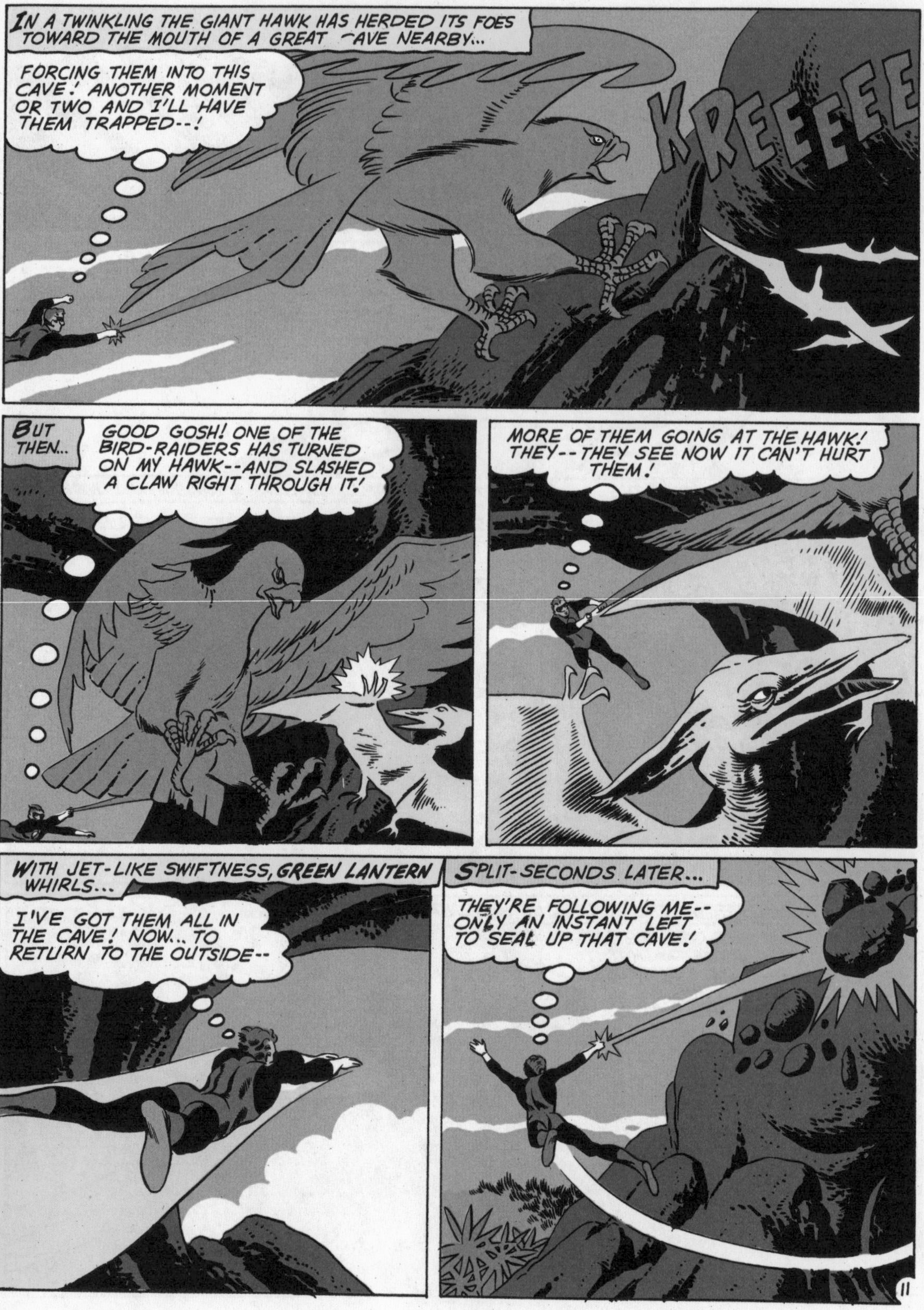
IN A TWINKLING THE GIANT HAWK HAS HERDED ITS FOES TOWARD THE MOUTH OF A GREAT CAVE NEARBY...
FORCING THEM INTO THIS CAVE! ANOTHER MOMENT OR TWO AND I'LL HAVE THEM TRAPPED--!
KREEEEE
BUT THEN...
GOOD GOSH! ONE OF THE BIRD-RAIDERS HAS TURNED ON MY HAWK--AND SLASHED A CLAW RIGHT THROUGH IT!
MORE OF THEM GOING AT THE HAWK! THEY--THEY SEE NOW IT CAN'T HURT THEM!
WITH JET-LIKE SWIFTNESS, GREEN LANTERN WHIRLS...
I'VE GOT THEM ALL IN THE CAVE! NOW... TO RETURN TO THE OUTSIDE--
SPLIT-SECONDS LATER...
THEY'RE FOLLOWING ME--ONLY AN INSTANT LEFT TO SEAL UP THAT CAVE!
11

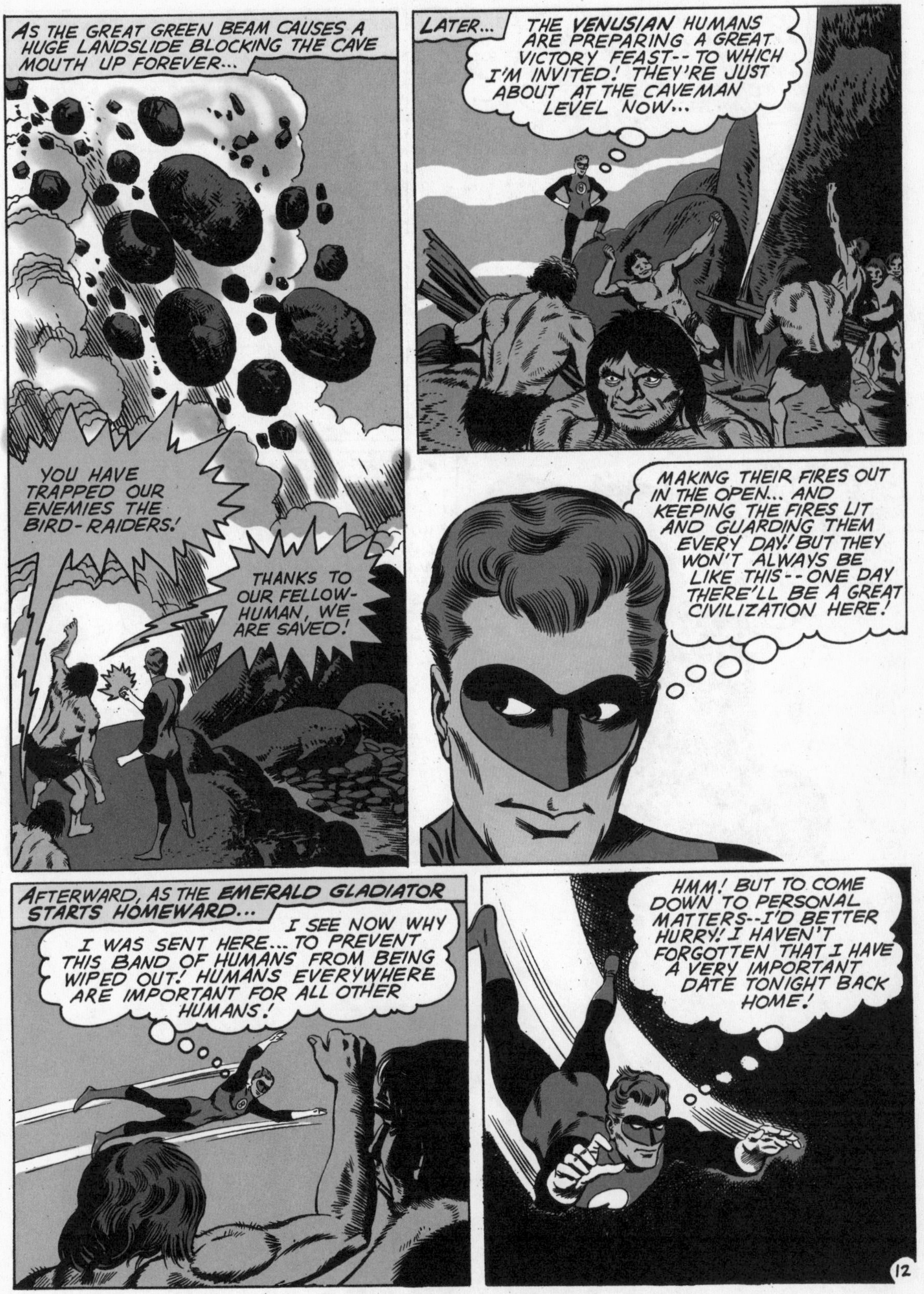
AS THE GREAT GREEN BEAM CAUSES A HUGE LANDSLIDE BLOCKING THE CAVE MOUTH UP FOREVER...
YOU HAVE TRAPPED OUR ENEMIES THE BIRD-RAIDERS!
THANKS TO OUR FELLOW-HUMAN, WE ARE SAVED!
LATER...
THE VENUSIAN HUMANS ARE PREPARING A GREAT VICTORY FEAST-- TO WHICH I'M INVITED! THEY'RE JUST ABOUT AT THE CAVEMAN LEVEL NOW...
MAKING THEIR FIRES OUT IN THE OPEN... AND KEEPING THE FIRES LIT AND GUARDING THEM EVERY DAY! BUT THEY WON'T ALWAYS BE LIKE THIS--ONE DAY THERE'LL BE A GREAT CIVILIZATION HERE!
AFTERWARD, AS THE EMERALD GLADIATOR STARTS HOMEWARD...
I SEE NOW WHY I WAS SENT HERE... TO PREVENT THIS BAND OF HUMANS FROM BEING WIPED OUT! HUMANS EVERYWHERE ARE IMPORTANT FOR ALL OTHER HUMANS!
HMM! BUT TO COME DOWN TO PERSONAL MATTERS--I'D BETTER HURRY! I HAVEN'T FORGOTTEN THAT I HAVE A VERY IMPORTANT DATE TONIGHT BACK HOME!
12

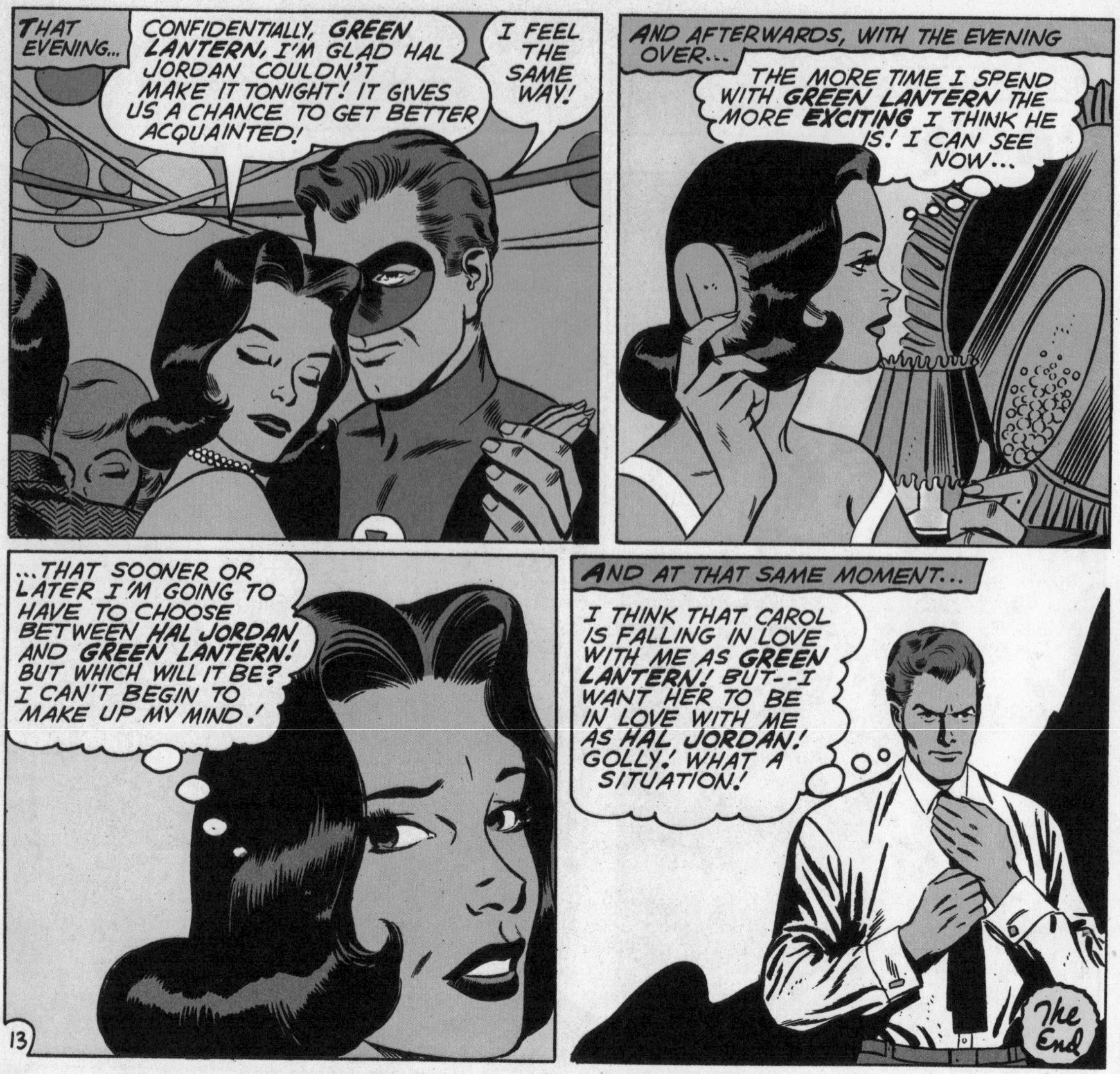
THAT EVENING...
CONFIDENTIALLY, GREEN LANTERN, I'M GLAD HAL JORDAN COULDN'T MAKE IT TONIGHT! IT GIVES US A CHANCE TO GET BETTER ACQUAINTED!
I FEEL THE SAME WAY!
AND AFTERWARDS, WITH THE EVENING OVER...
THE MORE TIME I SPEND WITH GREEN LANTERN THE MORE EXCITING I THINK HE IS! I CAN SEE NOW...
...THAT SOONER OR LATER I'M GOING TO HAVE TO CHOOSE BETWEEN HAL JORDAN AND GREEN LANTERN! BUT WHICH WILL IT BE? I CAN'T BEGIN TO MAKE UP MY MIND!
13
AND AT THAT SAME MOMENT...
I THINK THAT CAROL IS FALLING IN LOVE WITH ME AS GREEN LANTERN! BUT--I WANT HER TO BE IN LOVE WITH ME AS HAL JORDAN! GOLLY! WHAT A SITUATION!
The End

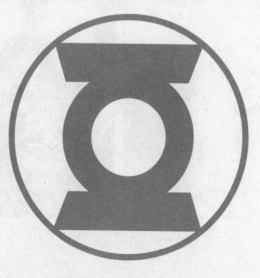

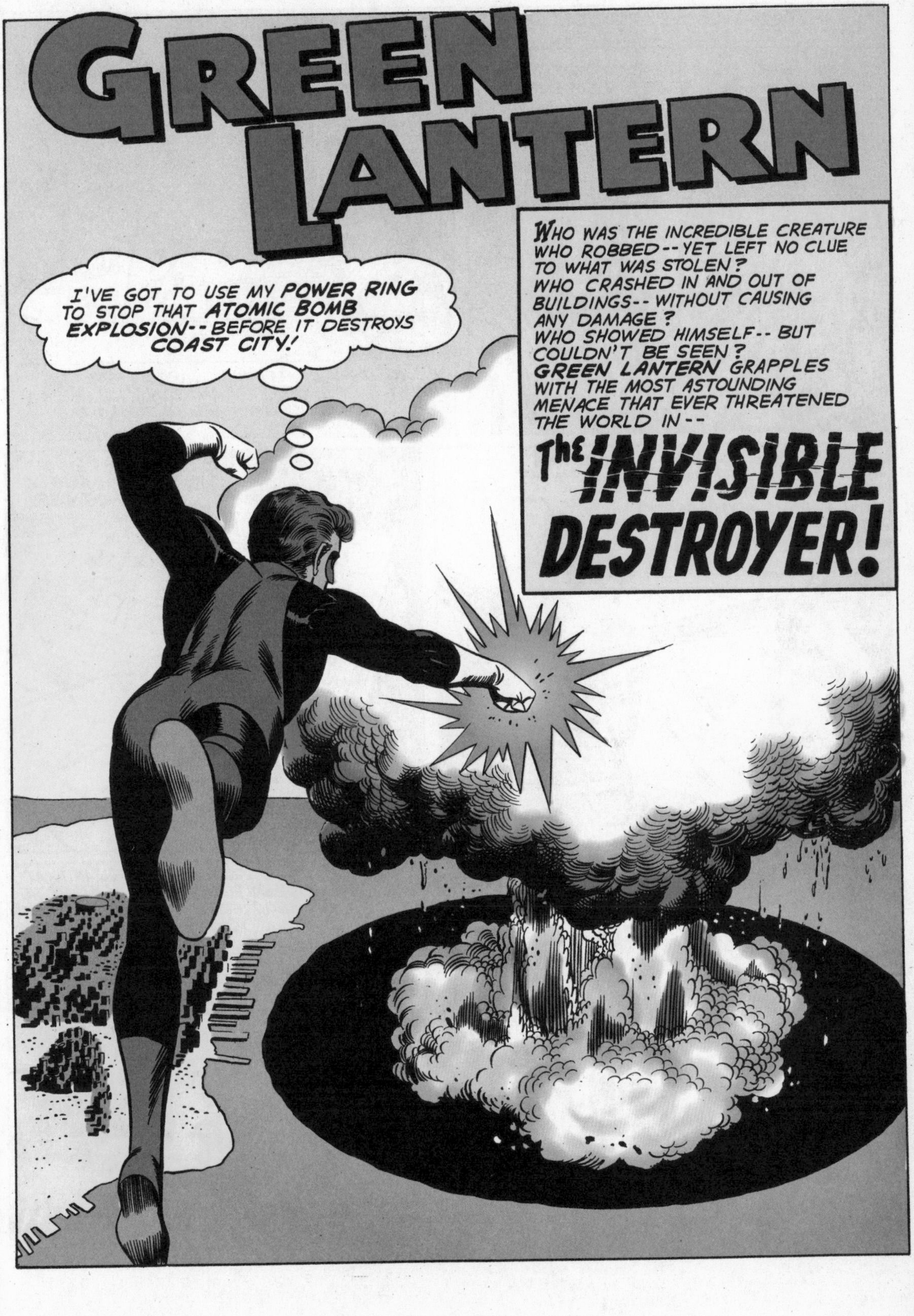
GREEN LANTERN
WHO WAS THE INCREDIBLE CREATURE WHO ROBBED--YET LEFT NO CLUE TO WHAT WAS STOLEN? WHO CRASHED IN AND OUT OF BUILDINGS--WITHOUT CAUSING ANY DAMAGE? WHO SHOWED HIMSELF--BUT COULDN'T BE SEEN? GREEN LANTERN GRAPPLES WITH THE MOST ASTOUNDING MENACE THAT EVER THREATENED THE WORLD IN--
THE INVISIBLE DESTROYER!
I'VE GOT TO USE MY POWER RING TO STOP THAT ATOMIC BOMB EXPLOSION--BEFORE IT DESTROYS COAST CITY!

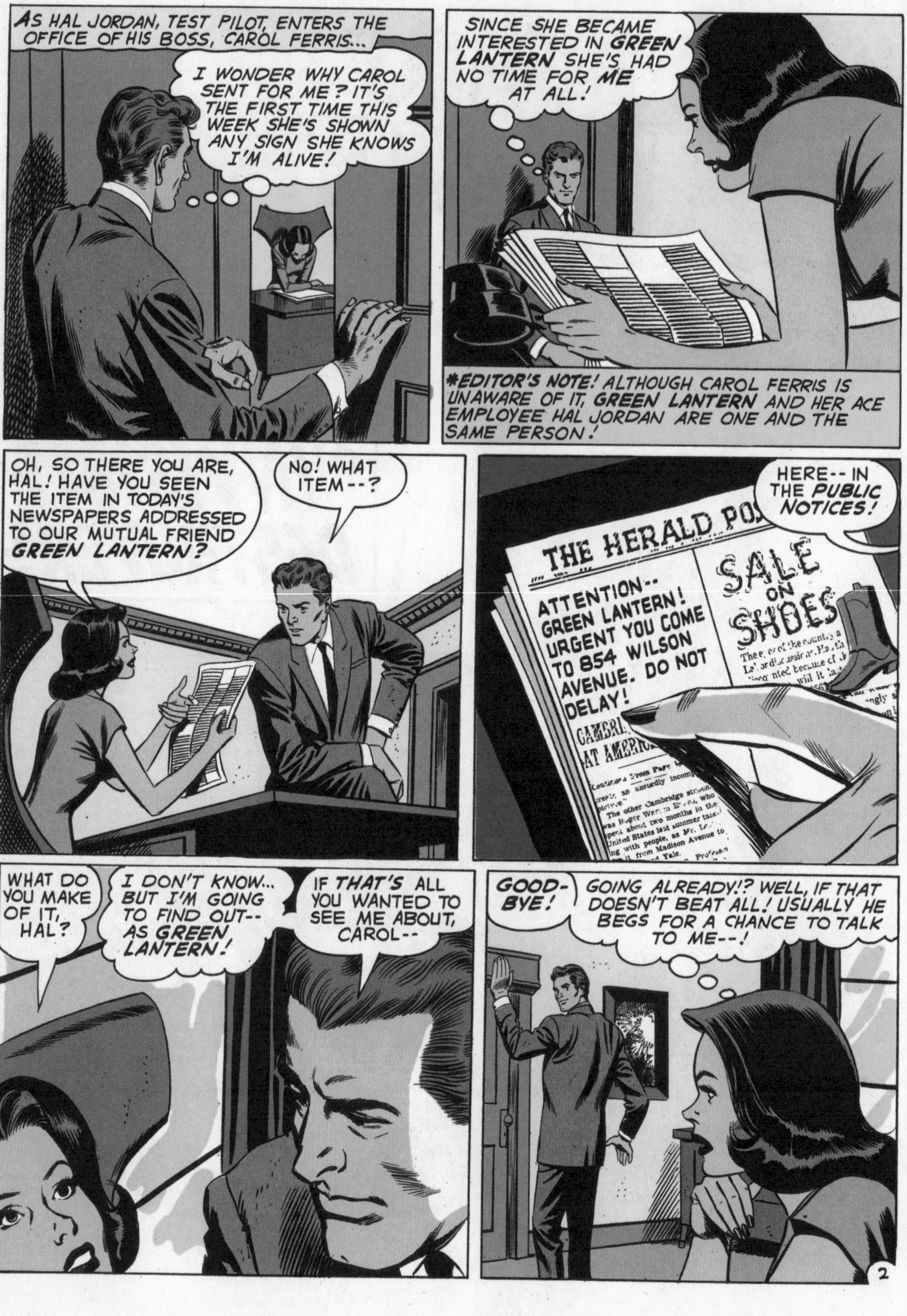
AS HAL JORDAN, TEST PILOT, ENTERS THE OFFICE OF HIS BOSS, CAROL FERRIS...
I WONDER WHY CAROL SENT FOR ME? IT'S THE FIRST TIME THIS WEEK SHE'S SHOWN ANY SIGN SHE KNOWS I'M ALIVE!
SINCE SHE BECAME INTERESTED IN GREEN LANTERN SHE'S HAD NO TIME FOR ME AT ALL!
*EDITOR'S NOTE! ALTHOUGH CAROL FERRIS IS UNAWARE OF IT, GREEN LANTERN AND HER ACE EMPLOYEE HAL JORDAN ARE ONE AND THE SAME PERSON!
OH, SO THERE YOU ARE, HAL! HAVE YOU SEEN THE ITEM IN TODAY'S NEWSPAPERS ADDRESSED TO OUR MUTUAL FRIEND GREEN LANTERN?
NO! WHAT ITEM--?
HERE-- IN THE PUBLIC NOTICES!
THE HERALD POS
ATTENTION-- GREEN LANTERN! URGENT YOU COME TO 854 WILSON AVENUE. DO NOT DELAY!
SALE ON SHOES
WHAT DO YOU MAKE OF IT, HAL?
I DON'T KNOW... BUT I'M GOING TO FIND OUT-- AS GREEN LANTERN!
IF THAT'S ALL YOU WANTED TO SEE ME ABOUT, CAROL--
GOOD-BYE!
GOING ALREADY!? WELL, IF THAT DOESN'T BEAT ALL! USUALLY HE BEGS FOR A CHANCE TO TALK TO ME--!
2

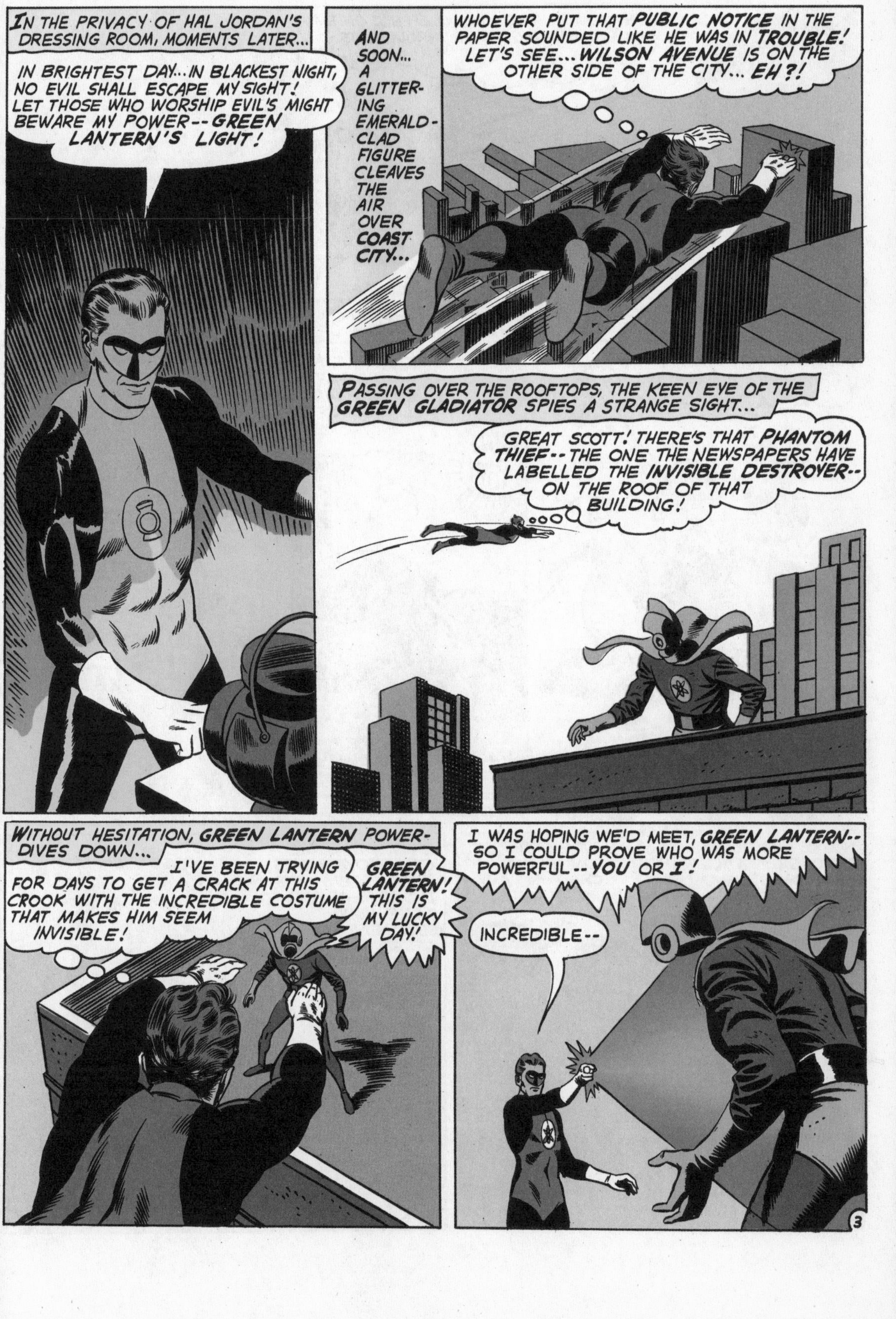
IN THE PRIVACY OF HAL JORDAN'S DRESSING ROOM, MOMENTS LATER...
IN BRIGHTEST DAY... IN BLACKEST NIGHT, NO EVIL SHALL ESCAPE MY SIGHT! LET THOSE WHO WORSHIP EVIL'S MIGHT BEWARE MY POWER -- GREEN LANTERN'S LIGHT!
AND SOON... A GLITTERING EMERALD-CLAD FIGURE CLEAVES THE AIR OVER COAST CITY...
WHOEVER PUT THAT PUBLIC NOTICE IN THE PAPER SOUNDED LIKE HE WAS IN TROUBLE! LET'S SEE... WILSON AVENUE IS ON THE OTHER SIDE OF THE CITY... EH?!
PASSING OVER THE ROOFTOPS, THE KEEN EYE OF THE GREEN GLADIATOR SPIES A STRANGE SIGHT...
GREAT SCOTT! THERE'S THAT PHANTOM THIEF -- THE ONE THE NEWSPAPERS HAVE LABELLED THE INVISIBLE DESTROYER -- ON THE ROOF OF THAT BUILDING!
WITHOUT HESITATION, GREEN LANTERN POWER-DIVES DOWN...
I'VE BEEN TRYING FOR DAYS TO GET A CRACK AT THIS CROOK WITH THE INCREDIBLE COSTUME THAT MAKES HIM SEEM INVISIBLE!
GREEN LANTERN! THIS IS MY LUCKY DAY!
I WAS HOPING WE'D MEET, GREEN LANTERN -- SO I COULD PROVE WHO WAS MORE POWERFUL -- YOU OR I!
INCREDIBLE --
3

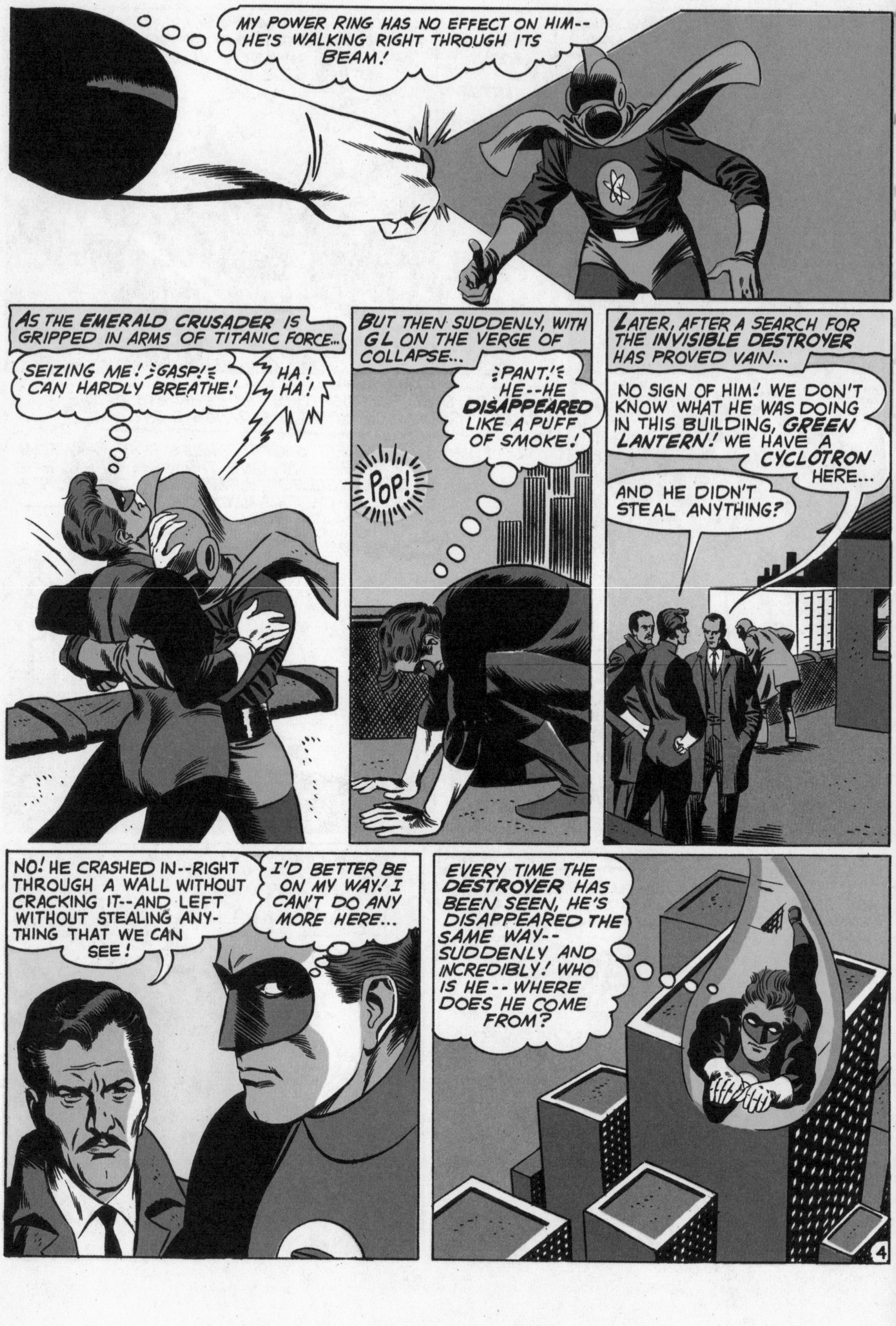

MY POWER RING HAS NO EFFECT ON HIM--HE'S WALKING RIGHT THROUGH ITS BEAM!
AS THE EMERALD CRUSADER IS GRIPPED IN ARMS OF TITANIC FORCE...
SEIZING ME! GASP! CAN HARDLY BREATHE!
HA! HA!
BUT THEN SUDDENLY, WITH GL ON THE VERGE OF COLLAPSE...
PANT! HE--HE DISAPPEARED LIKE A PUFF OF SMOKE!
POP!
LATER, AFTER A SEARCH FOR THE INVISIBLE DESTROYER HAS PROVED VAIN...
NO SIGN OF HIM! WE DON'T KNOW WHAT HE WAS DOING IN THIS BUILDING, GREEN LANTERN! WE HAVE A CYCLOTRON HERE...
AND HE DIDN'T STEAL ANYTHING?
NO! HE CRASHED IN--RIGHT THROUGH A WALL WITHOUT CRACKING IT--AND LEFT WITHOUT STEALING ANYTHING THAT WE CAN SEE!
I'D BETTER BE ON MY WAY! I CAN'T DO ANY MORE HERE...
EVERY TIME THE DESTROYER HAS BEEN SEEN, HE'S DISAPPEARED THE SAME WAY--SUDDENLY AND INCREDIBLY! WHO IS HE--WHERE DOES HE COME FROM?
4

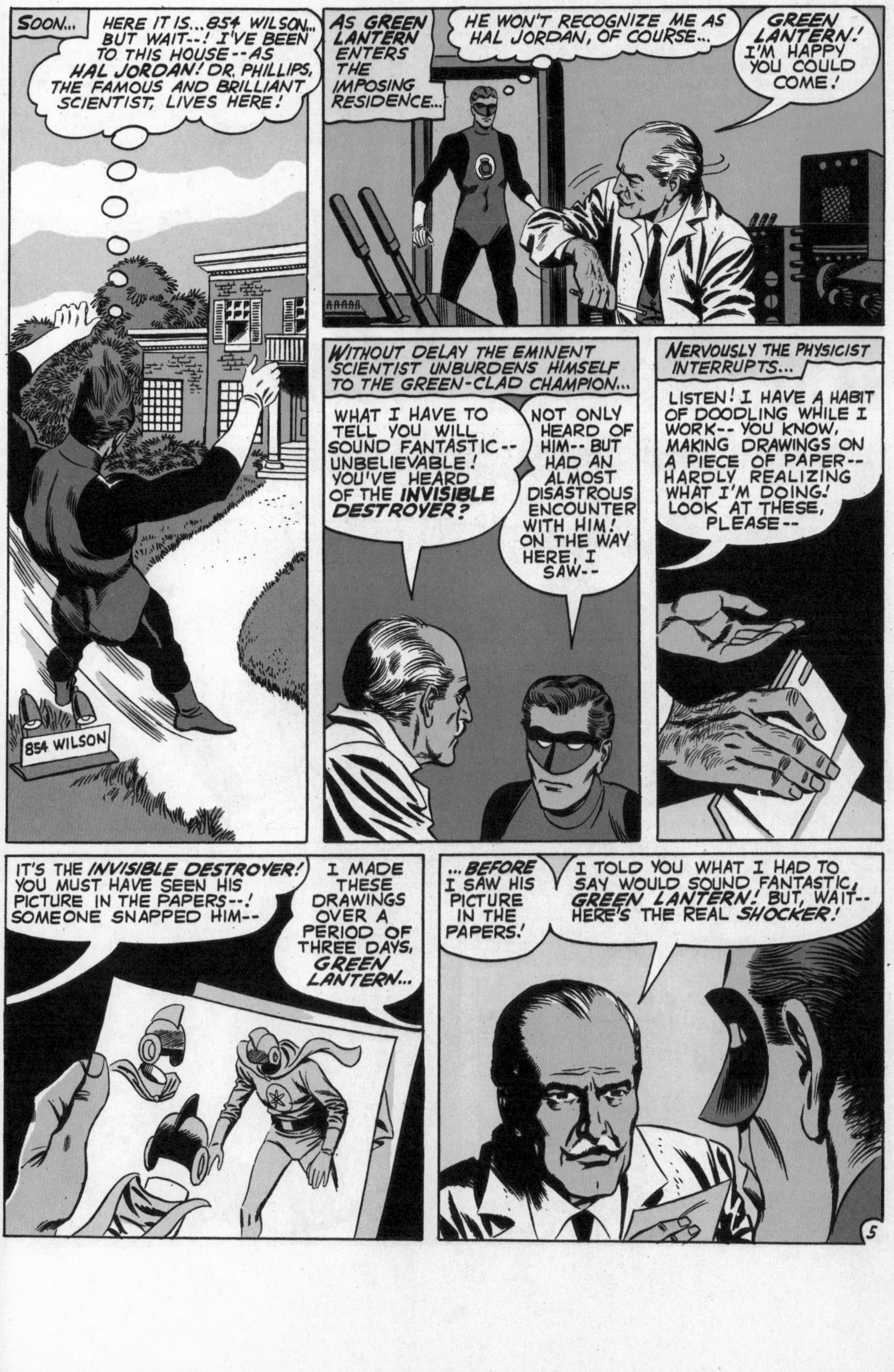
SOON...
HERE IT IS...854 WILSON... BUT WAIT--! I'VE BEEN TO THIS HOUSE--AS HAL JORDAN! DR. PHILLIPS, THE FAMOUS AND BRILLIANT SCIENTIST, LIVES HERE!
854 WILSON
AS GREEN LANTERN ENTERS THE IMPOSING RESIDENCE...
HE WON'T RECOGNIZE ME AS HAL JORDAN, OF COURSE...
GREEN LANTERN! I'M HAPPY YOU COULD COME!
WITHOUT DELAY THE EMINENT SCIENTIST UNBURDENS HIMSELF TO THE GREEN-CLAD CHAMPION...
WHAT I HAVE TO TELL YOU WILL SOUND FANTASTIC--UNBELIEVABLE! YOU'VE HEARD OF THE INVISIBLE DESTROYER?
NOT ONLY HEARD OF HIM--BUT HAD AN ALMOST DISASTROUS ENCOUNTER WITH HIM! ON THE WAY HERE, I SAW--
NERVOUSLY THE PHYSICIST INTERRUPTS...
LISTEN! I HAVE A HABIT OF DOODLING WHILE I WORK--YOU KNOW, MAKING DRAWINGS ON A PIECE OF PAPER--HARDLY REALIZING WHAT I'M DOING! LOOK AT THESE, PLEASE--
IT'S THE INVISIBLE DESTROYER! YOU MUST HAVE SEEN HIS PICTURE IN THE PAPERS--! SOMEONE SNAPPED HIM--
I MADE THESE DRAWINGS OVER A PERIOD OF THREE DAYS, GREEN LANTERN...
...BEFORE I SAW HIS PICTURE IN THE PAPERS!
I TOLD YOU WHAT I HAD TO SAY WOULD SOUND FANTASTIC, GREEN LANTERN! BUT, WAIT--HERE'S THE REAL SHOCKER!
5

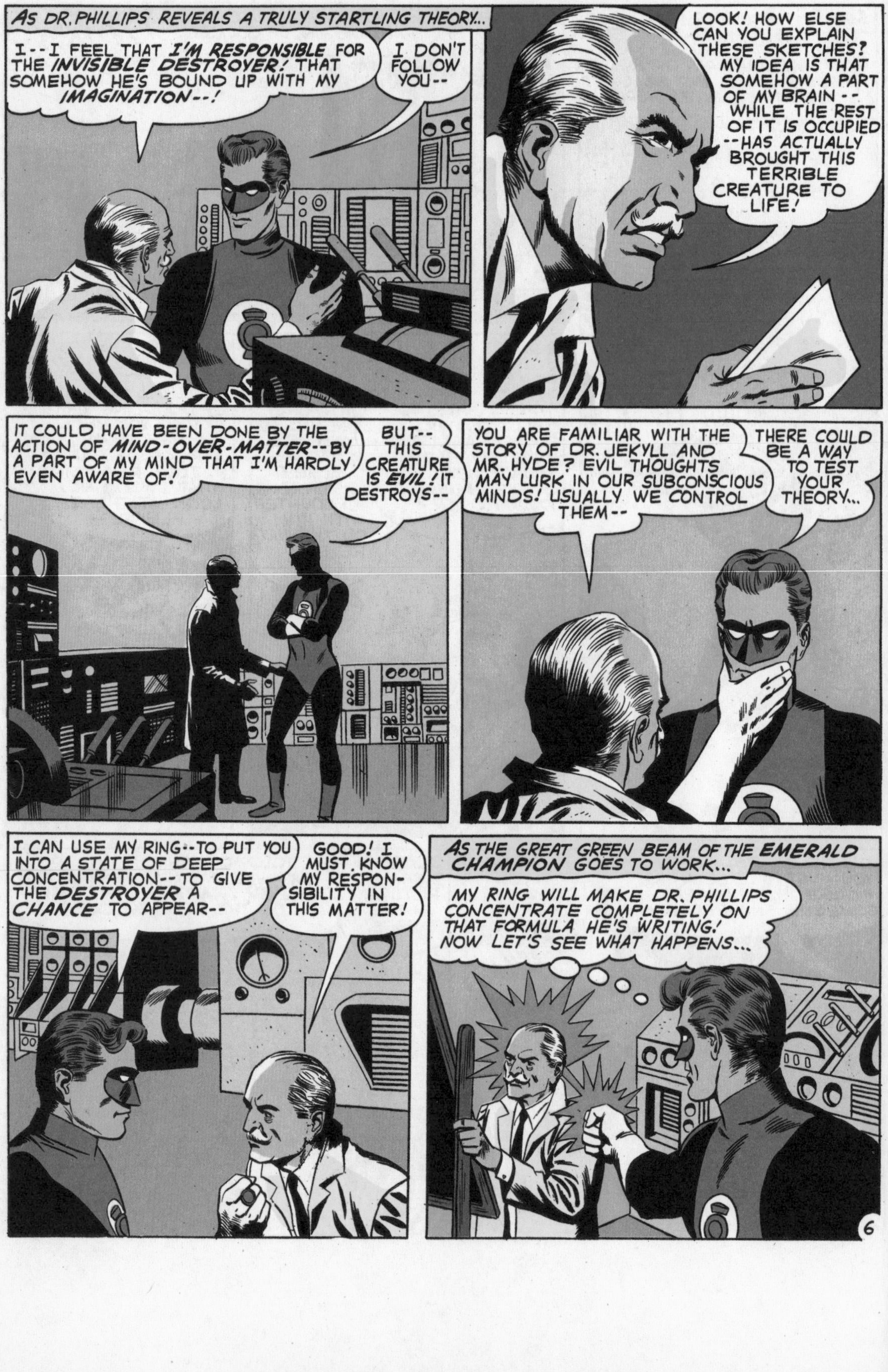

AS DR. PHILLIPS REVEALS A TRULY STARTLING THEORY...
I--I FEEL THAT I'M RESPONSIBLE FOR THE INVISIBLE DESTROYER! THAT SOMEHOW HE'S BOUND UP WITH MY IMAGINATION--!
I DON'T FOLLOW YOU--
LOOK! HOW ELSE CAN YOU EXPLAIN THESE SKETCHES? MY IDEA IS THAT SOMEHOW A PART OF MY BRAIN--WHILE THE REST OF IT IS OCCUPIED--HAS ACTUALLY BROUGHT THIS TERRIBLE CREATURE TO LIFE!
IT COULD HAVE BEEN DONE BY THE ACTION OF MIND-OVER-MATTER--BY A PART OF MY MIND THAT I'M HARDLY EVEN AWARE OF!
BUT--THIS CREATURE IS EVIL! IT DESTROYS--
YOU ARE FAMILIAR WITH THE STORY OF DR. JEKYLL AND MR. HYDE? EVIL THOUGHTS MAY LURK IN OUR SUBCONSCIOUS MINDS! USUALLY WE CONTROL THEM--
THERE COULD BE A WAY TO TEST YOUR THEORY...
I CAN USE MY RING--TO PUT YOU INTO A STATE OF DEEP CONCENTRATION--TO GIVE THE DESTROYER A CHANCE TO APPEAR--
GOOD! I MUST KNOW MY RESPONSIBILITY IN THIS MATTER!
AS THE GREAT GREEN BEAM OF THE EMERALD CHAMPION GOES TO WORK...
MY RING WILL MAKE DR. PHILLIPS CONCENTRATE COMPLETELY ON THAT FORMULA HE'S WRITING! NOW LET'S SEE WHAT HAPPENS...
6

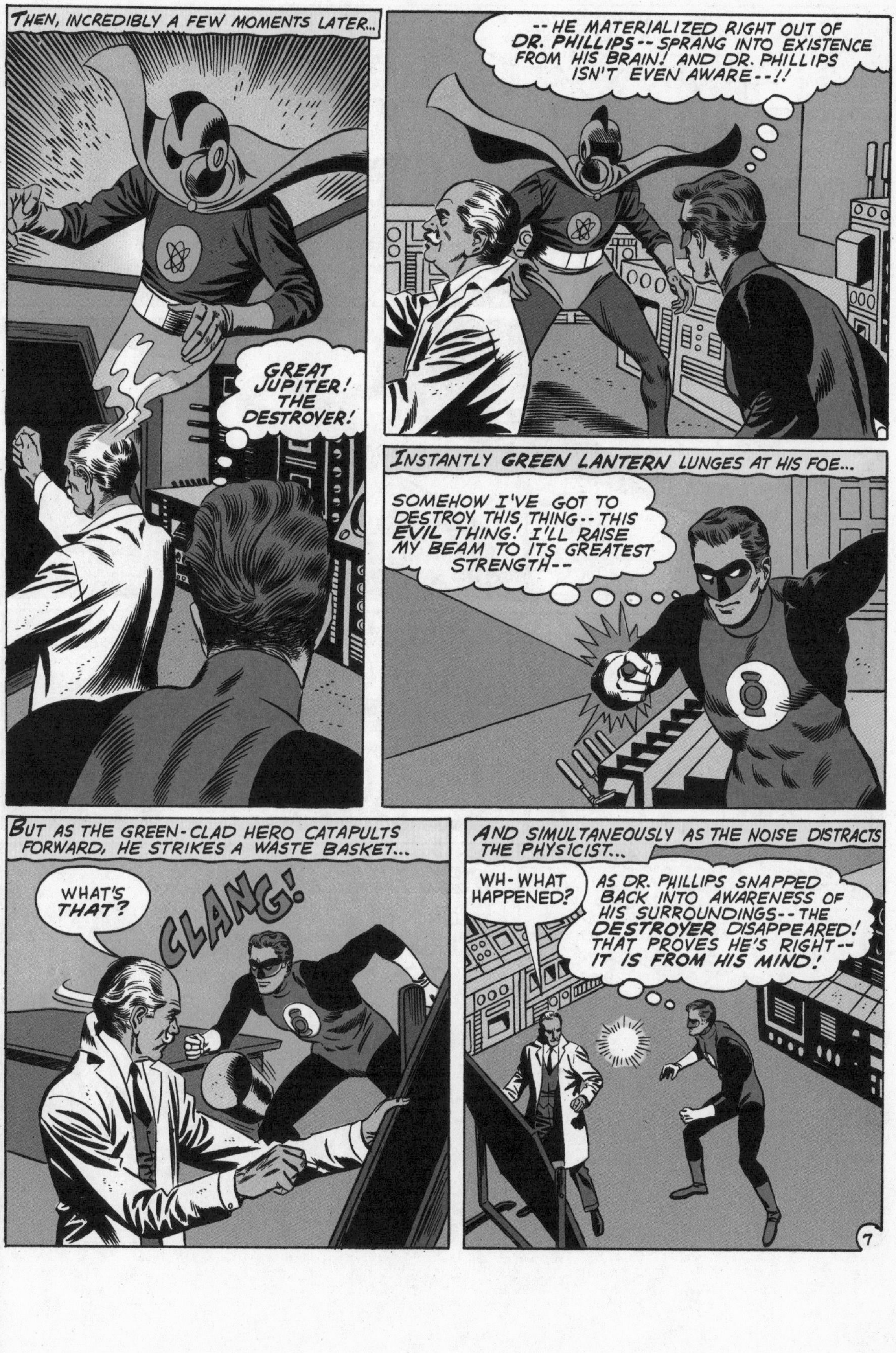
THEN, INCREDIBLY A FEW MOMENTS LATER...
GREAT JUPITER! THE DESTROYER!
-- HE MATERIALIZED RIGHT OUT OF DR. PHILLIPS -- SPRANG INTO EXISTENCE FROM HIS BRAIN! AND DR. PHILLIPS ISN'T EVEN AWARE--!!
INSTANTLY GREEN LANTERN LUNGES AT HIS FOE...
SOMEHOW I'VE GOT TO DESTROY THIS THING -- THIS EVIL THING! I'LL RAISE MY BEAM TO ITS GREATEST STRENGTH--
BUT AS THE GREEN-CLAD HERO CATAPULTS FORWARD, HE STRIKES A WASTE BASKET...
WHAT'S THAT?
CLANG!
AND SIMULTANEOUSLY AS THE NOISE DISTRACTS THE PHYSICIST...
WH-WHAT HAPPENED?
AS DR. PHILLIPS SNAPPED BACK INTO AWARENESS OF HIS SURROUNDINGS -- THE DESTROYER DISAPPEARED! THAT PROVES HE'S RIGHT -- IT IS FROM HIS MIND!
7

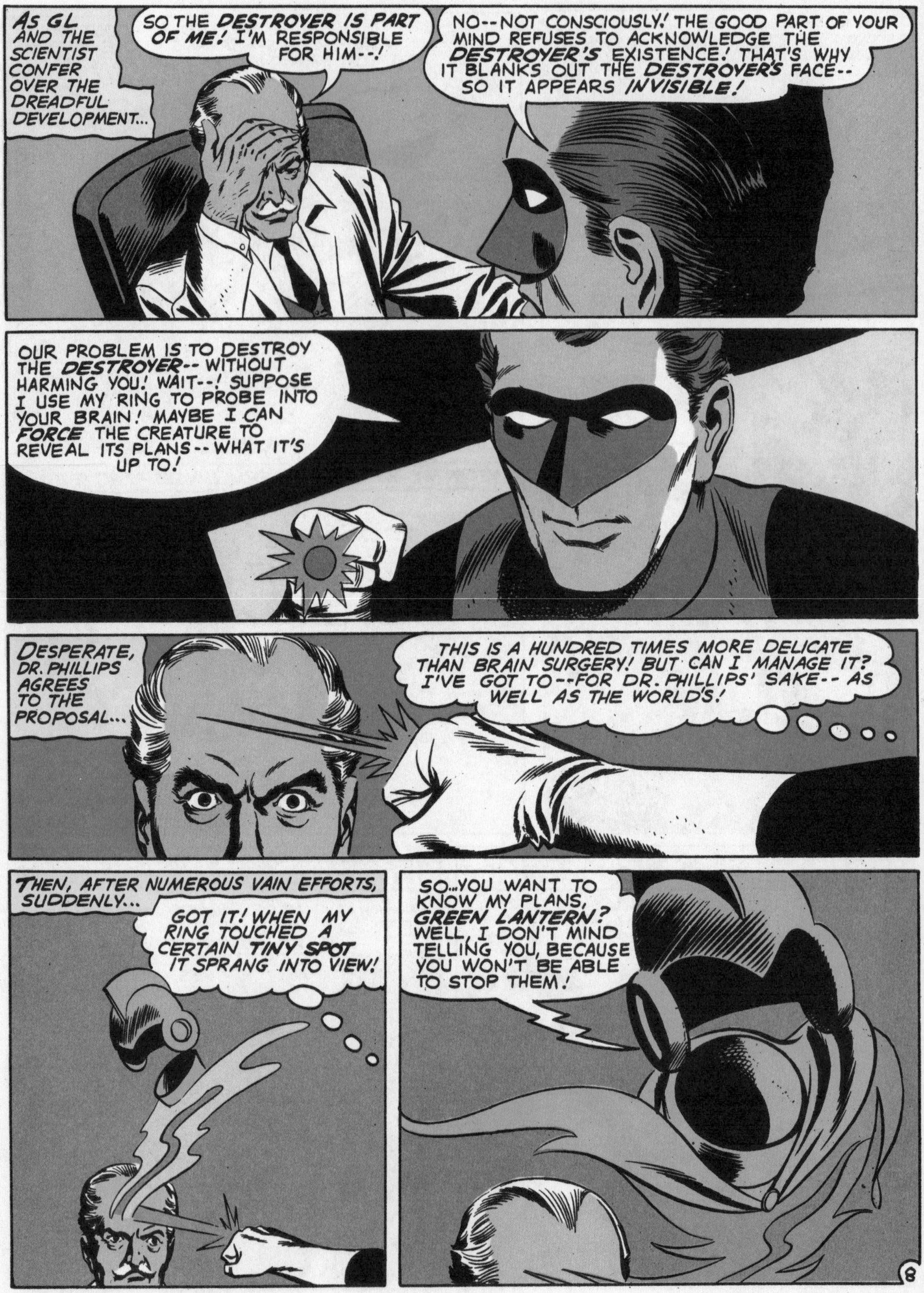

AS GL AND THE SCIENTIST CONFER OVER THE DREADFUL DEVELOPMENT...
SO THE DESTROYER IS PART OF ME! I'M RESPONSIBLE FOR HIM--!
NO--NOT CONSCIOUSLY! THE GOOD PART OF YOUR MIND REFUSES TO ACKNOWLEDGE THE DESTROYER'S EXISTENCE! THAT'S WHY IT BLANKS OUT THE DESTROYER'S FACE--SO IT APPEARS INVISIBLE!
OUR PROBLEM IS TO DESTROY THE DESTROYER--WITHOUT HARMING YOU! WAIT--! SUPPOSE I USE MY RING TO PROBE INTO YOUR BRAIN! MAYBE I CAN FORCE THE CREATURE TO REVEAL ITS PLANS--WHAT IT'S UP TO!
DESPERATE, DR. PHILLIPS AGREES TO THE PROPOSAL...
THIS IS A HUNDRED TIMES MORE DELICATE THAN BRAIN SURGERY! BUT CAN I MANAGE IT? I'VE GOT TO--FOR DR. PHILLIPS' SAKE--AS WELL AS THE WORLD'S!
THEN, AFTER NUMEROUS VAIN EFFORTS, SUDDENLY...
GOT IT! WHEN MY RING TOUCHED A CERTAIN TINY SPOT IT SPRANG INTO VIEW!
SO...YOU WANT TO KNOW MY PLANS, GREEN LANTERN? WELL, I DON'T MIND TELLING YOU, BECAUSE YOU WON'T BE ABLE TO STOP THEM!
8

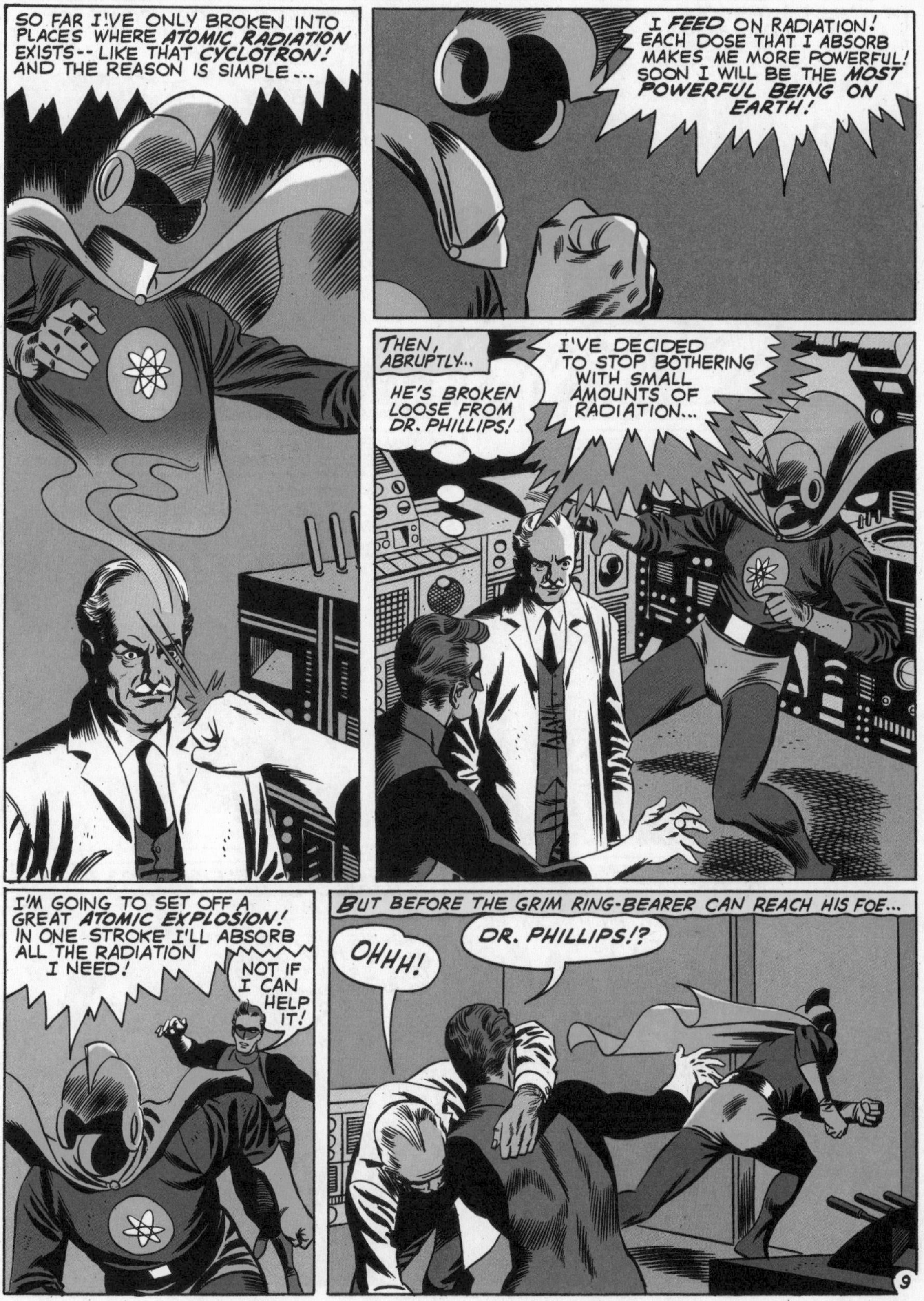
SO FAR I'VE ONLY BROKEN INTO PLACES WHERE ATOMIC RADIATION EXISTS-- LIKE THAT CYCLOTRON! AND THE REASON IS SIMPLE...
I FEED ON RADIATION! EACH DOSE THAT I ABSORB MAKES ME MORE POWERFUL! SOON I WILL BE THE MOST POWERFUL BEING ON EARTH!
THEN, ABRUPTLY...
I'VE DECIDED TO STOP BOTHERING WITH SMALL AMOUNTS OF RADIATION...
HE'S BROKEN LOOSE FROM DR. PHILLIPS!
I'M GOING TO SET OFF A GREAT ATOMIC EXPLOSION! IN ONE STROKE I'LL ABSORB ALL THE RADIATION I NEED!
NOT IF I CAN HELP IT!
BUT BEFORE THE GRIM RING-BEARER CAN REACH HIS FOE...
OHHH!
DR. PHILLIPS!?
9

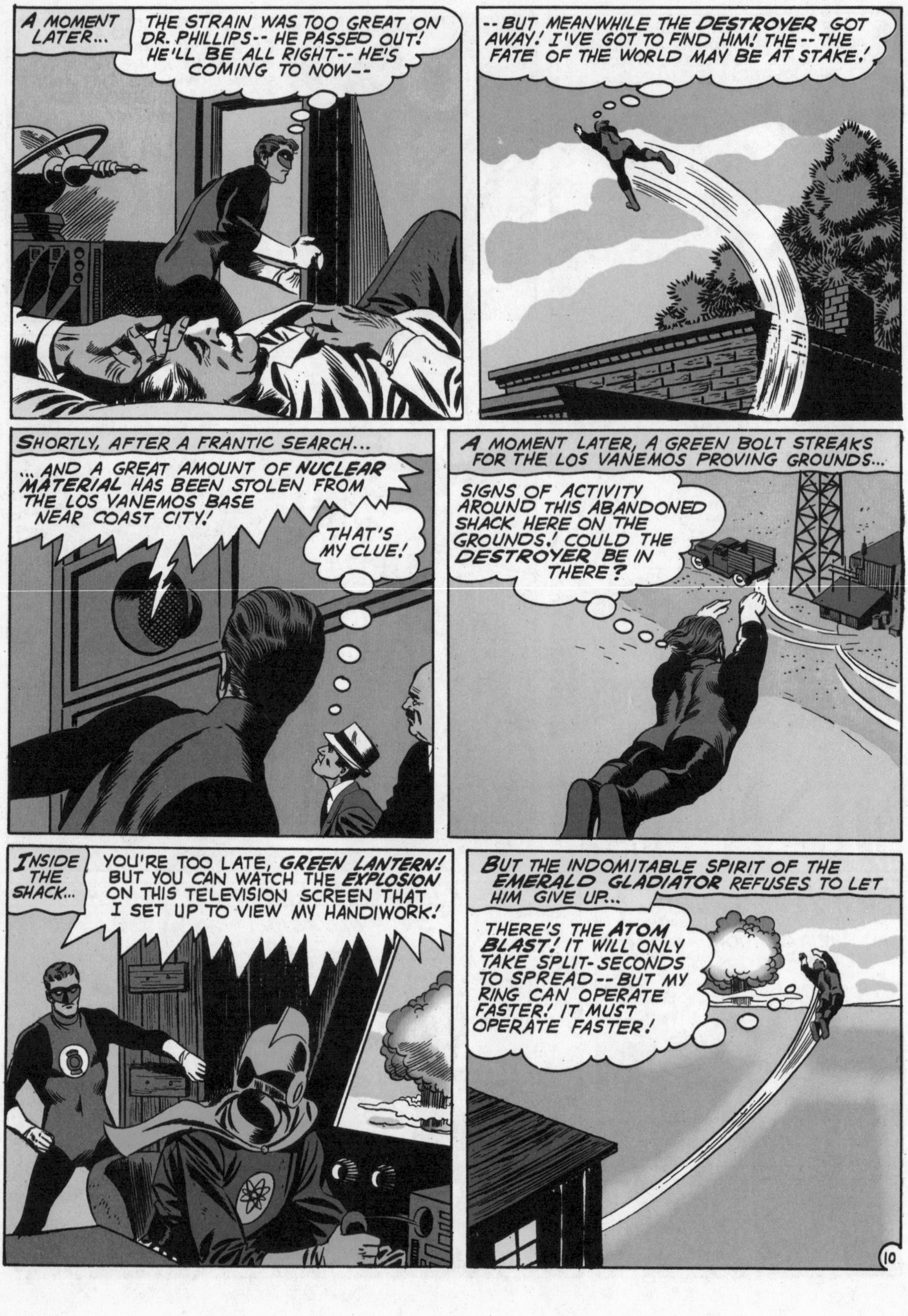
A MOMENT LATER...
THE STRAIN WAS TOO GREAT ON DR. PHILLIPS-- HE PASSED OUT! HE'LL BE ALL RIGHT-- HE'S COMING TO NOW--
--BUT MEANWHILE THE DESTROYER GOT AWAY! I'VE GOT TO FIND HIM! THE--THE FATE OF THE WORLD MAY BE AT STAKE!
SHORTLY, AFTER A FRANTIC SEARCH...
...AND A GREAT AMOUNT OF NUCLEAR MATERIAL HAS BEEN STOLEN FROM THE LOS VANEMOS BASE NEAR COAST CITY!
THAT'S MY CLUE!
A MOMENT LATER, A GREEN BOLT STREAKS FOR THE LOS VANEMOS PROVING GROUNDS...
SIGNS OF ACTIVITY AROUND THIS ABANDONED SHACK HERE ON THE GROUNDS! COULD THE DESTROYER BE IN THERE?
INSIDE THE SHACK...
YOU'RE TOO LATE, GREEN LANTERN! BUT YOU CAN WATCH THE EXPLOSION ON THIS TELEVISION SCREEN THAT I SET UP TO VIEW MY HANDIWORK!
BUT THE INDOMITABLE SPIRIT OF THE EMERALD GLADIATOR REFUSES TO LET HIM GIVE UP..
THERE'S THE ATOM BLAST! IT WILL ONLY TAKE SPLIT-SECONDS TO SPREAD--BUT MY RING CAN OPERATE FASTER! IT MUST OPERATE FASTER!
10

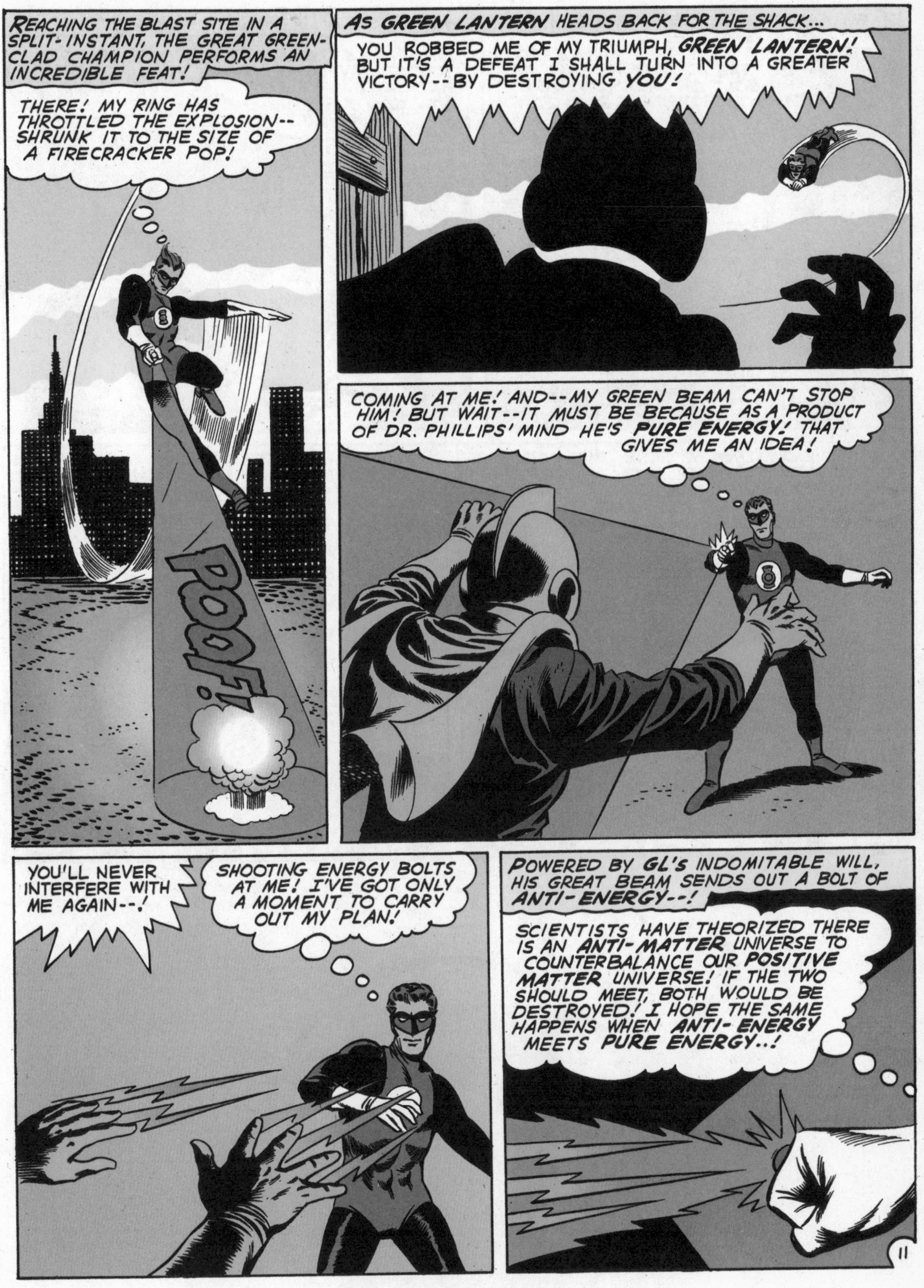
REACHING THE BLAST SITE IN A SPLIT-INSTANT, THE GREAT GREEN-CLAD CHAMPION PERFORMS AN INCREDIBLE FEAT!
THERE! MY RING HAS THROTTLED THE EXPLOSION-- SHRUNK IT TO THE SIZE OF A FIRECRACKER POP!
POOF!
AS GREEN LANTERN HEADS BACK FOR THE SHACK...
YOU ROBBED ME OF MY TRIUMPH, GREEN LANTERN! BUT IT'S A DEFEAT I SHALL TURN INTO A GREATER VICTORY--BY DESTROYING YOU!
COMING AT ME! AND--MY GREEN BEAM CAN'T STOP HIM! BUT WAIT--IT MUST BE BECAUSE AS A PRODUCT OF DR. PHILLIPS' MIND HE'S PURE ENERGY! THAT GIVES ME AN IDEA!
YOU'LL NEVER INTERFERE WITH ME AGAIN--!
SHOOTING ENERGY BOLTS AT ME! I'VE GOT ONLY A MOMENT TO CARRY OUT MY PLAN!
POWERED BY GL'S INDOMITABLE WILL, HIS GREAT BEAM SENDS OUT A BOLT OF ANTI-ENERGY--!
SCIENTISTS HAVE THEORIZED THERE IS AN ANTI-MATTER UNIVERSE TO COUNTERBALANCE OUR POSITIVE MATTER UNIVERSE! IF THE TWO SHOULD MEET, BOTH WOULD BE DESTROYED! I HOPE THE SAME HAPPENS WHEN ANTI-ENERGY MEETS PURE ENERGY..!
11

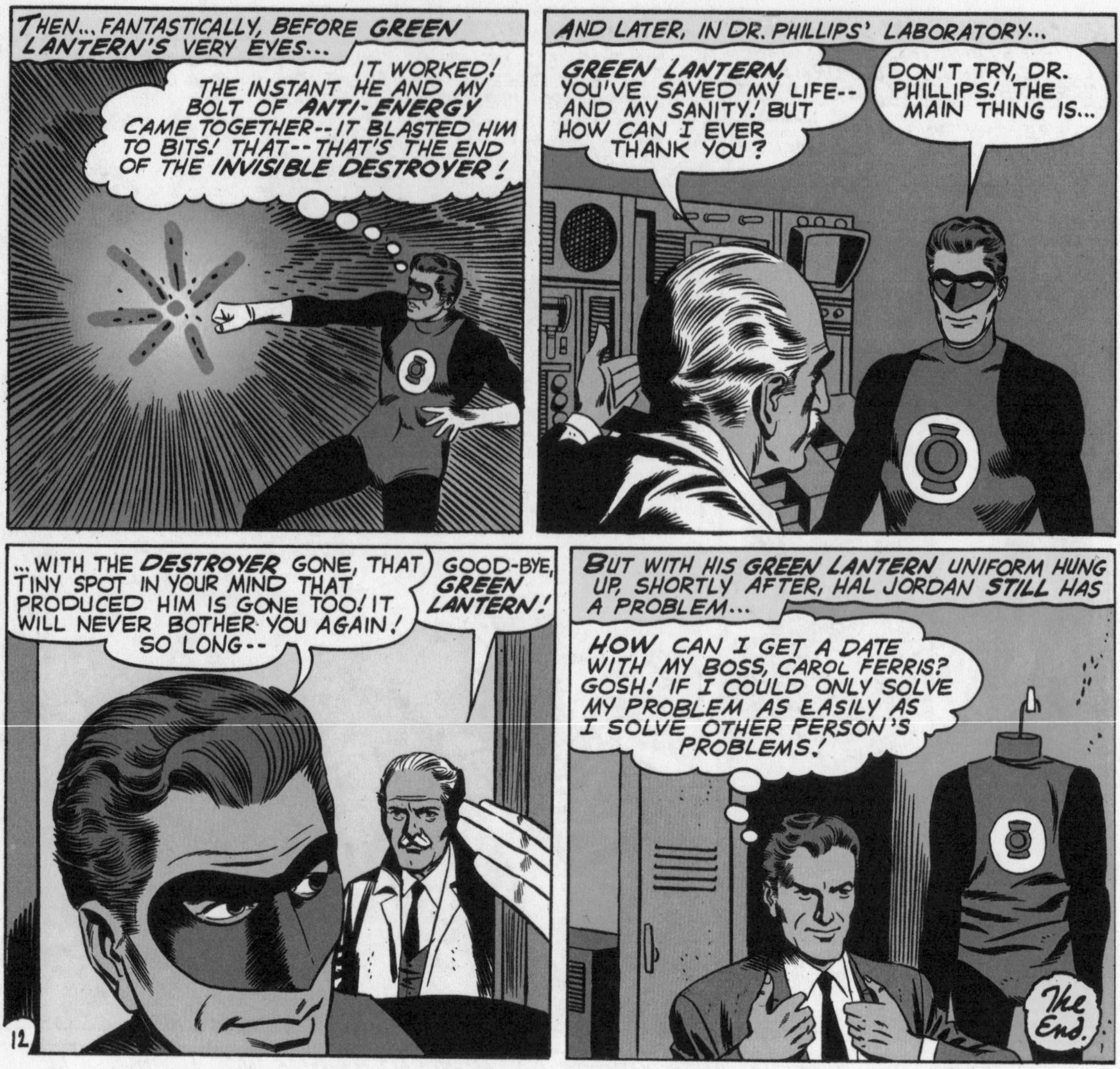
THEN... FANTASTICALLY, BEFORE GREEN LANTERN'S VERY EYES...
IT WORKED! THE INSTANT HE AND MY BOLT OF ANTI-ENERGY CAME TOGETHER--IT BLASTED HIM TO BITS! THAT--THAT'S THE END OF THE INVISIBLE DESTROYER!
AND LATER, IN DR. PHILLIPS' LABORATORY...
GREEN LANTERN, YOU'VE SAVED MY LIFE--AND MY SANITY! BUT HOW CAN I EVER THANK YOU?
DON'T TRY, DR. PHILLIPS! THE MAIN THING IS...
...WITH THE DESTROYER GONE, THAT TINY SPOT IN YOUR MIND THAT PRODUCED HIM IS GONE TOO! IT WILL NEVER BOTHER YOU AGAIN! SO LONG--
GOOD-BYE, GREEN LANTERN!
12
BUT WITH HIS GREEN LANTERN UNIFORM HUNG UP, SHORTLY AFTER, HAL JORDAN STILL HAS A PROBLEM...
HOW CAN I GET A DATE WITH MY BOSS, CAROL FERRIS? GOSH! IF I COULD ONLY SOLVE MY PROBLEM AS EASILY AS I SOLVE OTHER PERSON'S PROBLEMS!
The End.

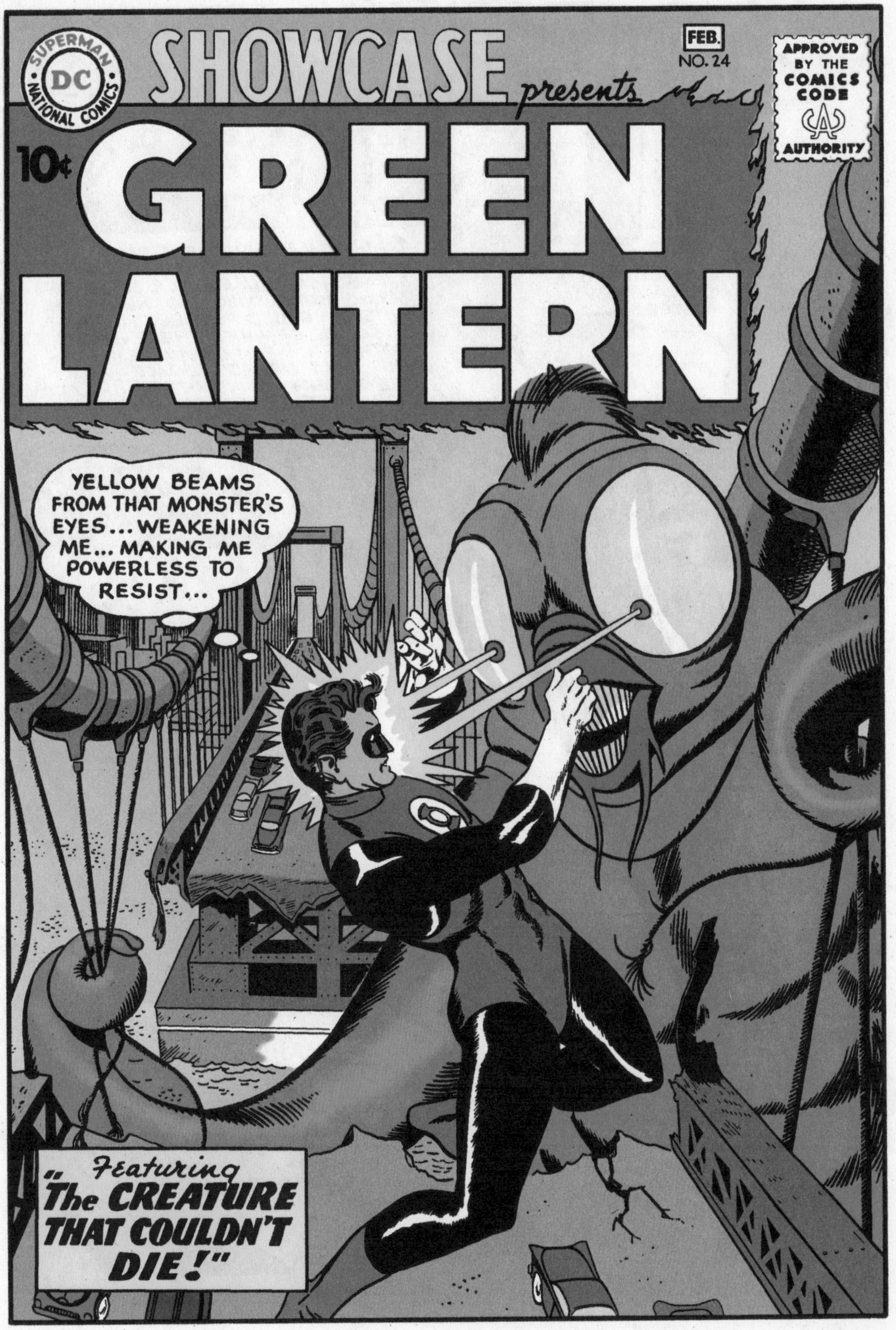
SUPERMAN DC NATIONAL COMICS
SHOWCASE presents
FEB. NO. 24
APPROVED BY THE COMICS CODE AUTHORITY
10¢
GREEN LANTERN
YELLOW BEAMS FROM THAT MONSTER'S EYES... WEAKENING ME... MAKING ME POWERLESS TO RESIST...
Featuring "The CREATURE THAT COULDN'T DIE!"

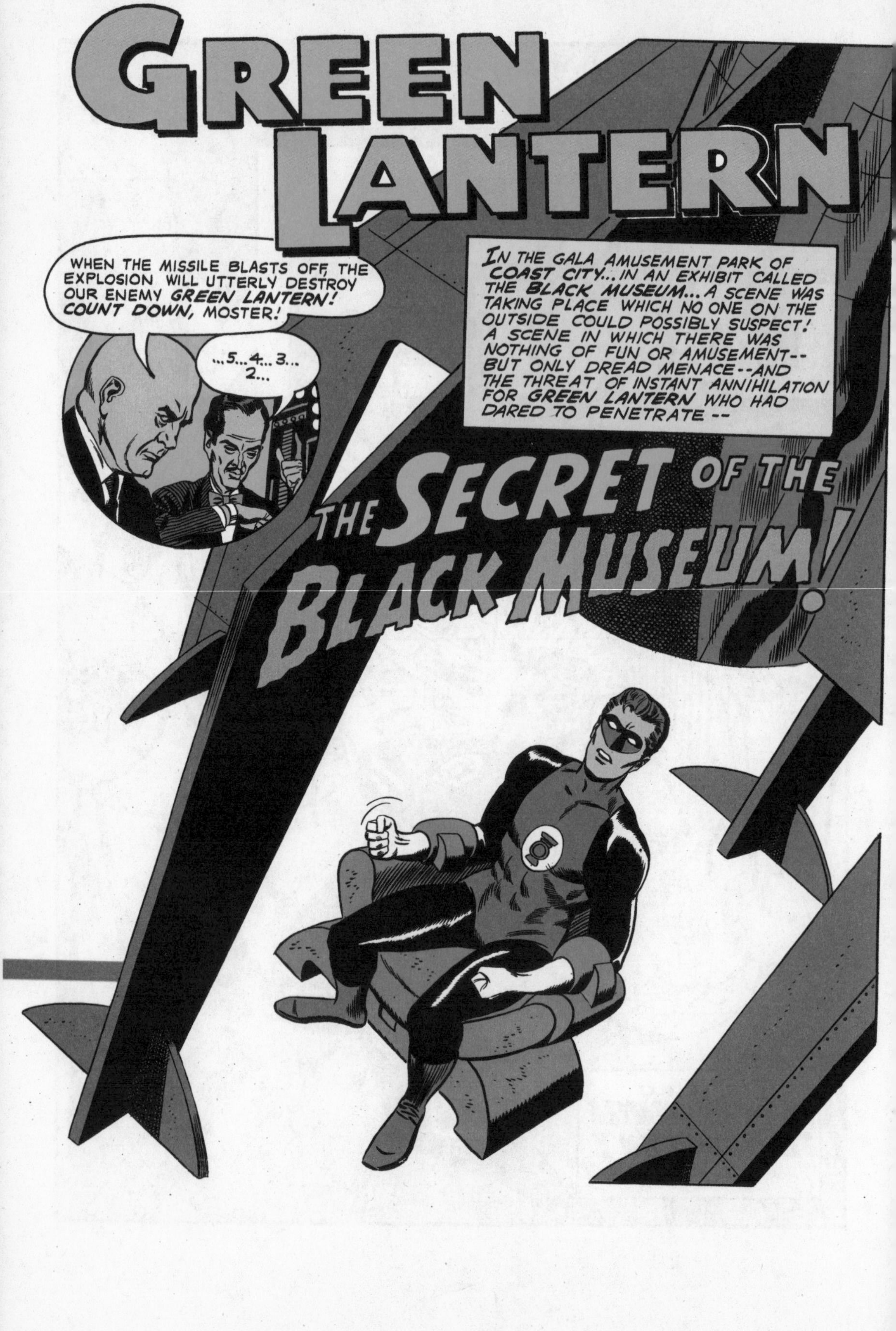
GREEN LANTERN
WHEN THE MISSILE BLASTS OFF, THE EXPLOSION WILL UTTERLY DESTROY OUR ENEMY GREEN LANTERN! COUNT DOWN, MOSTER!
...5...4...3... 2...
IN THE GALA AMUSEMENT PARK OF COAST CITY...IN AN EXHIBIT CALLED THE BLACK MUSEUM...A SCENE WAS TAKING PLACE WHICH NO ONE ON THE OUTSIDE COULD POSSIBLY SUSPECT! A SCENE IN WHICH THERE WAS NOTHING OF FUN OR AMUSEMENT--BUT ONLY DREAD MENACE--AND THE THREAT OF INSTANT ANNIHILATION FOR GREEN LANTERN WHO HAD DARED TO PENETRATE --
THE SECRET OF THE BLACK MUSEUM!

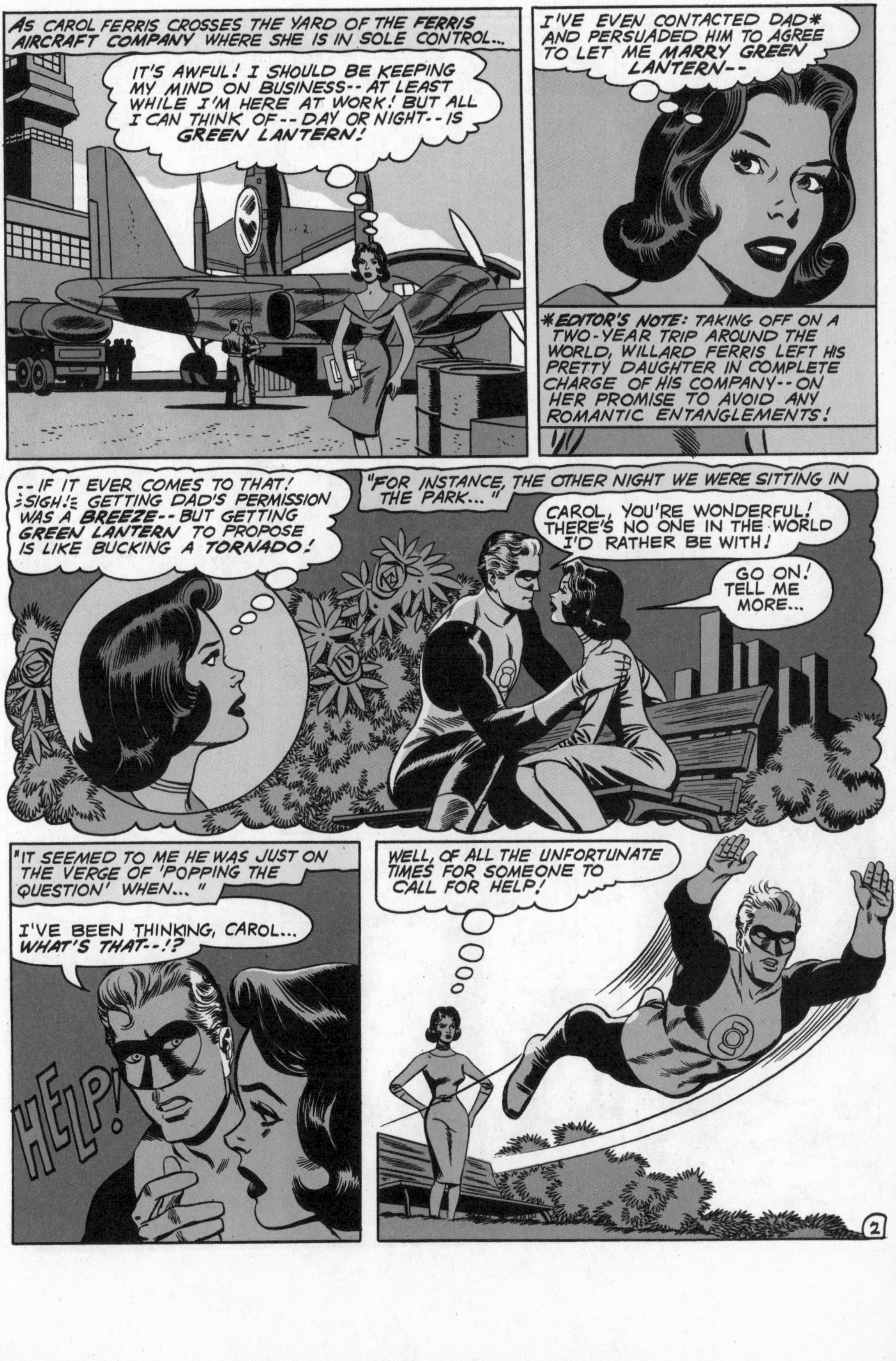

AS CAROL FERRIS CROSSES THE YARD OF THE FERRIS AIRCRAFT COMPANY WHERE SHE IS IN SOLE CONTROL...
IT'S AWFUL! I SHOULD BE KEEPING MY MIND ON BUSINESS-- AT LEAST WHILE I'M HERE AT WORK! BUT ALL I CAN THINK OF-- DAY OR NIGHT-- IS GREEN LANTERN!
I'VE EVEN CONTACTED DAD* AND PERSUADED HIM TO AGREE TO LET ME MARRY GREEN LANTERN--
*EDITOR'S NOTE: TAKING OFF ON A TWO-YEAR TRIP AROUND THE WORLD, WILLARD FERRIS LEFT HIS PRETTY DAUGHTER IN COMPLETE CHARGE OF HIS COMPANY--ON HER PROMISE TO AVOID ANY ROMANTIC ENTANGLEMENTS!
--IF IT EVER COMES TO THAT! SIGH! GETTING DAD'S PERMISSION WAS A BREEZE--BUT GETTING GREEN LANTERN TO PROPOSE IS LIKE BUCKING A TORNADO!
"FOR INSTANCE, THE OTHER NIGHT WE WERE SITTING IN THE PARK..."
CAROL, YOU'RE WONDERFUL! THERE'S NO ONE IN THE WORLD I'D RATHER BE WITH!
GO ON! TELL ME MORE...
"IT SEEMED TO ME HE WAS JUST ON THE VERGE OF 'POPPING THE QUESTION' WHEN..."
I'VE BEEN THINKING, CAROL... WHAT'S THAT--!?
HELP!
WELL, OF ALL THE UNFORTUNATE TIMES FOR SOMEONE TO CALL FOR HELP!
2

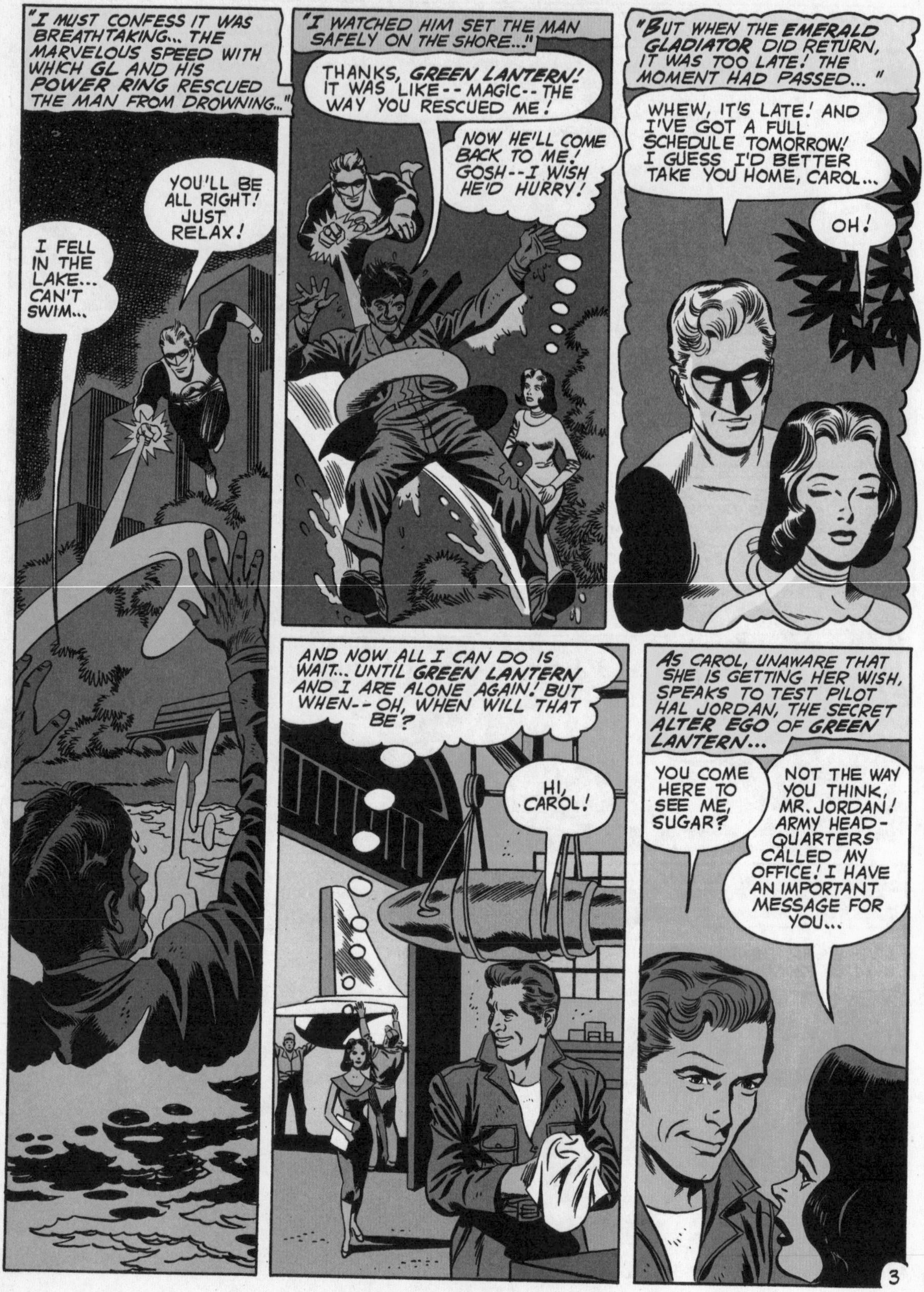
"I MUST CONFESS IT WAS BREATHTAKING... THE MARVELOUS SPEED WITH WHICH GL AND HIS POWER RING RESCUED THE MAN FROM DROWNING..."
YOU'LL BE ALL RIGHT! JUST RELAX!
I FELL IN THE LAKE... CAN'T SWIM...
"I WATCHED HIM SET THE MAN SAFELY ON THE SHORE..."
THANKS, GREEN LANTERN! IT WAS LIKE--MAGIC--THE WAY YOU RESCUED ME!
NOW HE'LL COME BACK TO ME! GOSH--I WISH HE'D HURRY!
"BUT WHEN THE EMERALD GLADIATOR DID RETURN, IT WAS TOO LATE! THE MOMENT HAD PASSED..."
WHEW, IT'S LATE! AND I'VE GOT A FULL SCHEDULE TOMORROW! I GUESS I'D BETTER TAKE YOU HOME, CAROL...
OH!
AND NOW ALL I CAN DO IS WAIT... UNTIL GREEN LANTERN AND I ARE ALONE AGAIN! BUT WHEN--OH, WHEN WILL THAT BE?
HI, CAROL!
AS CAROL, UNAWARE THAT SHE IS GETTING HER WISH, SPEAKS TO TEST PILOT HAL JORDAN, THE SECRET ALTER EGO OF GREEN LANTERN...
YOU COME HERE TO SEE ME, SUGAR?
NOT THE WAY YOU THINK, MR. JORDAN! ARMY HEAD-QUARTERS CALLED MY OFFICE! I HAVE AN IMPORTANT MESSAGE FOR YOU...
3

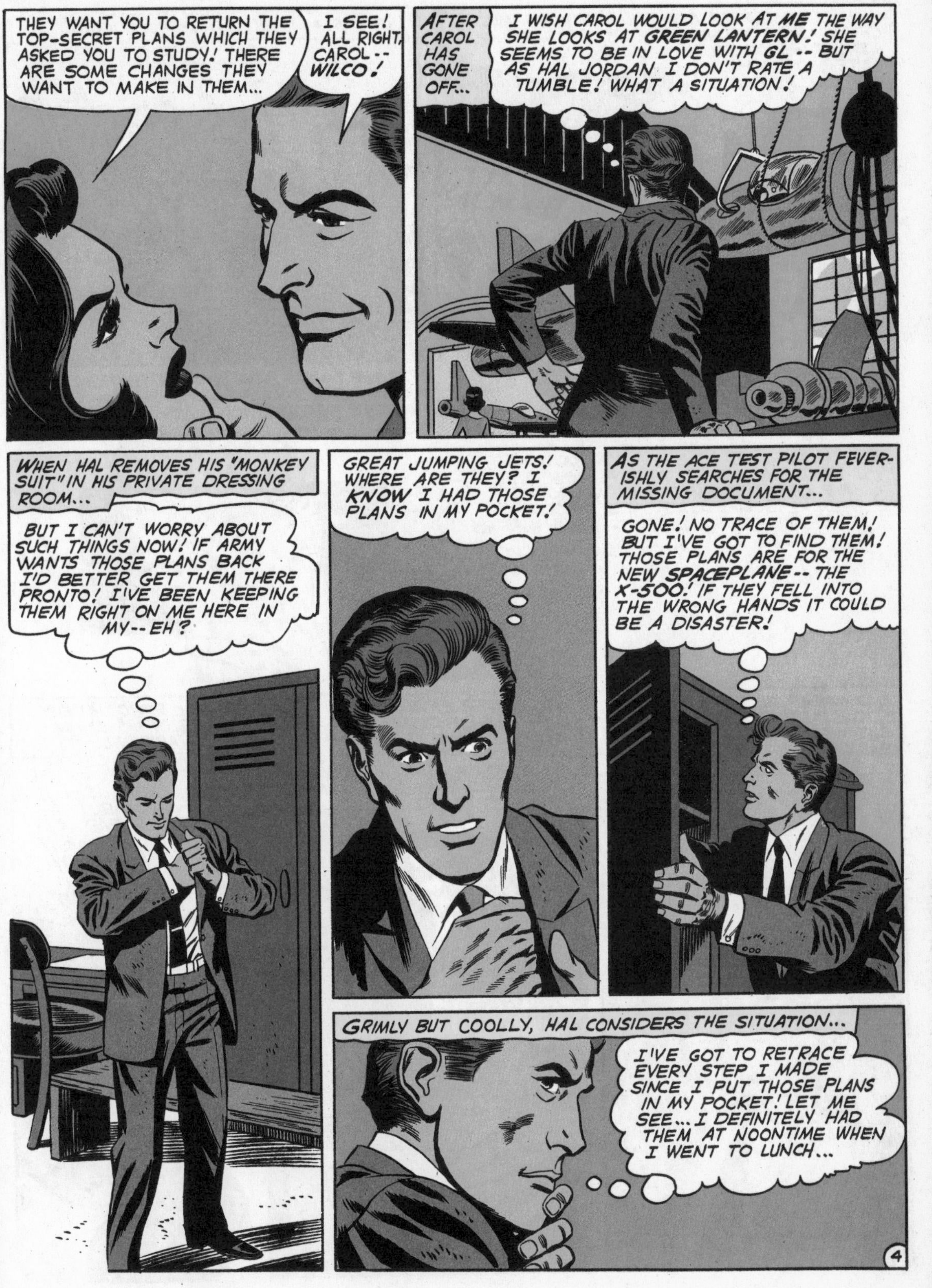
THEY WANT YOU TO RETURN THE TOP-SECRET PLANS WHICH THEY ASKED YOU TO STUDY! THERE ARE SOME CHANGES THEY WANT TO MAKE IN THEM...
I SEE! ALL RIGHT, CAROL -- WILCO!
AFTER CAROL HAS GONE OFF...
I WISH CAROL WOULD LOOK AT ME THE WAY SHE LOOKS AT GREEN LANTERN! SHE SEEMS TO BE IN LOVE WITH GL -- BUT AS HAL JORDAN I DON'T RATE A TUMBLE! WHAT A SITUATION!
WHEN HAL REMOVES HIS "MONKEY SUIT" IN HIS PRIVATE DRESSING ROOM...
BUT I CAN'T WORRY ABOUT SUCH THINGS NOW! IF ARMY WANTS THOSE PLANS BACK I'D BETTER GET THEM THERE PRONTO! I'VE BEEN KEEPING THEM RIGHT ON ME HERE IN MY-- EH?
GREAT JUMPING JETS! WHERE ARE THEY? I KNOW I HAD THOSE PLANS IN MY POCKET!
AS THE ACE TEST PILOT FEVERISHLY SEARCHES FOR THE MISSING DOCUMENT...
GONE! NO TRACE OF THEM! BUT I'VE GOT TO FIND THEM! THOSE PLANS ARE FOR THE NEW SPACEPLANE -- THE X-500! IF THEY FELL INTO THE WRONG HANDS IT COULD BE A DISASTER!
GRIMLY BUT COOLLY, HAL CONSIDERS THE SITUATION...
I'VE GOT TO RETRACE EVERY STEP I MADE SINCE I PUT THOSE PLANS IN MY POCKET! LET ME SEE... I DEFINITELY HAD THEM AT NOONTIME WHEN I WENT TO LUNCH...
4

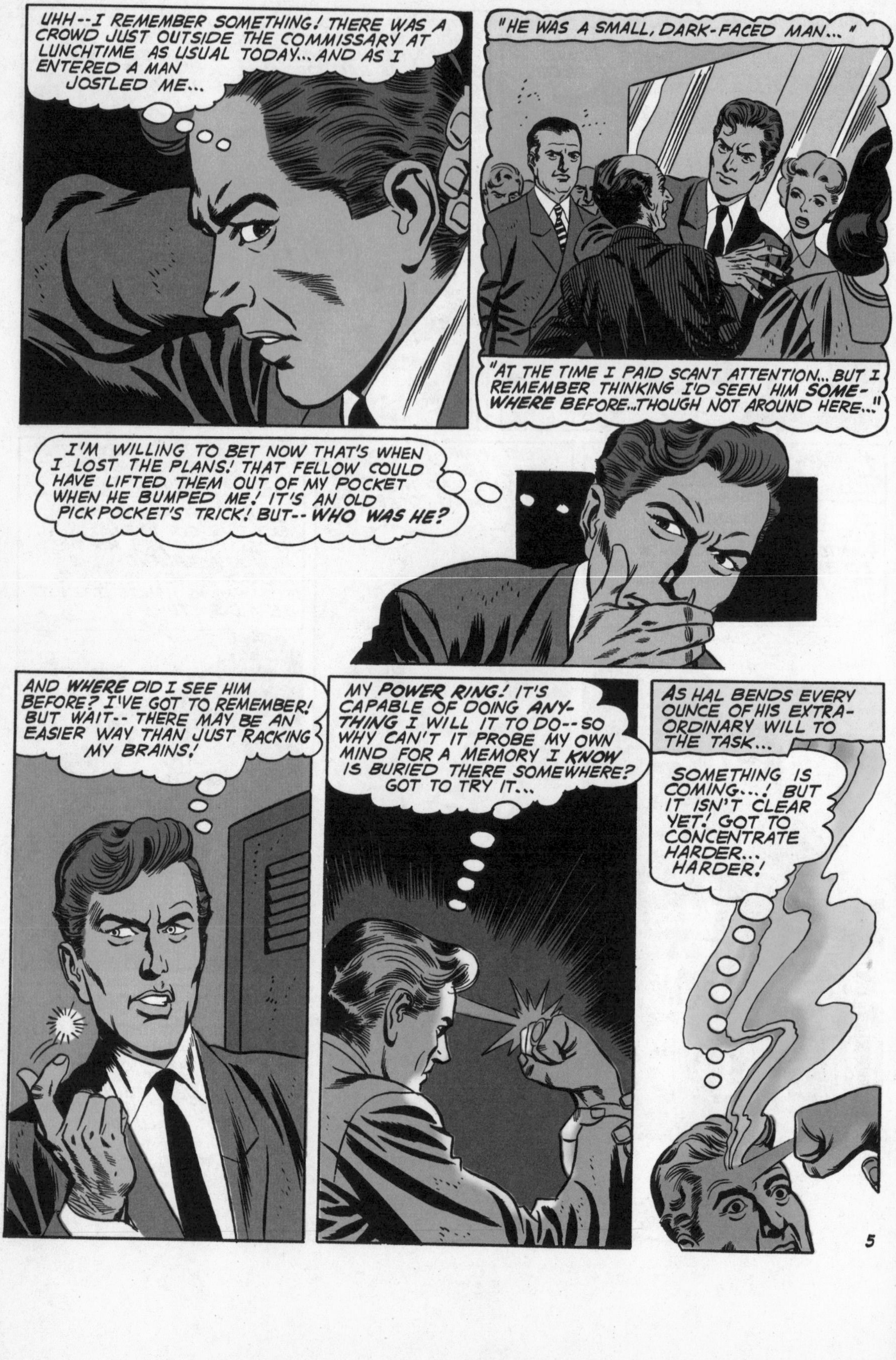

UHH--I REMEMBER SOMETHING! THERE WAS A CROWD JUST OUTSIDE THE COMMISSARY AT LUNCHTIME AS USUAL TODAY... AND AS I ENTERED A MAN JOSTLED ME...
"HE WAS A SMALL, DARK-FACED MAN..."
"AT THE TIME I PAID SCANT ATTENTION... BUT I REMEMBER THINKING I'D SEEN HIM SOMEWHERE BEFORE...THOUGH NOT AROUND HERE..."
I'M WILLING TO BET NOW THAT'S WHEN I LOST THE PLANS! THAT FELLOW COULD HAVE LIFTED THEM OUT OF MY POCKET WHEN HE BUMPED ME! IT'S AN OLD PICKPOCKET'S TRICK! BUT-- WHO WAS HE?
AND WHERE DID I SEE HIM BEFORE? I'VE GOT TO REMEMBER! BUT WAIT-- THERE MAY BE AN EASIER WAY THAN JUST RACKING MY BRAINS!
MY POWER RING! IT'S CAPABLE OF DOING ANYTHING I WILL IT TO DO-- SO WHY CAN'T IT PROBE MY OWN MIND FOR A MEMORY I KNOW IS BURIED THERE SOMEWHERE? GOT TO TRY IT...
AS HAL BENDS EVERY OUNCE OF HIS EXTRAORDINARY WILL TO THE TASK...
SOMETHING IS COMING...! BUT IT ISN'T CLEAR YET! GOT TO CONCENTRATE HARDER... HARDER!
5

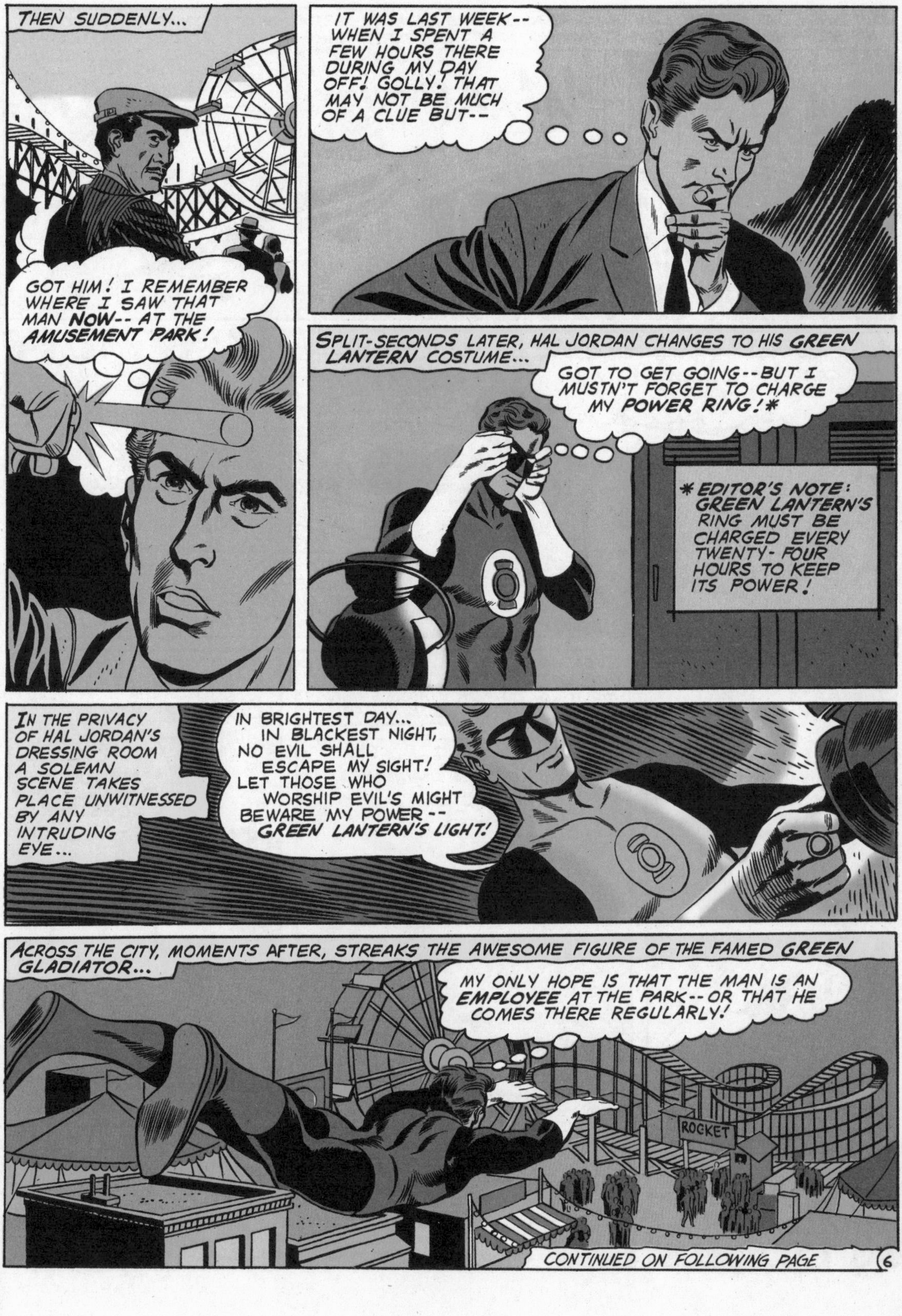
THEN SUDDENLY...
GOT HIM! I REMEMBER WHERE I SAW THAT MAN NOW-- AT THE AMUSEMENT PARK!
IT WAS LAST WEEK-- WHEN I SPENT A FEW HOURS THERE DURING MY DAY OFF! GOLLY! THAT MAY NOT BE MUCH OF A CLUE BUT--
SPLIT-SECONDS LATER, HAL JORDAN CHANGES TO HIS GREEN LANTERN COSTUME...
GOT TO GET GOING--BUT I MUSTN'T FORGET TO CHARGE MY POWER RING!*
*EDITOR'S NOTE: GREEN LANTERN'S RING MUST BE CHARGED EVERY TWENTY-FOUR HOURS TO KEEP ITS POWER!
IN THE PRIVACY OF HAL JORDAN'S DRESSING ROOM A SOLEMN SCENE TAKES PLACE UNWITNESSED BY ANY INTRUDING EYE...
IN BRIGHTEST DAY... IN BLACKEST NIGHT, NO EVIL SHALL ESCAPE MY SIGHT! LET THOSE WHO WORSHIP EVIL'S MIGHT BEWARE MY POWER-- GREEN LANTERN'S LIGHT!
ACROSS THE CITY, MOMENTS AFTER, STREAKS THE AWESOME FIGURE OF THE FAMED GREEN GLADIATOR...
MY ONLY HOPE IS THAT THE MAN IS AN EMPLOYEE AT THE PARK--OR THAT HE COMES THERE REGULARLY!
ROCKET
CONTINUED ON FOLLOWING PAGE
6

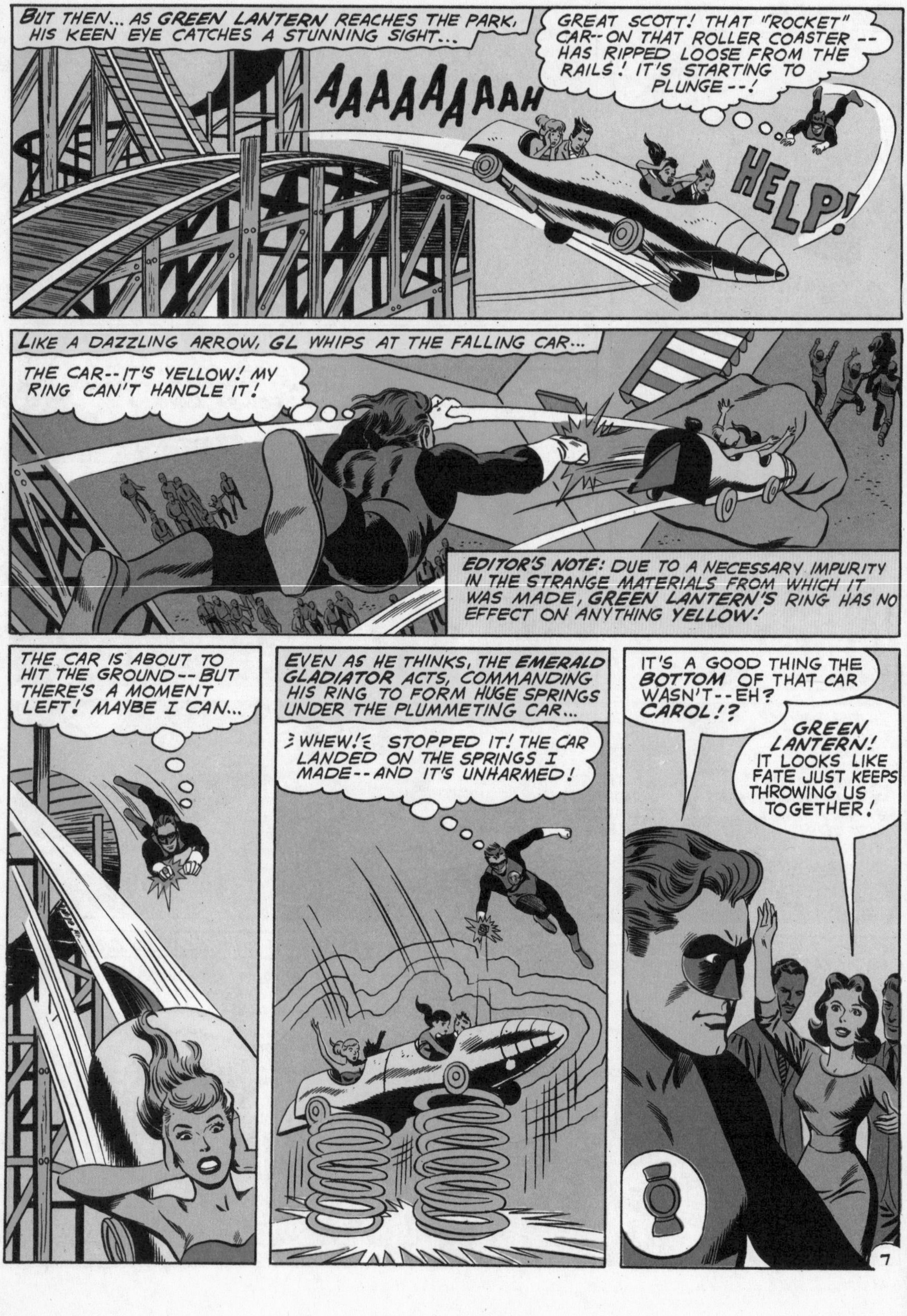
BUT THEN... AS GREEN LANTERN REACHES THE PARK, HIS KEEN EYE CATCHES A STUNNING SIGHT...
GREAT SCOTT! THAT "ROCKET" CAR--ON THAT ROLLER COASTER --HAS RIPPED LOOSE FROM THE RAILS! IT'S STARTING TO PLUNGE--!
AAAAAAAAAH
HELP!
LIKE A DAZZLING ARROW, GL WHIPS AT THE FALLING CAR...
THE CAR--IT'S YELLOW! MY RING CAN'T HANDLE IT!
EDITOR'S NOTE: DUE TO A NECESSARY IMPURITY IN THE STRANGE MATERIALS FROM WHICH IT WAS MADE, GREEN LANTERN'S RING HAS NO EFFECT ON ANYTHING YELLOW!
THE CAR IS ABOUT TO HIT THE GROUND--BUT THERE'S A MOMENT LEFT! MAYBE I CAN...
EVEN AS HE THINKS, THE EMERALD GLADIATOR ACTS, COMMANDING HIS RING TO FORM HUGE SPRINGS UNDER THE PLUMMETING CAR...
WHEW! STOPPED IT! THE CAR LANDED ON THE SPRINGS I MADE--AND IT'S UNHARMED!
IT'S A GOOD THING THE BOTTOM OF THAT CAR WASN'T--EH? CAROL!?
GREEN LANTERN! IT LOOKS LIKE FATE JUST KEEPS THROWING US TOGETHER!
7

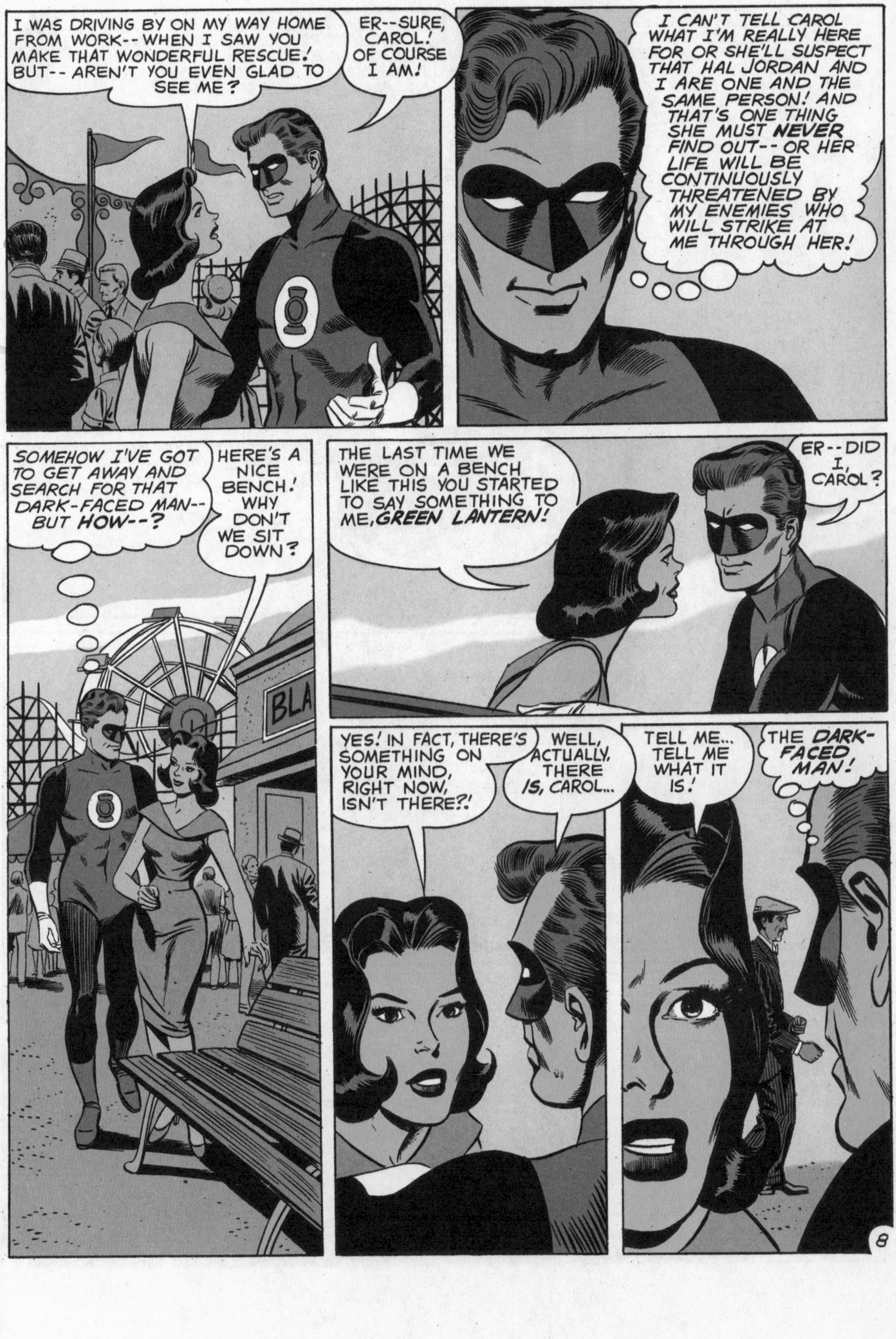
I WAS DRIVING BY ON MY WAY HOME FROM WORK-- WHEN I SAW YOU MAKE THAT WONDERFUL RESCUE! BUT-- AREN'T YOU EVEN GLAD TO SEE ME?
ER--SURE, CAROL! OF COURSE I AM!
I CAN'T TELL CAROL WHAT I'M REALLY HERE FOR OR SHE'LL SUSPECT THAT HAL JORDAN AND I ARE ONE AND THE SAME PERSON! AND THAT'S ONE THING SHE MUST NEVER FIND OUT-- OR HER LIFE WILL BE CONTINUOUSLY THREATENED BY MY ENEMIES WHO WILL STRIKE AT ME THROUGH HER!
SOMEHOW I'VE GOT TO GET AWAY AND SEARCH FOR THAT DARK-FACED MAN-- BUT HOW--?
HERE'S A NICE BENCH! WHY DON'T WE SIT DOWN?
BLA
THE LAST TIME WE WERE ON A BENCH LIKE THIS YOU STARTED TO SAY SOMETHING TO ME, GREEN LANTERN!
ER--DID I, CAROL?
YES! IN FACT, THERE'S SOMETHING ON YOUR MIND, RIGHT NOW, ISN'T THERE?!
WELL, ACTUALLY, THERE IS, CAROL...
TELL ME... TELL ME WHAT IT IS!
THE DARK-FACED MAN!
8

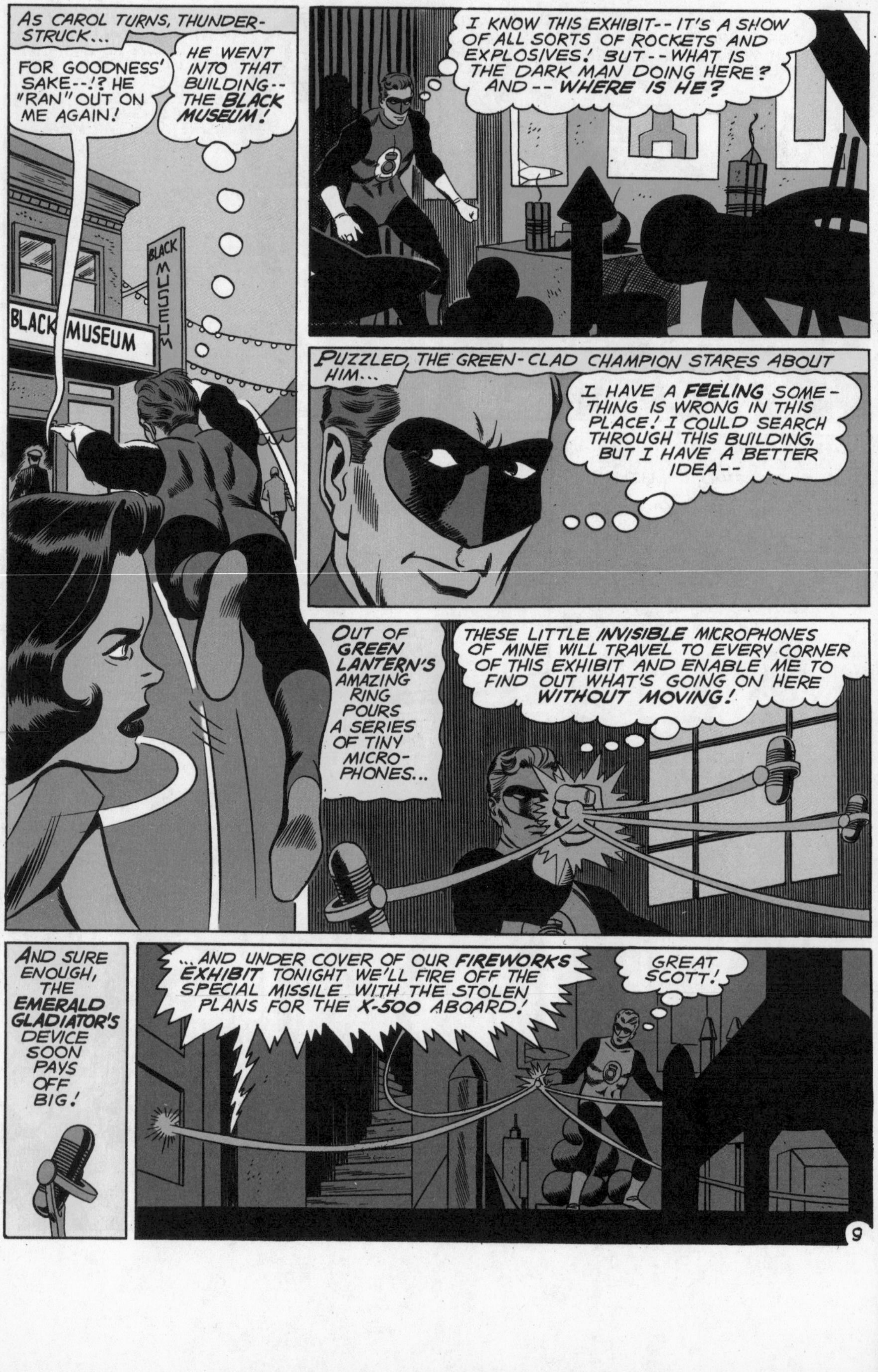
AS CAROL TURNS, THUNDER-STRUCK...
FOR GOODNESS' SAKE--!? HE "RAN" OUT ON ME AGAIN!
HE WENT INTO THAT BUILDING-- THE BLACK MUSEUM!
BLACK MUSEUM
BLACK MUSEUM
I KNOW THIS EXHIBIT-- IT'S A SHOW OF ALL SORTS OF ROCKETS AND EXPLOSIVES! BUT--WHAT IS THE DARK MAN DOING HERE? AND-- WHERE IS HE?
PUZZLED, THE GREEN-CLAD CHAMPION STARES ABOUT HIM...
I HAVE A FEELING SOMETHING IS WRONG IN THIS PLACE! I COULD SEARCH THROUGH THIS BUILDING, BUT I HAVE A BETTER IDEA--
OUT OF GREEN LANTERN'S AMAZING RING POURS A SERIES OF TINY MICRO-PHONES...
THESE LITTLE INVISIBLE MICROPHONES OF MINE WILL TRAVEL TO EVERY CORNER OF THIS EXHIBIT AND ENABLE ME TO FIND OUT WHAT'S GOING ON HERE WITHOUT MOVING!
AND SURE ENOUGH, THE EMERALD GLADIATOR'S DEVICE SOON PAYS OFF BIG!
...AND UNDER COVER OF OUR FIREWORKS EXHIBIT TONIGHT WE'LL FIRE OFF THE SPECIAL MISSILE WITH THE STOLEN PLANS FOR THE X-500 ABOARD!
GREAT SCOTT!
9

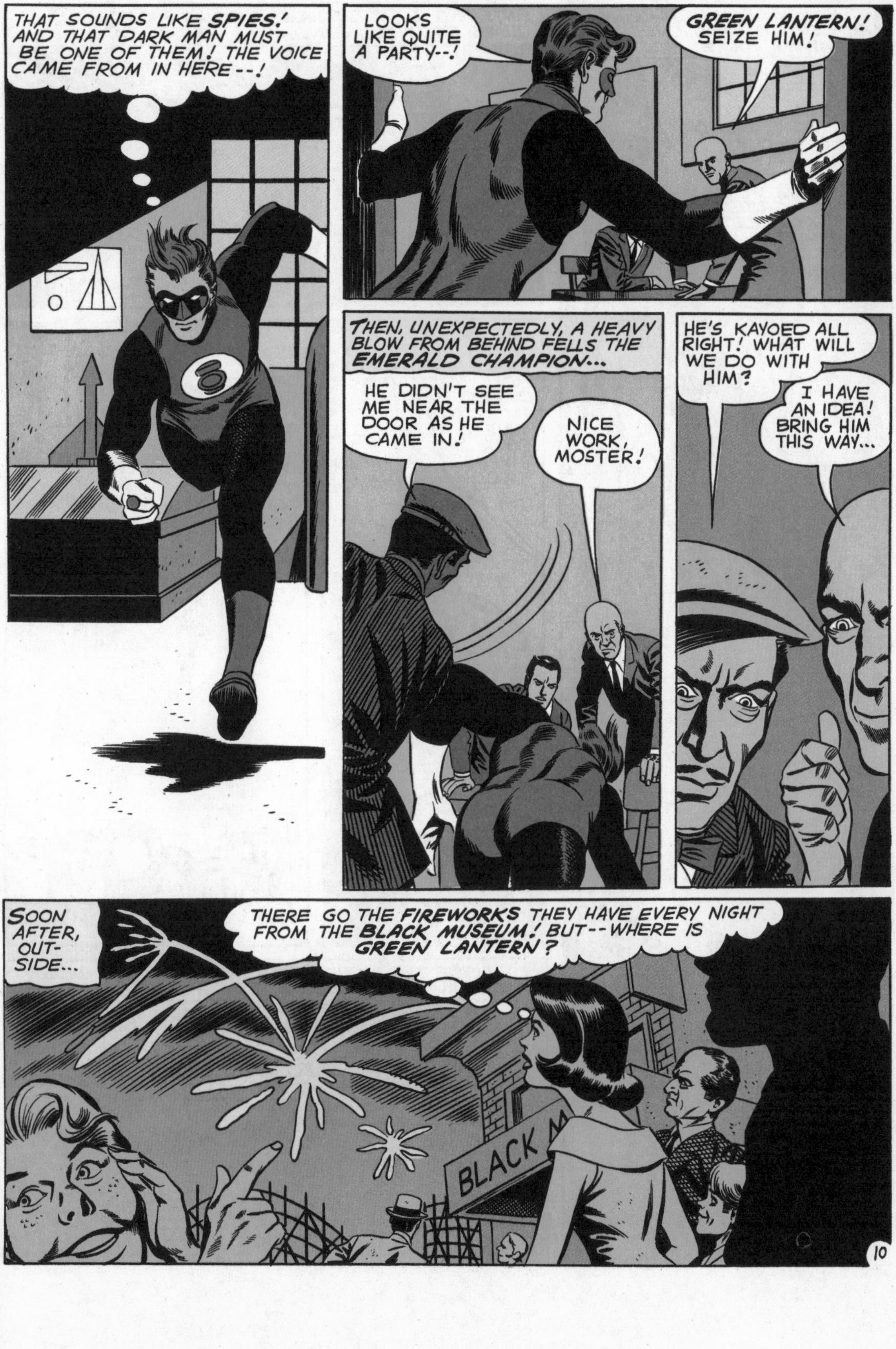
THAT SOUNDS LIKE SPIES! AND THAT DARK MAN MUST BE ONE OF THEM! THE VOICE CAME FROM IN HERE--!
LOOKS LIKE QUITE A PARTY--!
GREEN LANTERN! SEIZE HIM!
THEN, UNEXPECTEDLY, A HEAVY BLOW FROM BEHIND FELLS THE EMERALD CHAMPION...
HE DIDN'T SEE ME NEAR THE DOOR AS HE CAME IN!
NICE WORK, MOSTER!
HE'S KAYOED ALL RIGHT! WHAT WILL WE DO WITH HIM?
I HAVE AN IDEA! BRING HIM THIS WAY...
SOON AFTER, OUT-SIDE...
THERE GO THE FIREWORKS THEY HAVE EVERY NIGHT FROM THE BLACK MUSEUM! BUT--WHERE IS GREEN LANTERN?
BLACK M
10

Panel 1: AND A MOMENT LATER AS THE *GREAT GLADIATOR* RECOVERS HIS STRENGTH...

HE--HE'S USING HIS *POWER RING* TO MELT THE *CLAMPS* AND FREE HIMSELF!

THAT ROCKET BLAST--IT DIDN'T HURT HIM!

Panel 2: IN A MOMENT, GL'S RING HAS THE GROUP *CORRALLED*...

FIRST I'VE GOT TO MAKE SURE THESE SPIES ARE HERE WHEN I GET BACK-- AND THIS BIG JAIL CELL FORMED BY MY RING WILL HOLD THEM!

Panel 3: THEN, SHOOTING UP THROUGH THE ROOF OF THE MUSEUM...

NOW TO GET AFTER THAT MISSILE!

Panel 4: IT'S TRAVELING AT A FANTASTIC RATE! BUT I'VE *GOT* TO OVERTAKE IT!

Panel 5: AS GREEN LANTERN'S AMAZING BEAM, BACKED BY HIS INDOMITABLE WILL, OUTSPEEDS THE HURTLING *PROJECTILE*...

DID IT! NOW TO RECOVER THE PLANS-- AND THEN GO BACK AND TURN THOSE SPIES OVER TO THE AUTHORITIES!

12

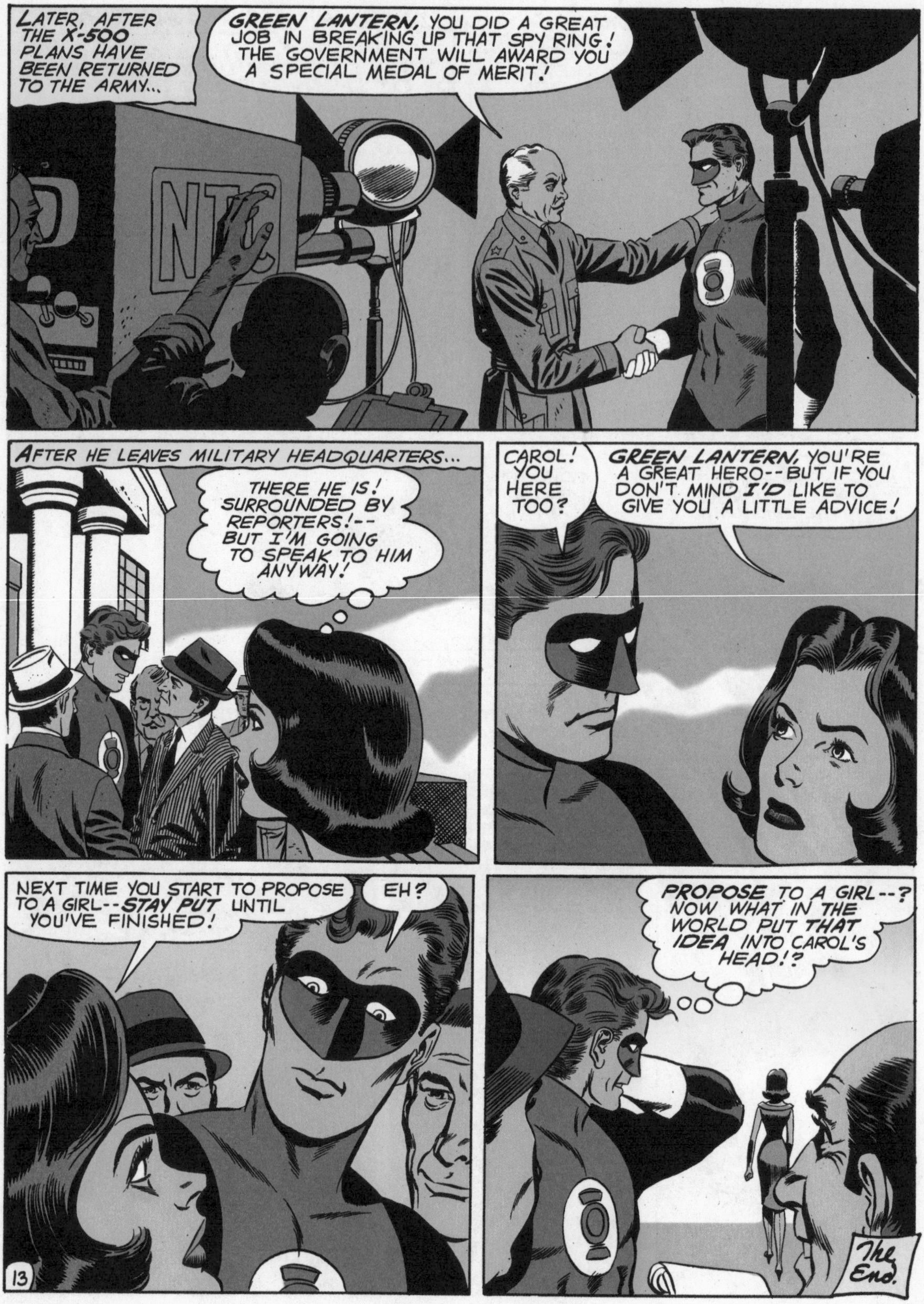
LATER, AFTER THE X-500 PLANS HAVE BEEN RETURNED TO THE ARMY...
GREEN LANTERN, YOU DID A GREAT JOB IN BREAKING UP THAT SPY RING! THE GOVERNMENT WILL AWARD YOU A SPECIAL MEDAL OF MERIT!
NTC
AFTER HE LEAVES MILITARY HEADQUARTERS...
THERE HE IS! SURROUNDED BY REPORTERS!-- BUT I'M GOING TO SPEAK TO HIM ANYWAY!
CAROL! YOU HERE TOO?
GREEN LANTERN, YOU'RE A GREAT HERO--BUT IF YOU DON'T MIND I'D LIKE TO GIVE YOU A LITTLE ADVICE!
NEXT TIME YOU START TO PROPOSE TO A GIRL--STAY PUT UNTIL YOU'VE FINISHED!
EH?
13
PROPOSE TO A GIRL--? NOW WHAT IN THE WORLD PUT THAT IDEA INTO CAROL'S HEAD!?
The End.

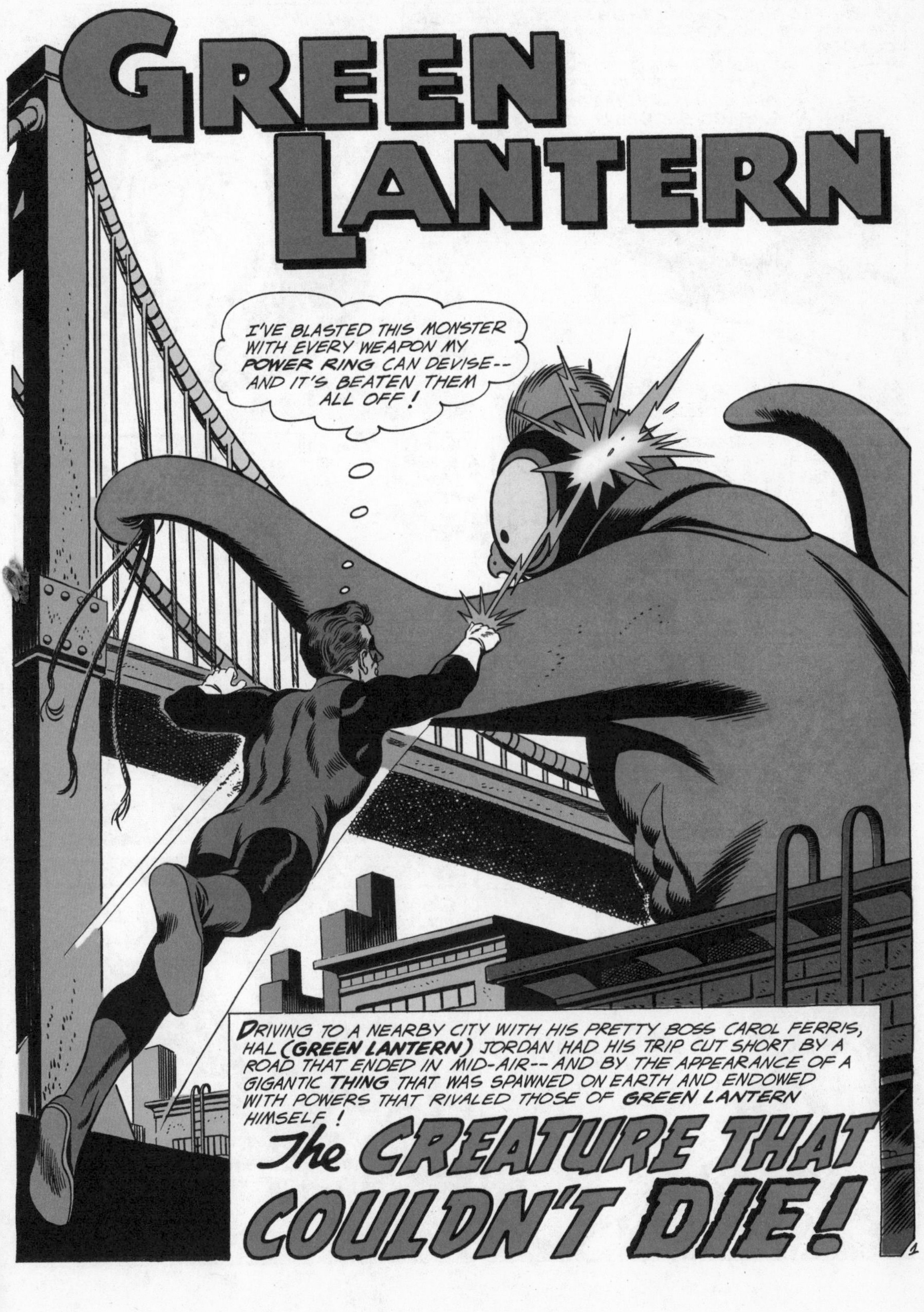
GREEN LANTERN
I'VE BLASTED THIS MONSTER WITH EVERY WEAPON MY POWER RING CAN DEVISE-- AND IT'S BEATEN THEM ALL OFF!
DRIVING TO A NEARBY CITY WITH HIS PRETTY BOSS CAROL FERRIS, HAL (GREEN LANTERN) JORDAN HAD HIS TRIP CUT SHORT BY A ROAD THAT ENDED IN MID-AIR-- AND BY THE APPEARANCE OF A GIGANTIC THING THAT WAS SPAWNED ON EARTH AND ENDOWED WITH POWERS THAT RIVALED THOSE OF GREEN LANTERN HIMSELF!
The CREATURE THAT COULDN'T DIE!
1

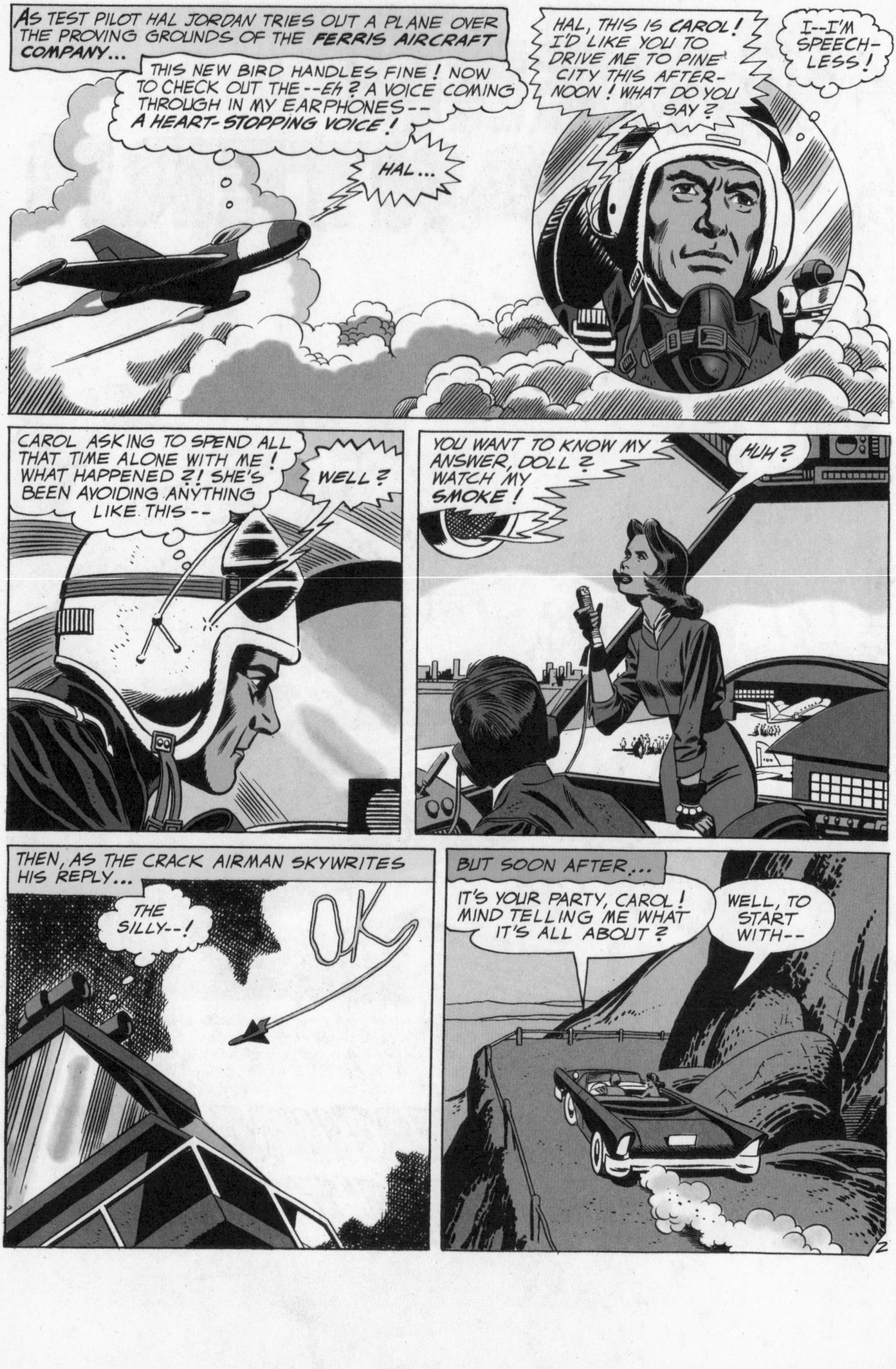
AS TEST PILOT HAL JORDAN TRIES OUT A PLANE OVER THE PROVING GROUNDS OF THE FERRIS AIRCRAFT COMPANY...
THIS NEW BIRD HANDLES FINE! NOW TO CHECK OUT THE--Eh? A VOICE COMING THROUGH IN MY EARPHONES-- A HEART-STOPPING VOICE!
HAL...
HAL, THIS IS CAROL! I'D LIKE YOU TO DRIVE ME TO PINE CITY THIS AFTERNOON! WHAT DO YOU SAY?
I--I'M SPEECHLESS!
CAROL ASKING TO SPEND ALL THAT TIME ALONE WITH ME! WHAT HAPPENED?! SHE'S BEEN AVOIDING ANYTHING LIKE THIS--
WELL?
YOU WANT TO KNOW MY ANSWER, DOLL? WATCH MY SMOKE!
HUH?
THEN, AS THE CRACK AIRMAN SKYWRITES HIS REPLY...
THE SILLY--!
OK
BUT SOON AFTER...
IT'S YOUR PARTY, CAROL! MIND TELLING ME WHAT IT'S ALL ABOUT?
WELL, TO START WITH--
2

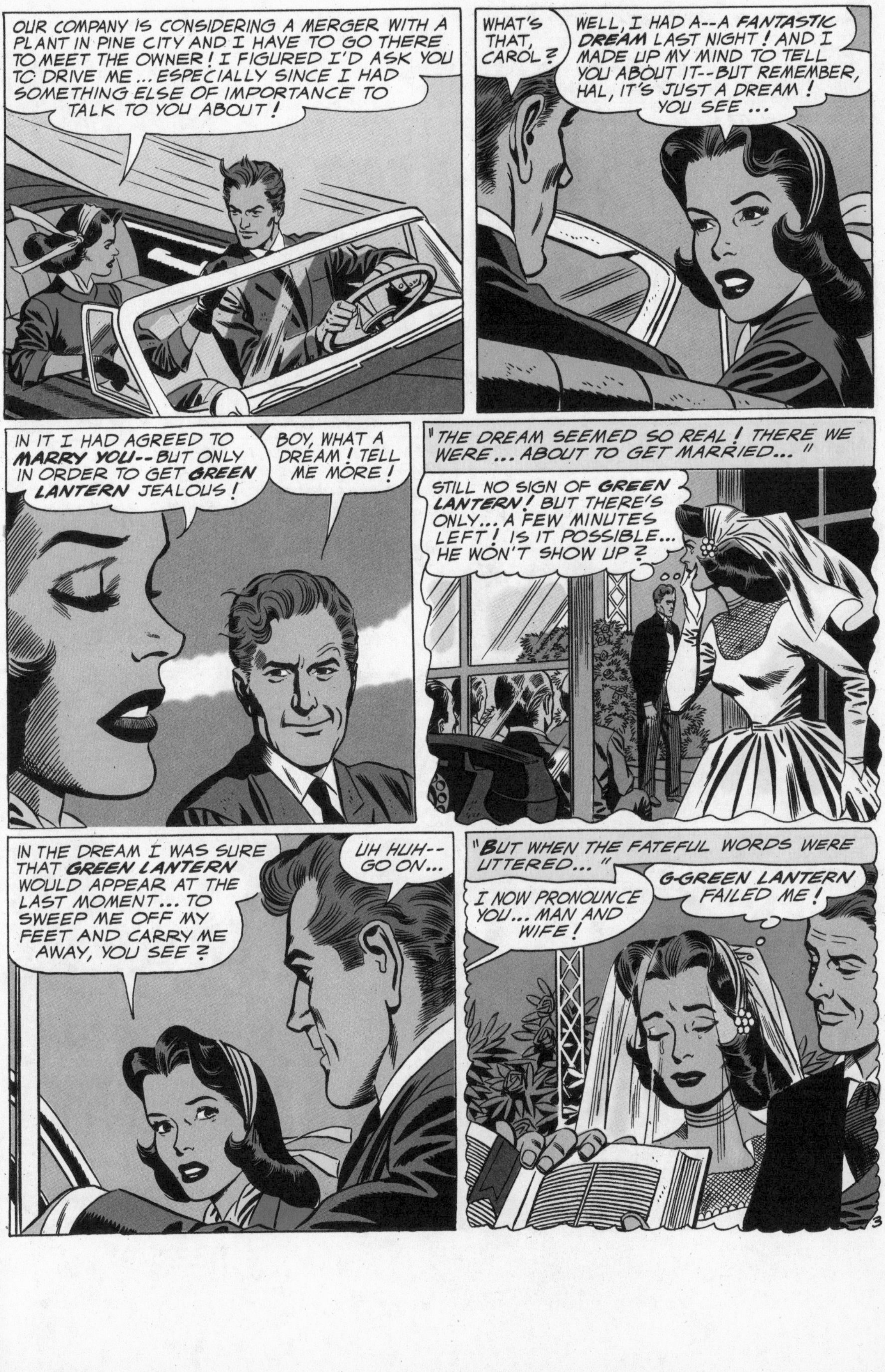
OUR COMPANY IS CONSIDERING A MERGER WITH A PLANT IN PINE CITY AND I HAVE TO GO THERE TO MEET THE OWNER! I FIGURED I'D ASK YOU TO DRIVE ME... ESPECIALLY SINCE I HAD SOMETHING ELSE OF IMPORTANCE TO TALK TO YOU ABOUT!
WHAT'S THAT, CAROL?
WELL, I HAD A--A FANTASTIC DREAM LAST NIGHT! AND I MADE UP MY MIND TO TELL YOU ABOUT IT--BUT REMEMBER, HAL, IT'S JUST A DREAM! YOU SEE...
IN IT I HAD AGREED TO MARRY YOU--BUT ONLY IN ORDER TO GET GREEN LANTERN JEALOUS!
BOY, WHAT A DREAM! TELL ME MORE!
"THE DREAM SEEMED SO REAL! THERE WE WERE... ABOUT TO GET MARRIED..."
STILL NO SIGN OF GREEN LANTERN! BUT THERE'S ONLY... A FEW MINUTES LEFT! IS IT POSSIBLE... HE WON'T SHOW UP?
IN THE DREAM I WAS SURE THAT GREEN LANTERN WOULD APPEAR AT THE LAST MOMENT... TO SWEEP ME OFF MY FEET AND CARRY ME AWAY, YOU SEE?
UH HUH-- GO ON...
"BUT WHEN THE FATEFUL WORDS WERE UTTERED..."
I NOW PRONOUNCE YOU... MAN AND WIFE!
G-GREEN LANTERN FAILED ME!
3

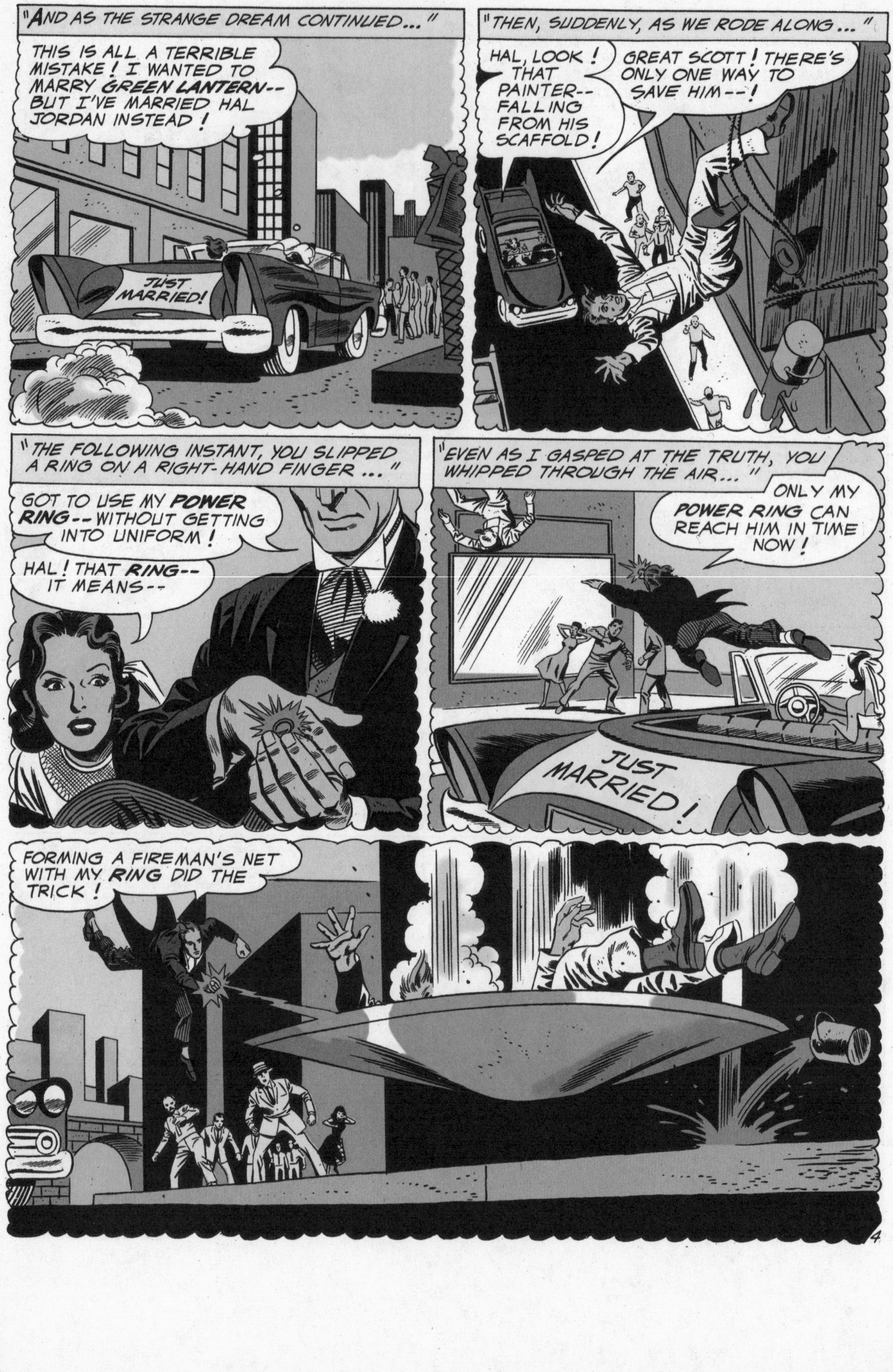
"AND AS THE STRANGE DREAM CONTINUED..."
THIS IS ALL A TERRIBLE MISTAKE! I WANTED TO MARRY GREEN LANTERN--BUT I'VE MARRIED HAL JORDAN INSTEAD!
JUST MARRIED!
"THEN, SUDDENLY, AS WE RODE ALONG..."
HAL, LOOK! THAT PAINTER--FALLING FROM HIS SCAFFOLD!
GREAT SCOTT! THERE'S ONLY ONE WAY TO SAVE HIM--!
"THE FOLLOWING INSTANT, YOU SLIPPED A RING ON A RIGHT-HAND FINGER..."
GOT TO USE MY POWER RING--WITHOUT GETTING INTO UNIFORM!
HAL! THAT RING--IT MEANS--
"EVEN AS I GASPED AT THE TRUTH, YOU WHIPPED THROUGH THE AIR..."
ONLY MY POWER RING CAN REACH HIM IN TIME NOW!
JUST MARRIED!
FORMING A FIREMAN'S NET WITH MY RING DID THE TRICK!
4

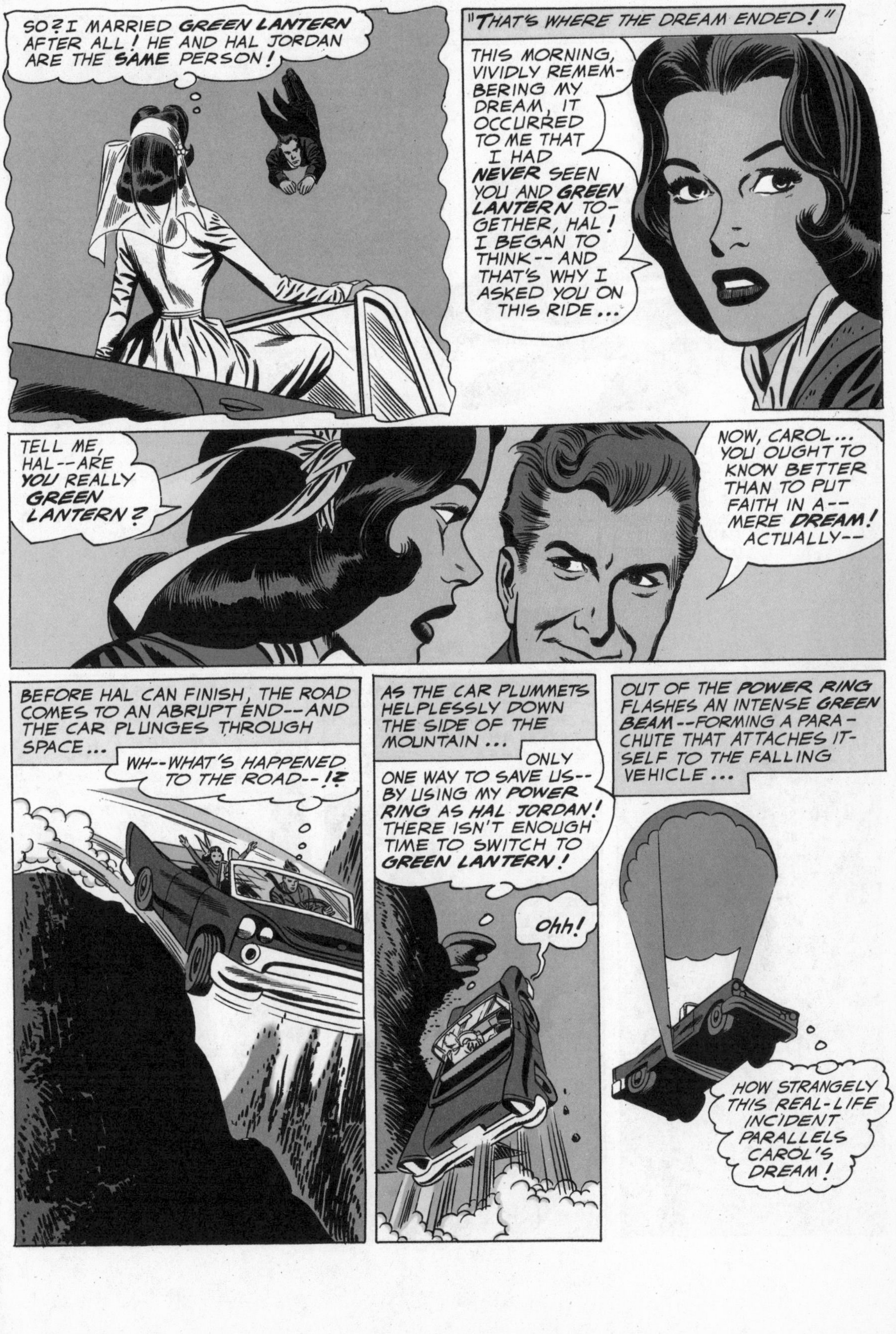
SO? I MARRIED GREEN LANTERN AFTER ALL! HE AND HAL JORDAN ARE THE SAME PERSON!
"THAT'S WHERE THE DREAM ENDED!"
THIS MORNING, VIVIDLY REMEMBERING MY DREAM, IT OCCURRED TO ME THAT I HAD NEVER SEEN YOU AND GREEN LANTERN TOGETHER, HAL! I BEGAN TO THINK-- AND THAT'S WHY I ASKED YOU ON THIS RIDE...
TELL ME, HAL--ARE YOU REALLY GREEN LANTERN?
NOW, CAROL... YOU OUGHT TO KNOW BETTER THAN TO PUT FAITH IN A-- MERE DREAM! ACTUALLY--
BEFORE HAL CAN FINISH, THE ROAD COMES TO AN ABRUPT END--AND THE CAR PLUNGES THROUGH SPACE...
WH--WHAT'S HAPPENED TO THE ROAD--!?
AS THE CAR PLUMMETS HELPLESSLY DOWN THE SIDE OF THE MOUNTAIN...
ONLY ONE WAY TO SAVE US-- BY USING MY POWER RING AS HAL JORDAN! THERE ISN'T ENOUGH TIME TO SWITCH TO GREEN LANTERN!
OHH!
OUT OF THE POWER RING FLASHES AN INTENSE GREEN BEAM--FORMING A PARACHUTE THAT ATTACHES ITSELF TO THE FALLING VEHICLE...
HOW STRANGELY THIS REAL-LIFE INCIDENT PARALLELS CAROL'S DREAM!

SOON, NOT FAR FROM THE ACCIDENT-SCENE...

THOSE MEN IN THAT JEEP--WAVING FRANTICALLY AT ME!

GREEN LANTERN--STOP! WE'VE GOT TO TALK TO YOU!

MOMENTS LATER, AS THE MEN IN THE CAR POUR OUT WILD WORDS TO THE GREEN-CLAD CHAMPION...

WE'RE SCIENTISTS--FROM THE DULONG EXPERIMENTAL STATION ON TOP OF THE MOUNTAIN--!

SOMETHING TERRIBLE HAS HAPPENED!

CALM DOWN! WE'VE GOT TO EXPLAIN! LISTEN, GREEN LANTERN--OUR WORK IN THE DULONG STATION HAS BEEN THE INVESTIGATION OF THE EFFECTS OF COSMIC RAYS ON VARIOUS TYPES OF MATTER...

"UP TO YESTERDAY WE HAD NO IMPORTANT RESULTS....BUT THEN THIS MORNING ..."

GREAT STARS! WHAT'S HAPPENING TO THE BLOB I PLACED IN THIS TEST TUBE?

A--A SHAPE MATERIALIZING INSIDE!

"WITHIN MOMENTS, THE THING SPROUTED BEFORE MY EYES--UNTIL ..."

RUN! IT'S GROWING WILD! WE CAN'T CONTROL IT--!

I'VE TRIED TO SHOOT IT--!

WE COULD DO NOTHING, GREEN LANTERN! THE THING GREW TO ENORMOUS SIZE! WE'RE TRYING TO ALARM THE COUNTRY-SIDE--! IT MAY KILL--DESTROY THOUSANDS OF PEOPLE!

YOU KEEP GOING--SPREAD THE WARNING!

⑦

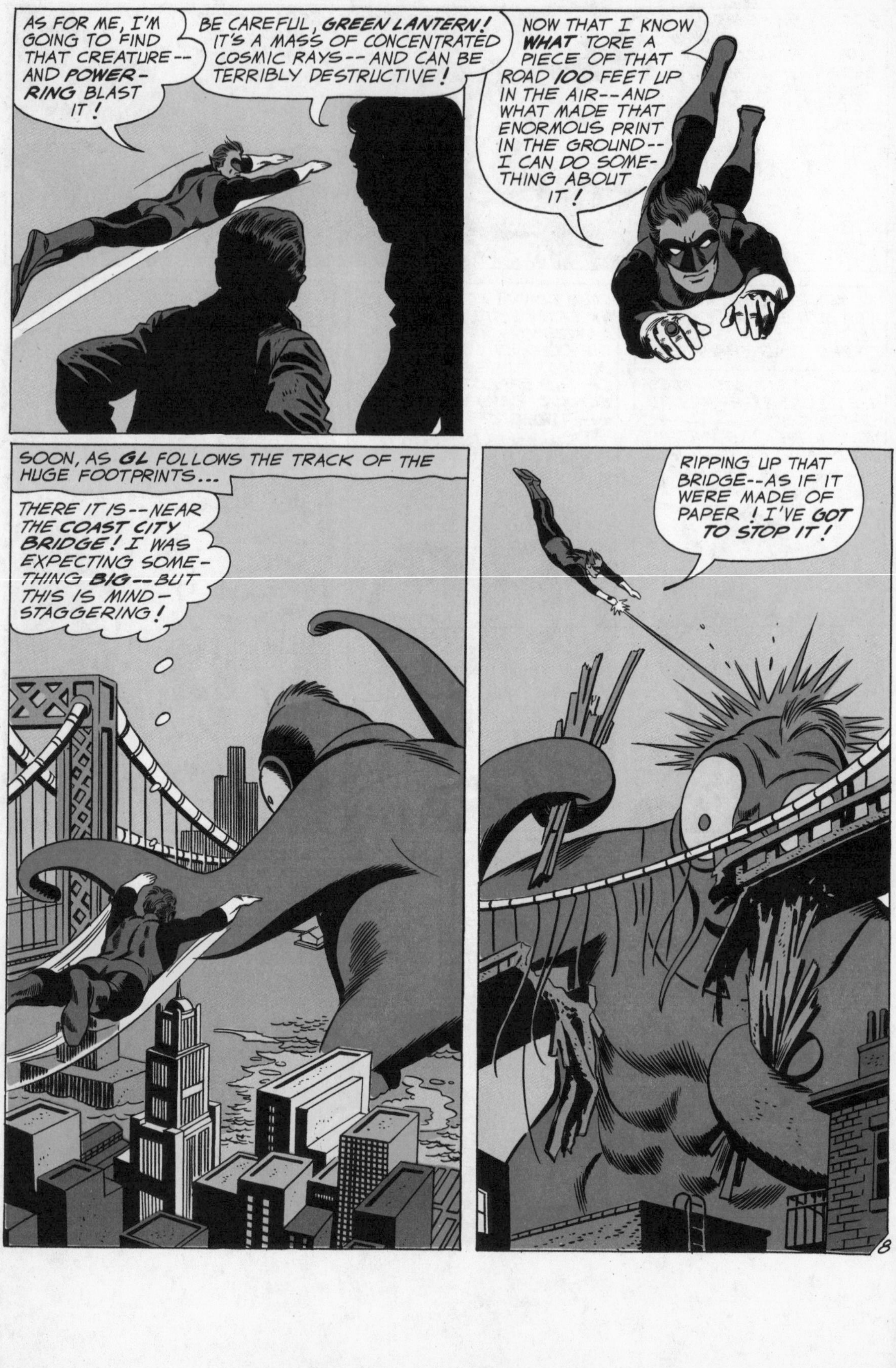
AS FOR ME, I'M GOING TO FIND THAT CREATURE -- AND POWER-RING BLAST IT!
BE CAREFUL, GREEN LANTERN! IT'S A MASS OF CONCENTRATED COSMIC RAYS -- AND CAN BE TERRIBLY DESTRUCTIVE!
NOW THAT I KNOW WHAT TORE A PIECE OF THAT ROAD 100 FEET UP IN THE AIR -- AND WHAT MADE THAT ENORMOUS PRINT IN THE GROUND -- I CAN DO SOMETHING ABOUT IT!
SOON, AS GL FOLLOWS THE TRACK OF THE HUGE FOOTPRINTS...
THERE IT IS -- NEAR THE COAST CITY BRIDGE! I WAS EXPECTING SOMETHING BIG -- BUT THIS IS MIND-STAGGERING!
RIPPING UP THAT BRIDGE -- AS IF IT WERE MADE OF PAPER! I'VE GOT TO STOP IT!
8

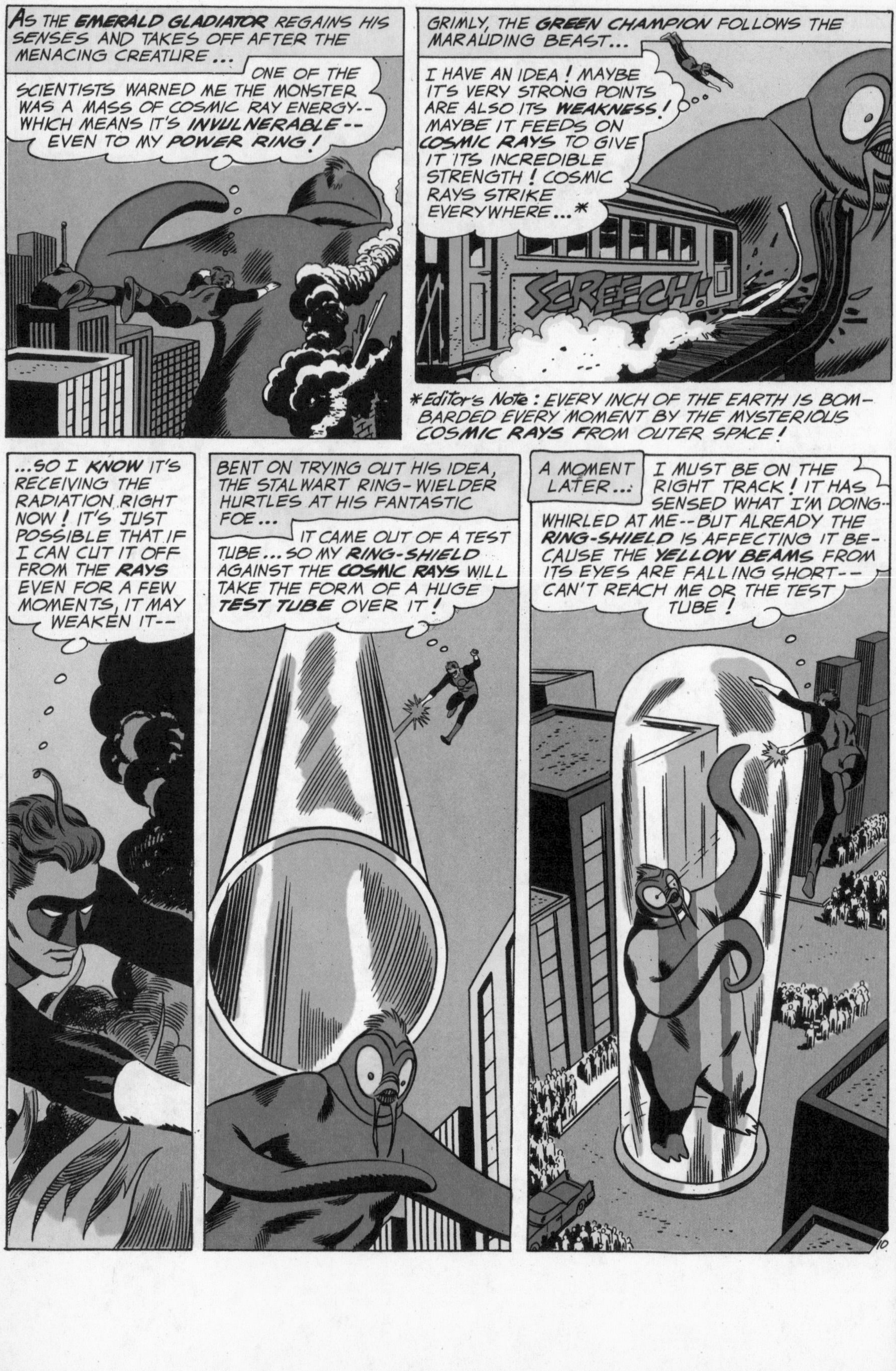

AS THE EMERALD GLADIATOR REGAINS HIS SENSES AND TAKES OFF AFTER THE MENACING CREATURE ...
ONE OF THE SCIENTISTS WARNED ME THE MONSTER WAS A MASS OF COSMIC RAY ENERGY-- WHICH MEANS IT'S INVULNERABLE -- EVEN TO MY POWER RING!
GRIMLY, THE GREEN CHAMPION FOLLOWS THE MARAUDING BEAST...
I HAVE AN IDEA! MAYBE IT'S VERY STRONG POINTS ARE ALSO ITS WEAKNESS! MAYBE IT FEEDS ON COSMIC RAYS TO GIVE IT ITS INCREDIBLE STRENGTH! COSMIC RAYS STRIKE EVERYWHERE...*
SCREECH!
*Editor's Note: EVERY INCH OF THE EARTH IS BOMBARDED EVERY MOMENT BY THE MYSTERIOUS COSMIC RAYS FROM OUTER SPACE!
...SO I KNOW IT'S RECEIVING THE RADIATION RIGHT NOW! IT'S JUST POSSIBLE THAT IF I CAN CUT IT OFF FROM THE RAYS EVEN FOR A FEW MOMENTS, IT MAY WEAKEN IT--
BENT ON TRYING OUT HIS IDEA, THE STALWART RING-WIELDER HURTLES AT HIS FANTASTIC FOE...
IT CAME OUT OF A TEST TUBE... SO MY RING-SHIELD AGAINST THE COSMIC RAYS WILL TAKE THE FORM OF A HUGE TEST TUBE OVER IT!
A MOMENT LATER...
I MUST BE ON THE RIGHT TRACK! IT HAS SENSED WHAT I'M DOING-- WHIRLED AT ME--BUT ALREADY THE RING-SHIELD IS AFFECTING IT BECAUSE THE YELLOW BEAMS FROM ITS EYES ARE FALLING SHORT-- CAN'T REACH ME OR THE TEST TUBE!
10

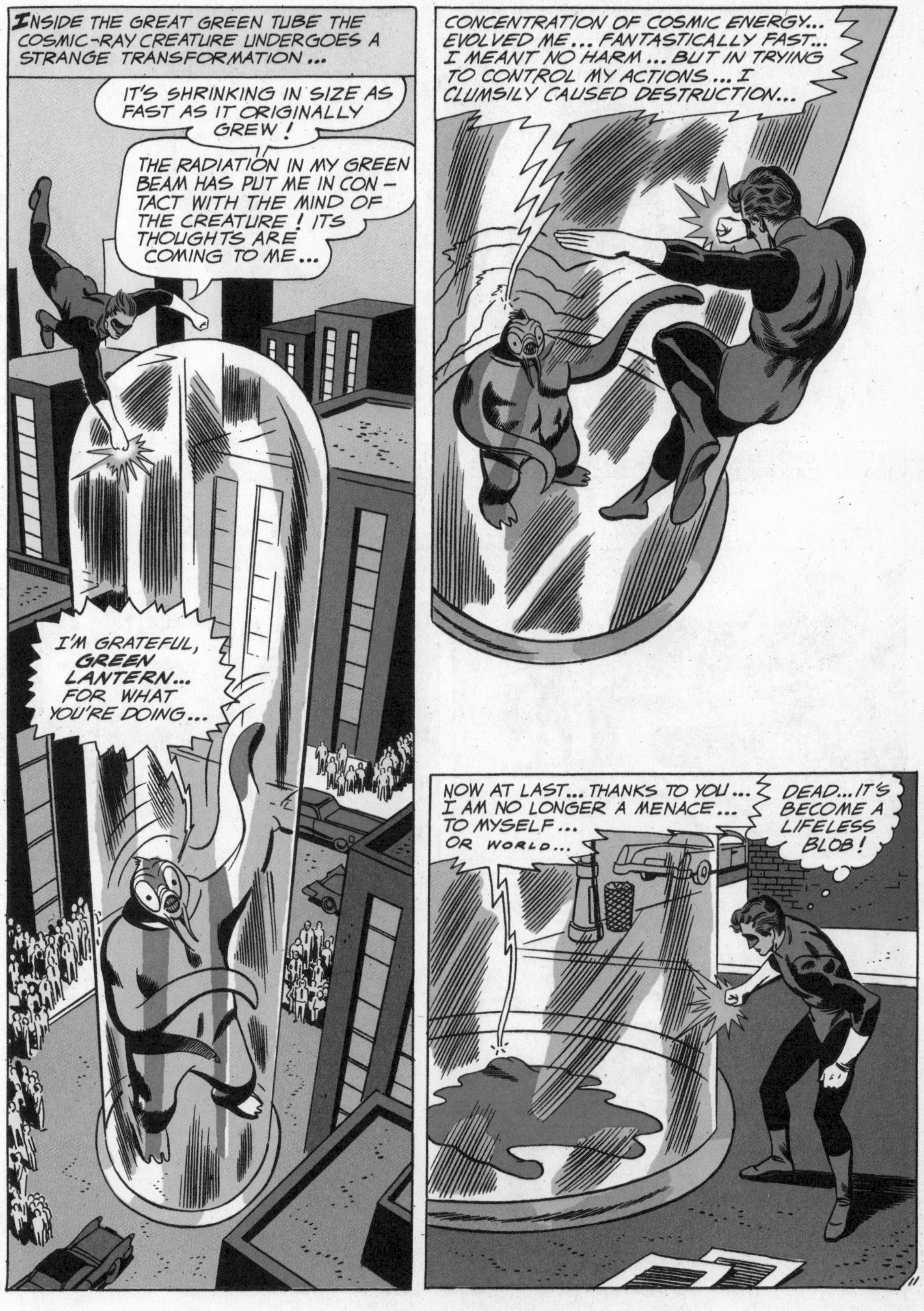
INSIDE THE GREAT GREEN TUBE THE COSMIC-RAY CREATURE UNDERGOES A STRANGE TRANSFORMATION...
IT'S SHRINKING IN SIZE AS FAST AS IT ORIGINALLY GREW!
THE RADIATION IN MY GREEN BEAM HAS PUT ME IN CON-TACT WITH THE MIND OF THE CREATURE! ITS THOUGHTS ARE COMING TO ME...
I'M GRATEFUL, GREEN LANTERN... FOR WHAT YOU'RE DOING...
CONCENTRATION OF COSMIC ENERGY... EVOLVED ME... FANTASTICALLY FAST... I MEANT NO HARM... BUT IN TRYING TO CONTROL MY ACTIONS... I CLUMSILY CAUSED DESTRUCTION...
NOW AT LAST... THANKS TO YOU... I AM NO LONGER A MENACE... TO MYSELF... OR WORLD...
DEAD... IT'S BECOME A LIFELESS BLOB!
11

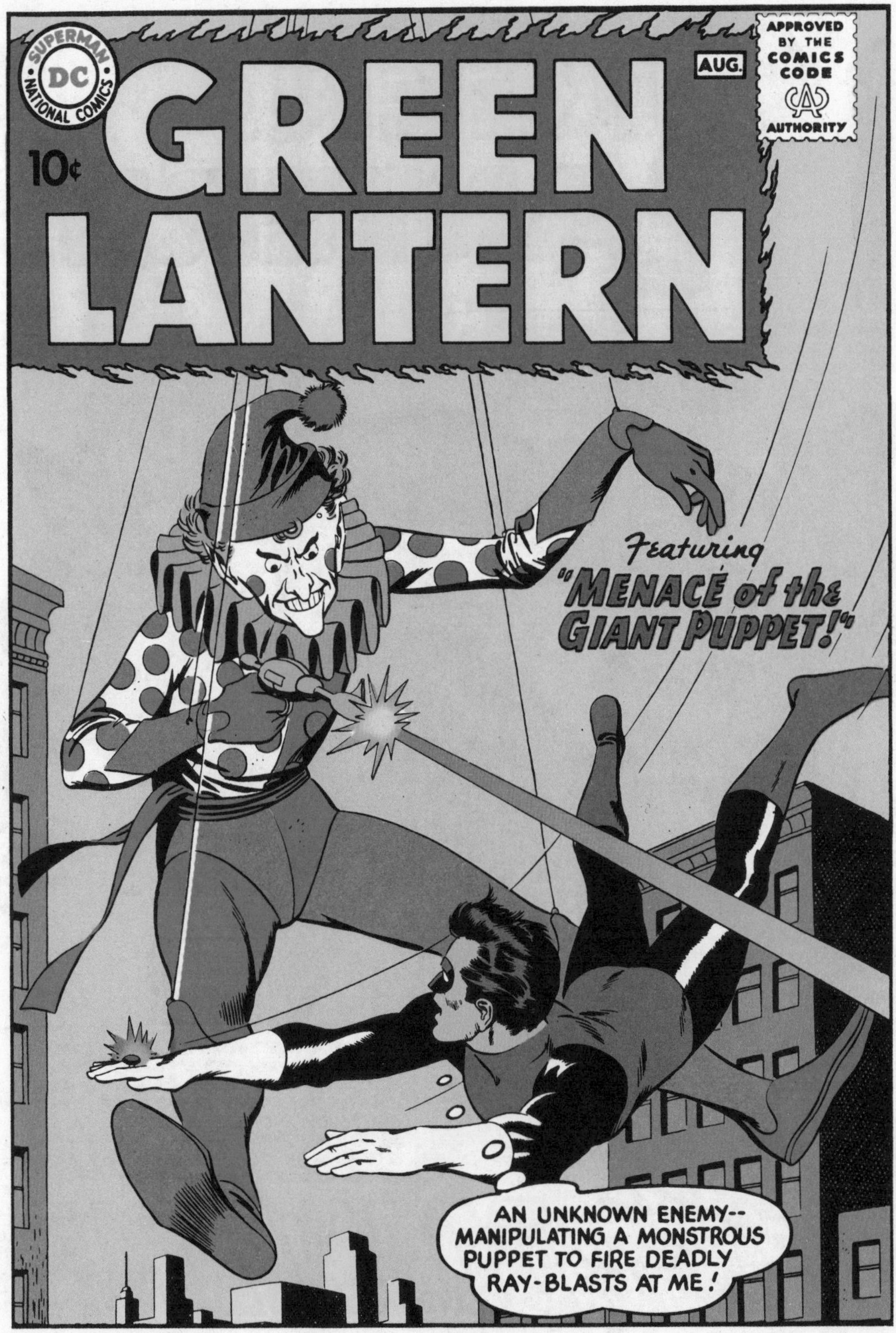
SUPERMAN DC NATIONAL COMICS
GREEN LANTERN
10¢
AUG.
APPROVED BY THE COMICS CODE AUTHORITY
Featuring "MENACE of the GIANT PUPPET!"
AN UNKNOWN ENEMY-- MANIPULATING A MONSTROUS PUPPET TO FIRE DEADLY RAY-BLASTS AT ME!

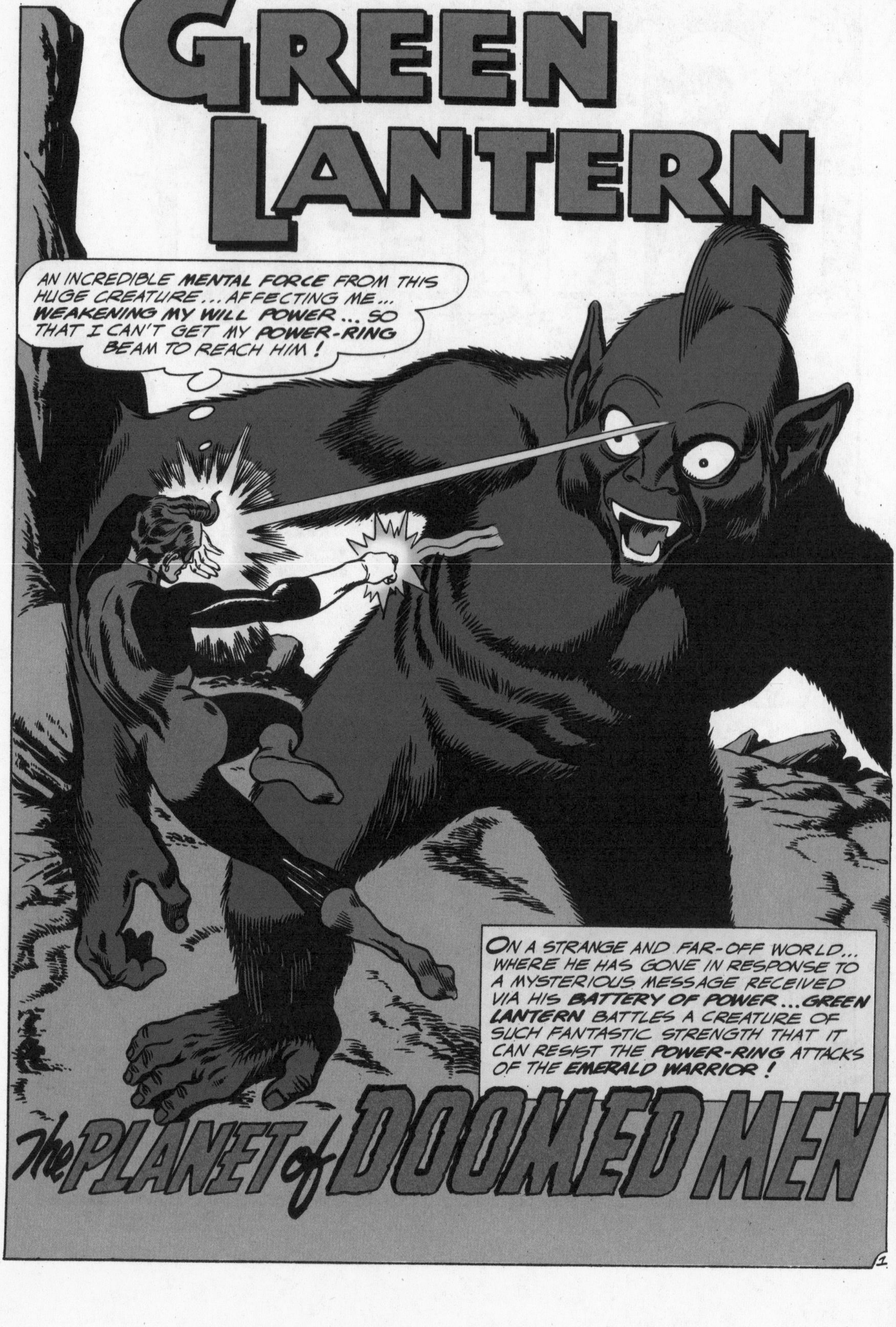

GREEN LANTERN
AN INCREDIBLE MENTAL FORCE FROM THIS HUGE CREATURE... AFFECTING ME... WEAKENING MY WILL POWER... SO THAT I CAN'T GET MY POWER-RING BEAM TO REACH HIM!
ON A STRANGE AND FAR-OFF WORLD... WHERE HE HAS GONE IN RESPONSE TO A MYSTERIOUS MESSAGE RECEIVED VIA HIS BATTERY OF POWER... GREEN LANTERN BATTLES A CREATURE OF SUCH FANTASTIC STRENGTH THAT IT CAN RESIST THE POWER-RING ATTACKS OF THE EMERALD WARRIOR!
The PLANET of DOOMED MEN
1

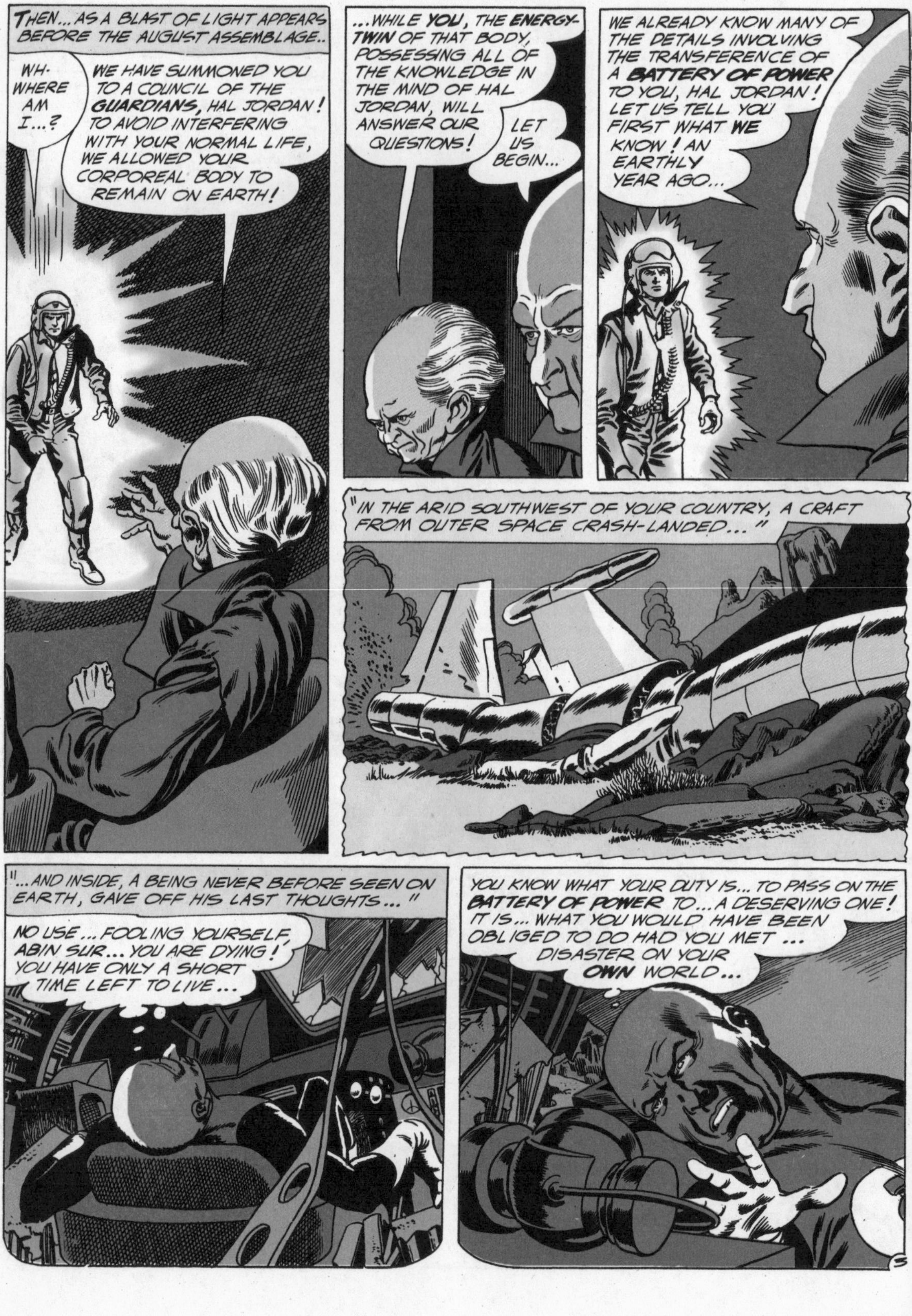
THEN...AS A BLAST OF LIGHT APPEARS BEFORE THE AUGUST ASSEMBLAGE..
WH- WHERE AM I...?
WE HAVE SUMMONED YOU TO A COUNCIL OF THE GUARDIANS, HAL JORDAN! TO AVOID INTERFERING WITH YOUR NORMAL LIFE, WE ALLOWED YOUR CORPOREAL BODY TO REMAIN ON EARTH!
...WHILE YOU, THE ENERGY-TWIN OF THAT BODY, POSSESSING ALL OF THE KNOWLEDGE IN THE MIND OF HAL JORDAN, WILL ANSWER OUR QUESTIONS!
LET US BEGIN...
WE ALREADY KNOW MANY OF THE DETAILS INVOLVING THE TRANSFERENCE OF A BATTERY OF POWER TO YOU, HAL JORDAN! LET US TELL YOU FIRST WHAT WE KNOW! AN EARTHLY YEAR AGO...
"IN THE ARID SOUTHWEST OF YOUR COUNTRY, A CRAFT FROM OUTER SPACE CRASH-LANDED..."
"...AND INSIDE, A BEING NEVER BEFORE SEEN ON EARTH, GAVE OFF HIS LAST THOUGHTS..."
NO USE...FOOLING YOURSELF, ABIN SUR...YOU ARE DYING! YOU HAVE ONLY A SHORT TIME LEFT TO LIVE...
YOU KNOW WHAT YOUR DUTY IS...TO PASS ON THE BATTERY OF POWER TO...A DESERVING ONE! IT IS...WHAT YOU WOULD HAVE BEEN OBLIGED TO DO HAD YOU MET...DISASTER ON YOUR OWN WORLD...
5

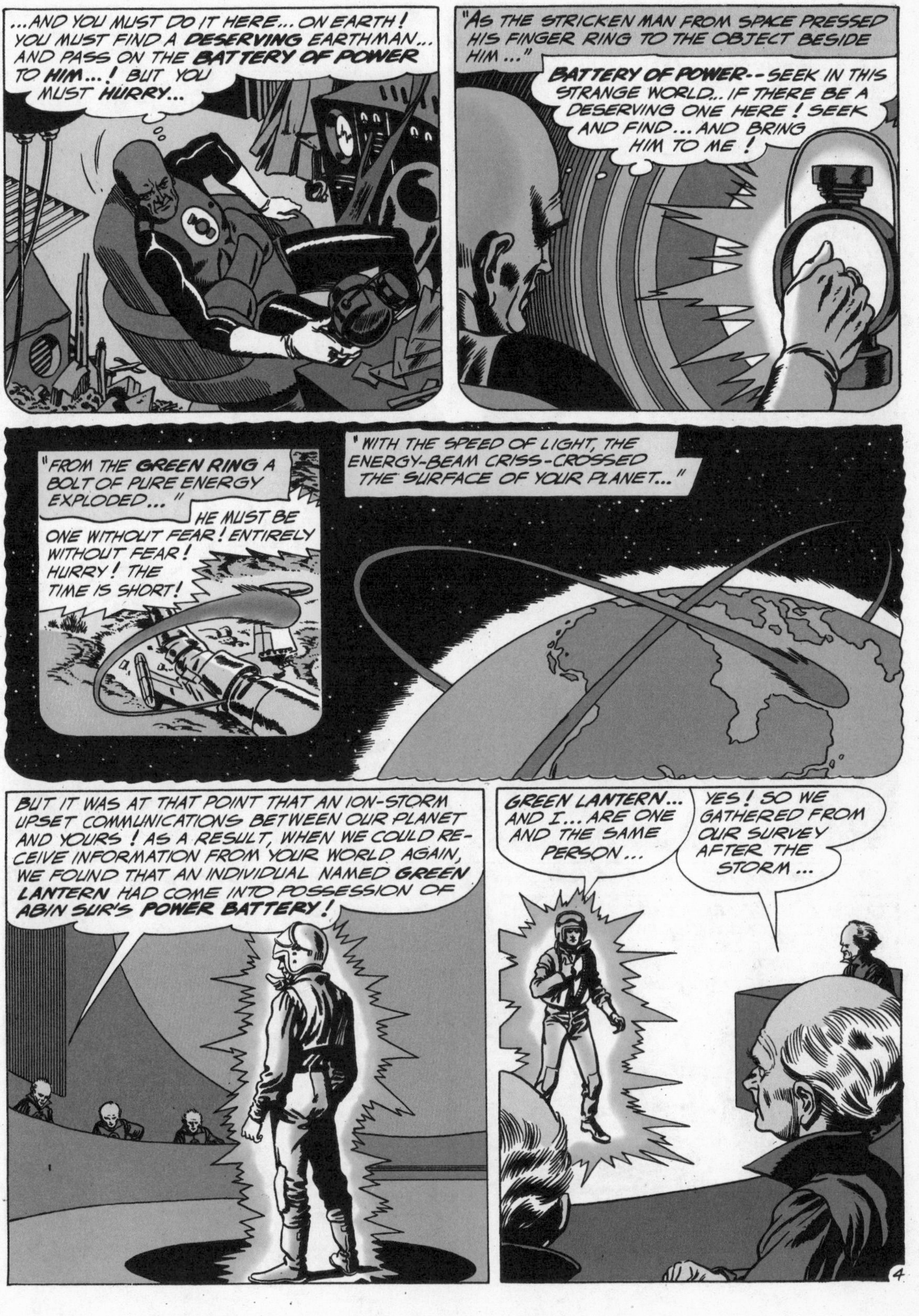
...AND YOU MUST DO IT HERE... ON EARTH! YOU MUST FIND A DESERVING EARTHMAN... AND PASS ON THE BATTERY OF POWER TO HIM...! BUT YOU MUST HURRY...
"AS THE STRICKEN MAN FROM SPACE PRESSED HIS FINGER RING TO THE OBJECT BESIDE HIM..."
BATTERY OF POWER--SEEK IN THIS STRANGE WORLD... IF THERE BE A DESERVING ONE HERE! SEEK AND FIND... AND BRING HIM TO ME!
"FROM THE GREEN RING A BOLT OF PURE ENERGY EXPLODED..."
HE MUST BE ONE WITHOUT FEAR! ENTIRELY WITHOUT FEAR! HURRY! THE TIME IS SHORT!
"WITH THE SPEED OF LIGHT, THE ENERGY-BEAM CRISS-CROSSED THE SURFACE OF YOUR PLANET..."
BUT IT WAS AT THAT POINT THAT AN ION-STORM UPSET COMMUNICATIONS BETWEEN OUR PLANET AND YOURS! AS A RESULT, WHEN WE COULD RE-CEIVE INFORMATION FROM YOUR WORLD AGAIN, WE FOUND THAT AN INDIVIDUAL NAMED GREEN LANTERN HAD COME INTO POSSESSION OF ABIN SUR'S POWER BATTERY!
GREEN LANTERN... AND I... ARE ONE AND THE SAME PERSON...
YES! SO WE GATHERED FROM OUR SURVEY AFTER THE STORM...
4

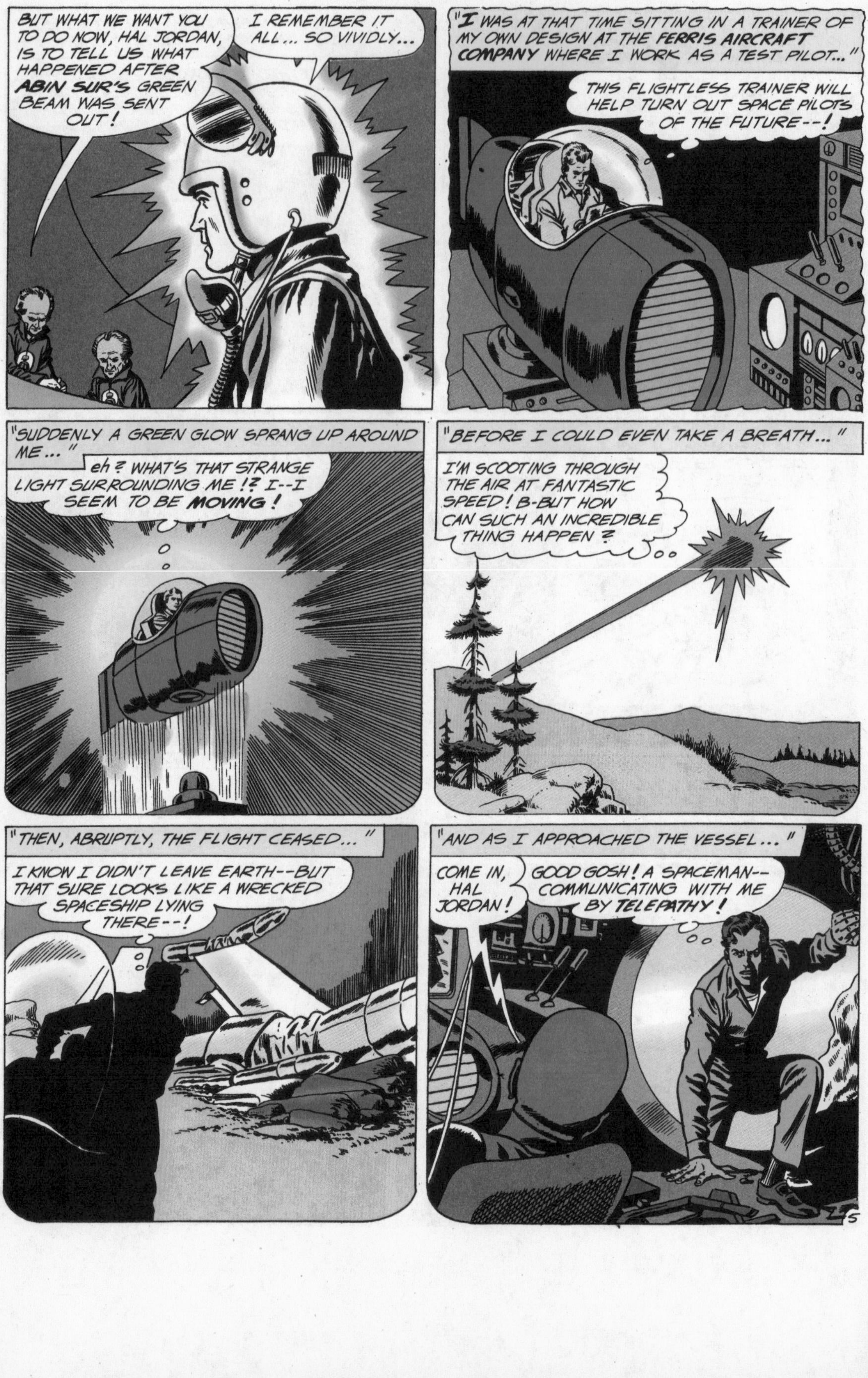
BUT WHAT WE WANT YOU TO DO NOW, HAL JORDAN, IS TO TELL US WHAT HAPPENED AFTER ABIN SUR'S GREEN BEAM WAS SENT OUT!
I REMEMBER IT ALL... SO VIVIDLY...
"I WAS AT THAT TIME SITTING IN A TRAINER OF MY OWN DESIGN AT THE FERRIS AIRCRAFT COMPANY WHERE I WORK AS A TEST PILOT..."
THIS FLIGHTLESS TRAINER WILL HELP TURN OUT SPACE PILOTS OF THE FUTURE--!
"SUDDENLY A GREEN GLOW SPRANG UP AROUND ME..."
eh? WHAT'S THAT STRANGE LIGHT SURROUNDING ME!? I--I SEEM TO BE MOVING!
"BEFORE I COULD EVEN TAKE A BREATH..."
I'M SCOOTING THROUGH THE AIR AT FANTASTIC SPEED! B-BUT HOW CAN SUCH AN INCREDIBLE THING HAPPEN?
"THEN, ABRUPTLY, THE FLIGHT CEASED..."
I KNOW I DIDN'T LEAVE EARTH--BUT THAT SURE LOOKS LIKE A WRECKED SPACESHIP LYING THERE--!
"AND AS I APPROACHED THE VESSEL..."
COME IN, HAL JORDAN!
GOOD GOSH! A SPACEMAN--COMMUNICATING WITH ME BY TELEPATHY!
5

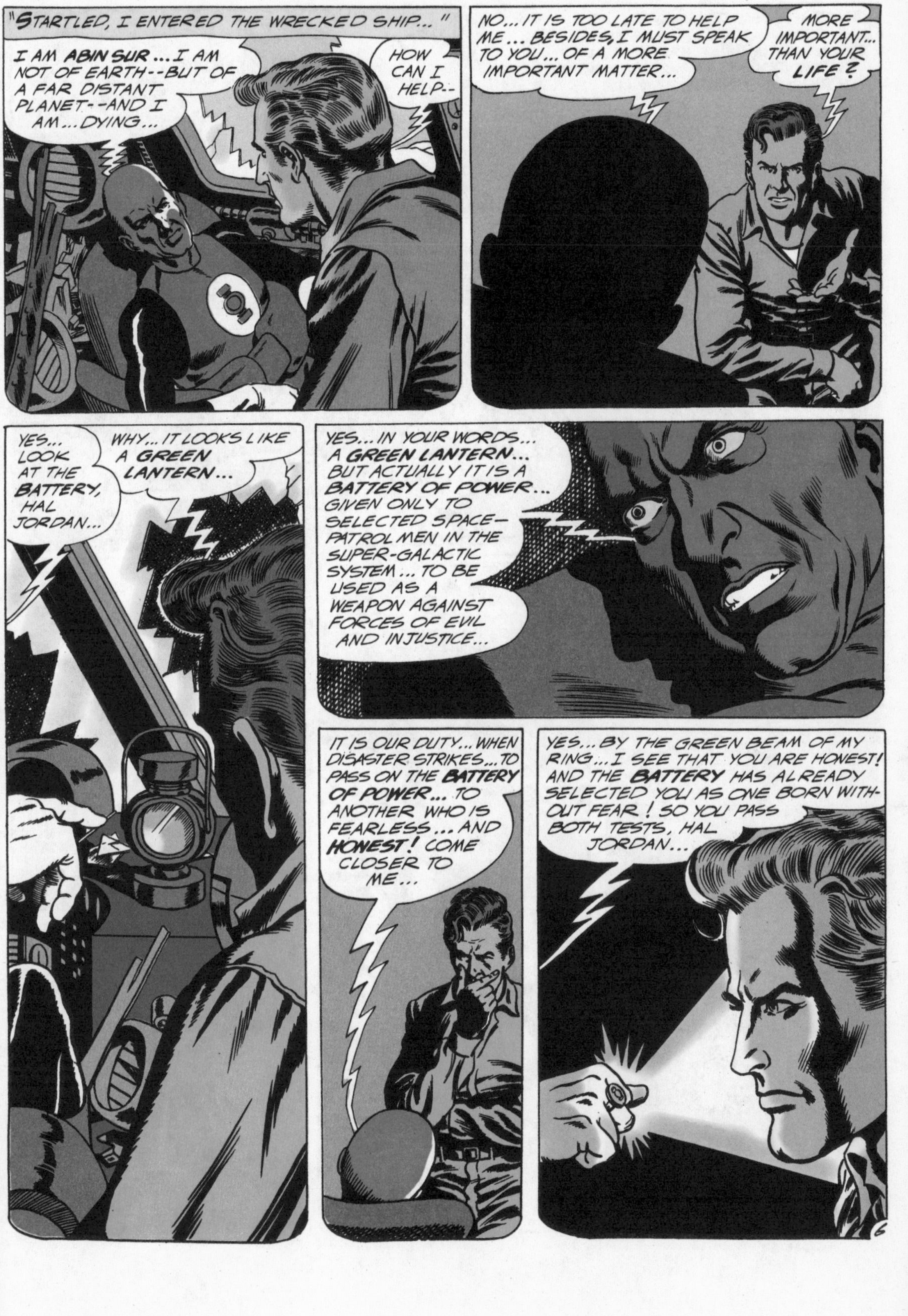
"STARTLED, I ENTERED THE WRECKED SHIP..."
I AM ABIN SUR... I AM NOT OF EARTH--BUT OF A FAR DISTANT PLANET--AND I AM... DYING...
HOW CAN I HELP--
NO... IT IS TOO LATE TO HELP ME... BESIDES, I MUST SPEAK TO YOU... OF A MORE IMPORTANT MATTER...
MORE IMPORTANT... THAN YOUR LIFE?
YES... LOOK AT THE BATTERY, HAL JORDAN...
WHY... IT LOOKS LIKE A GREEN LANTERN...
YES... IN YOUR WORDS... A GREEN LANTERN... BUT ACTUALLY IT IS A BATTERY OF POWER... GIVEN ONLY TO SELECTED SPACE-PATROLMEN IN THE SUPER-GALACTIC SYSTEM... TO BE USED AS A WEAPON AGAINST FORCES OF EVIL AND INJUSTICE...
IT IS OUR DUTY... WHEN DISASTER STRIKES... TO PASS ON THE BATTERY OF POWER... TO ANOTHER WHO IS FEARLESS... AND HONEST! COME CLOSER TO ME...
YES... BY THE GREEN BEAM OF MY RING... I SEE THAT YOU ARE HONEST! AND THE BATTERY HAS ALREADY SELECTED YOU AS ONE BORN WITHOUT FEAR! SO YOU PASS BOTH TESTS, HAL JORDAN...
6

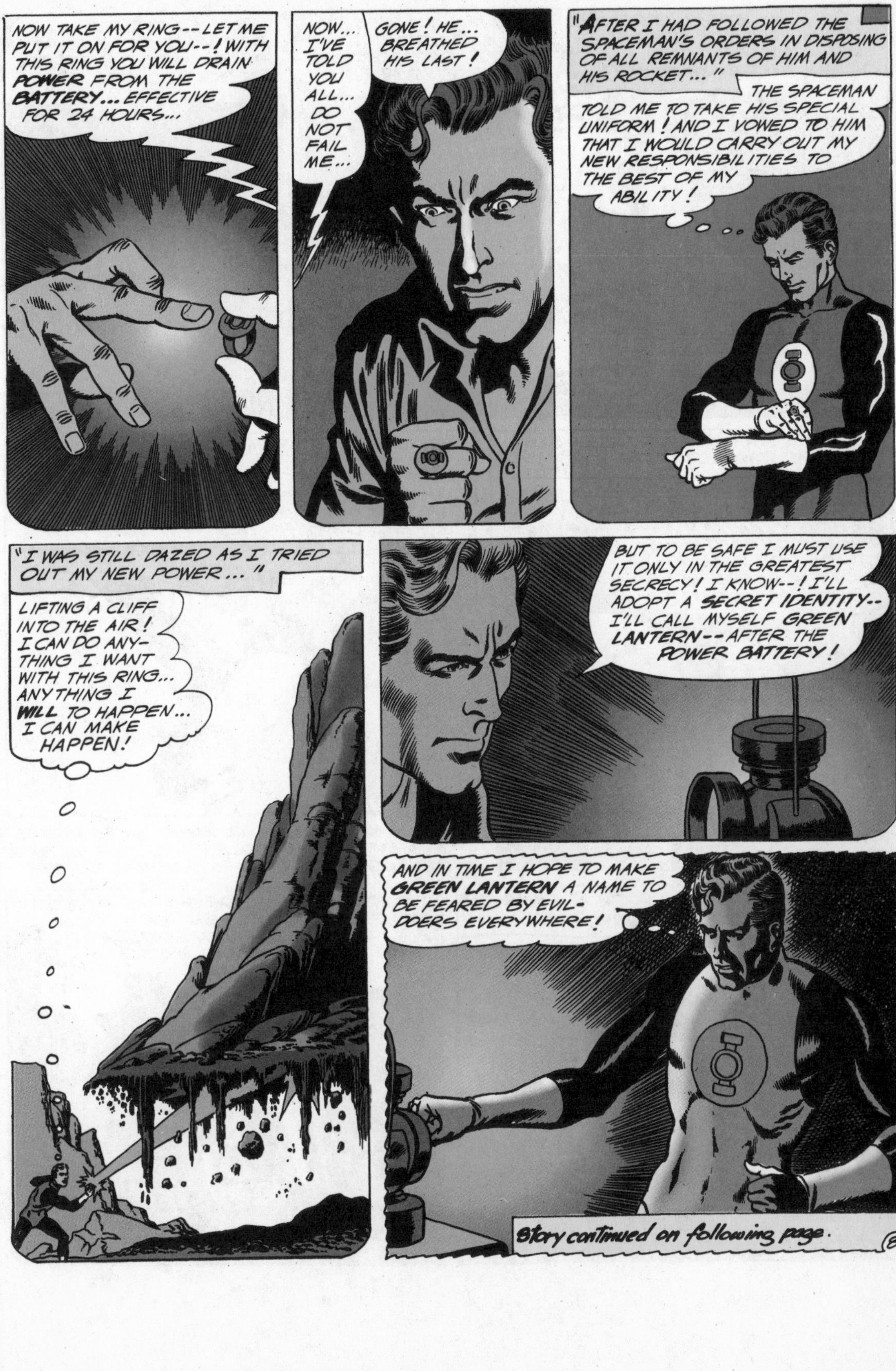
NOW TAKE MY RING--LET ME PUT IT ON FOR YOU--! WITH THIS RING YOU WILL DRAIN POWER FROM THE BATTERY... EFFECTIVE FOR 24 HOURS...
NOW... I'VE TOLD YOU ALL... DO NOT FAIL ME...
GONE! HE... BREATHED HIS LAST!
"AFTER I HAD FOLLOWED THE SPACEMAN'S ORDERS IN DISPOSING OF ALL REMNANTS OF HIM AND HIS ROCKET..."
THE SPACEMAN TOLD ME TO TAKE HIS SPECIAL UNIFORM! AND I VOWED TO HIM THAT I WOULD CARRY OUT MY NEW RESPONSIBILITIES TO THE BEST OF MY ABILITY!
"I WAS STILL DAZED AS I TRIED OUT MY NEW POWER..."
LIFTING A CLIFF INTO THE AIR! I CAN DO ANYTHING I WANT WITH THIS RING... ANYTHING I WILL TO HAPPEN... I CAN MAKE HAPPEN!
BUT TO BE SAFE I MUST USE IT ONLY IN THE GREATEST SECRECY! I KNOW--! I'LL ADOPT A SECRET IDENTITY-- I'LL CALL MYSELF GREEN LANTERN--AFTER THE POWER BATTERY!
AND IN TIME I HOPE TO MAKE GREEN LANTERN A NAME TO BE FEARED BY EVIL-DOERS EVERYWHERE!
Story continued on following page.
8

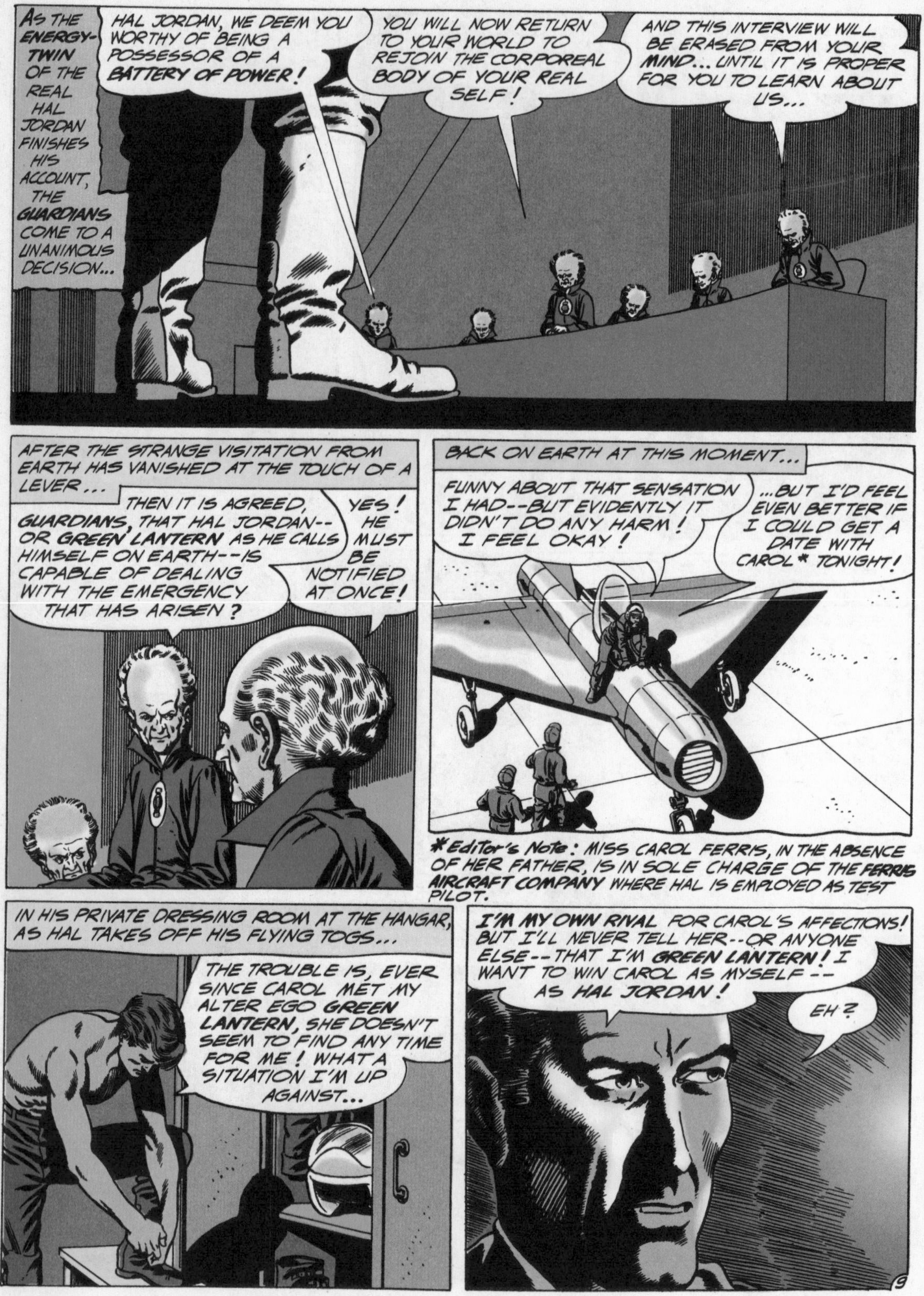
AS THE ENERGY-TWIN OF THE REAL HAL JORDAN FINISHES HIS ACCOUNT, THE GUARDIANS COME TO A UNANIMOUS DECISION...
HAL JORDAN, WE DEEM YOU WORTHY OF BEING A POSSESSOR OF A BATTERY OF POWER!
YOU WILL NOW RETURN TO YOUR WORLD TO REJOIN THE CORPOREAL BODY OF YOUR REAL SELF!
AND THIS INTERVIEW WILL BE ERASED FROM YOUR MIND... UNTIL IT IS PROPER FOR YOU TO LEARN ABOUT US...
AFTER THE STRANGE VISITATION FROM EARTH HAS VANISHED AT THE TOUCH OF A LEVER...
THEN IT IS AGREED, GUARDIANS, THAT HAL JORDAN-- OR GREEN LANTERN AS HE CALLS HIMSELF ON EARTH--IS CAPABLE OF DEALING WITH THE EMERGENCY THAT HAS ARISEN?
YES! HE MUST BE NOTIFIED AT ONCE!
BACK ON EARTH AT THIS MOMENT...
FUNNY ABOUT THAT SENSATION I HAD--BUT EVIDENTLY IT DIDN'T DO ANY HARM! I FEEL OKAY!
...BUT I'D FEEL EVEN BETTER IF I COULD GET A DATE WITH CAROL* TONIGHT!
*Editor's Note: MISS CAROL FERRIS, IN THE ABSENCE OF HER FATHER, IS IN SOLE CHARGE OF THE FERRIS AIRCRAFT COMPANY WHERE HAL IS EMPLOYED AS TEST PILOT.
IN HIS PRIVATE DRESSING ROOM AT THE HANGAR, AS HAL TAKES OFF HIS FLYING TOGS...
THE TROUBLE IS, EVER SINCE CAROL MET MY ALTER EGO GREEN LANTERN, SHE DOESN'T SEEM TO FIND ANY TIME FOR ME! WHAT A SITUATION I'M UP AGAINST...
I'M MY OWN RIVAL FOR CAROL'S AFFECTIONS! BUT I'LL NEVER TELL HER--OR ANYONE ELSE--THAT I'M GREEN LANTERN! I WANT TO WIN CAROL AS MYSELF-- AS HAL JORDAN!
EH?
9

TURNING HIS EYES TO A CORNER OF THE ROOM, THE ACE TEST PILOT SEES...

A GREEN GLOW COMING THROUGH THE INVISIBILITY SHIELD PROTECTING MY POWER BATTERY!*

*Editor's Note: HAL (GREEN LANTERN) JORDAN HAS CREATED THE INVISIBILITY SHIELD TO PREVENT THE POWER BATTERY FROM BEING SEEN OR TOUCHED BY ANYONE BUT HIMSELF!

THE BATTERY IS SIGNALING ME AGAIN--PROJECTING THOUGHTS AT ME!

WIELDER OF THE GREEN BEAM OF POWER, YOU MUST TAKE CARE OF AN EMERGENCY IN YOUR SECTOR...

...ON THE WORLD OF CALOR, THE THIRD PLANET IN THE STAR-SYSTEM CLOSEST TO YOURS, A RACE OF HUMAN-TYPE BEINGS IS IN DANGER!

HE ACTS WITH COMMENDABLE SPEED... CHARGING HIS POWER RING...

IN BRIGHTEST DAY... IN BLACKEST NIGHT, NO EVIL SHALL ESCAPE MY SIGHT! LET THOSE WHO WORSHIP EVIL'S MIGHT BEWARE MY POWER-- GREEN LANTERN'S LIGHT!

...REPEATING HIS SOLEMN OATH...

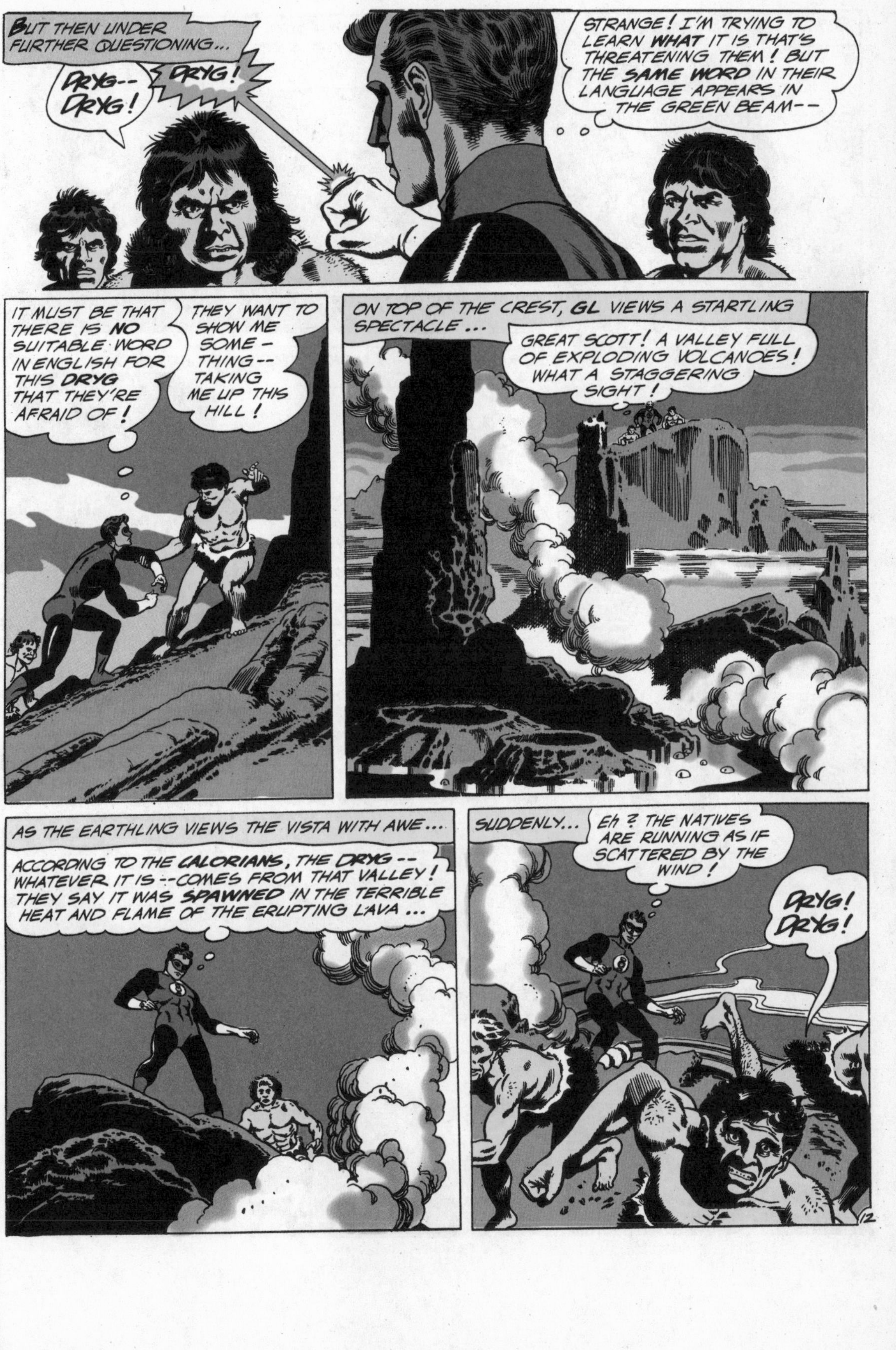

BUT THEN UNDER FURTHER QUESTIONING...
DRYG-- DRYG!
DRYG!
STRANGE! I'M TRYING TO LEARN WHAT IT IS THAT'S THREATENING THEM! BUT THE SAME WORD IN THEIR LANGUAGE APPEARS IN THE GREEN BEAM--
IT MUST BE THAT THERE IS NO SUITABLE WORD IN ENGLISH FOR THIS DRYG THAT THEY'RE AFRAID OF!
THEY WANT TO SHOW ME SOME-THING-- TAKING ME UP THIS HILL!
ON TOP OF THE CREST, GL VIEWS A STARTLING SPECTACLE...
GREAT SCOTT! A VALLEY FULL OF EXPLODING VOLCANOES! WHAT A STAGGERING SIGHT!
AS THE EARTHLING VIEWS THE VISTA WITH AWE...
ACCORDING TO THE CALORIANS, THE DRYG -- WHATEVER IT IS--COMES FROM THAT VALLEY! THEY SAY IT WAS SPAWNED IN THE TERRIBLE HEAT AND FLAME OF THE ERUPTING LAVA...
SUDDENLY...
Eh? THE NATIVES ARE RUNNING AS IF SCATTERED BY THE WIND!
DRYG! DRYG!
12

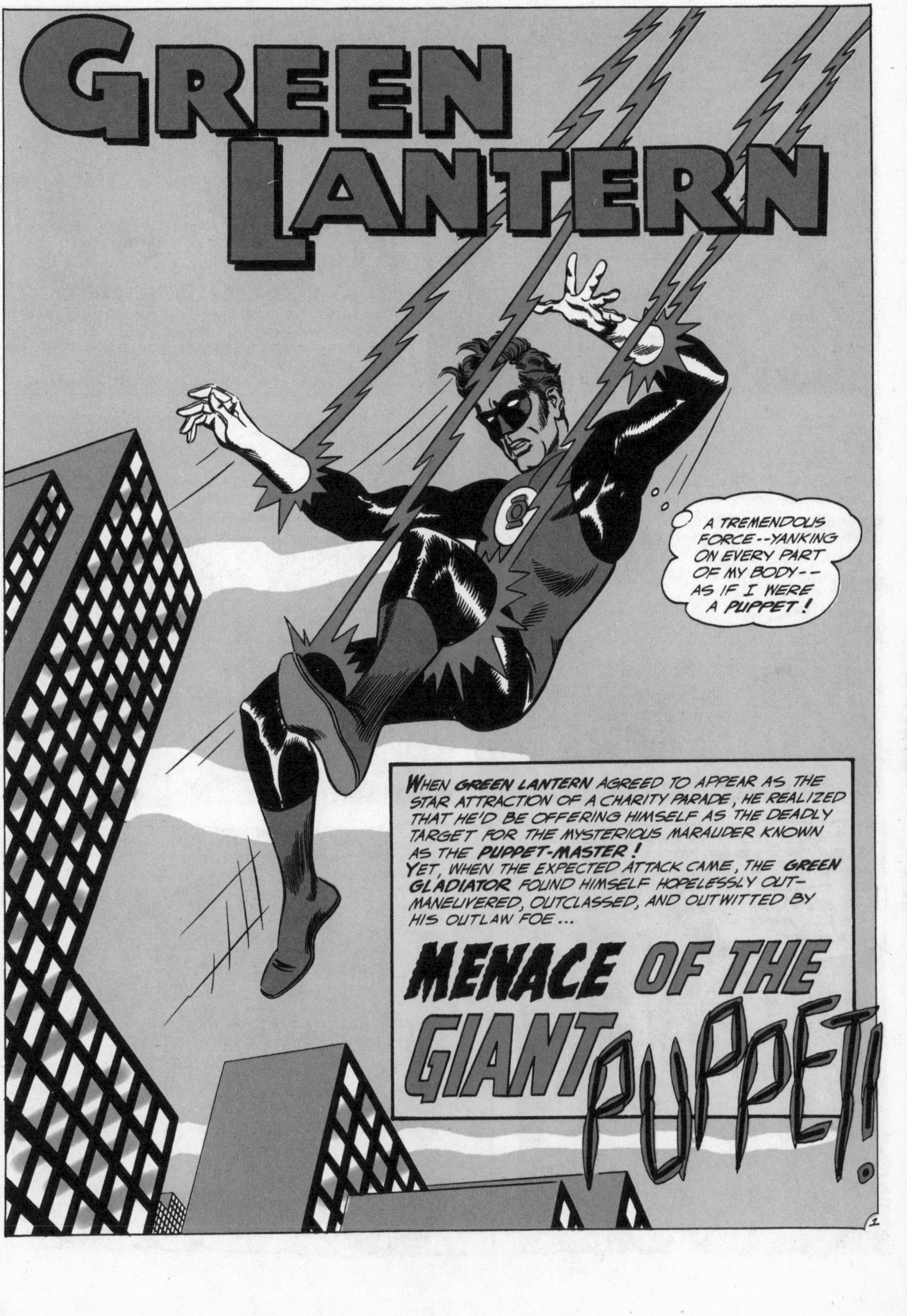
GREEN LANTERN
A TREMENDOUS FORCE--YANKING ON EVERY PART OF MY BODY--AS IF I WERE A PUPPET!
WHEN GREEN LANTERN AGREED TO APPEAR AS THE STAR ATTRACTION OF A CHARITY PARADE, HE REALIZED THAT HE'D BE OFFERING HIMSELF AS THE DEADLY TARGET FOR THE MYSTERIOUS MARAUDER KNOWN AS THE PUPPET-MASTER!
YET, WHEN THE EXPECTED ATTACK CAME, THE GREEN GLADIATOR FOUND HIMSELF HOPELESSLY OUT-MANEUVERED, OUTCLASSED, AND OUTWITTED BY HIS OUTLAW FOE...
MENACE OF THE GIANT PUPPET!
1

98

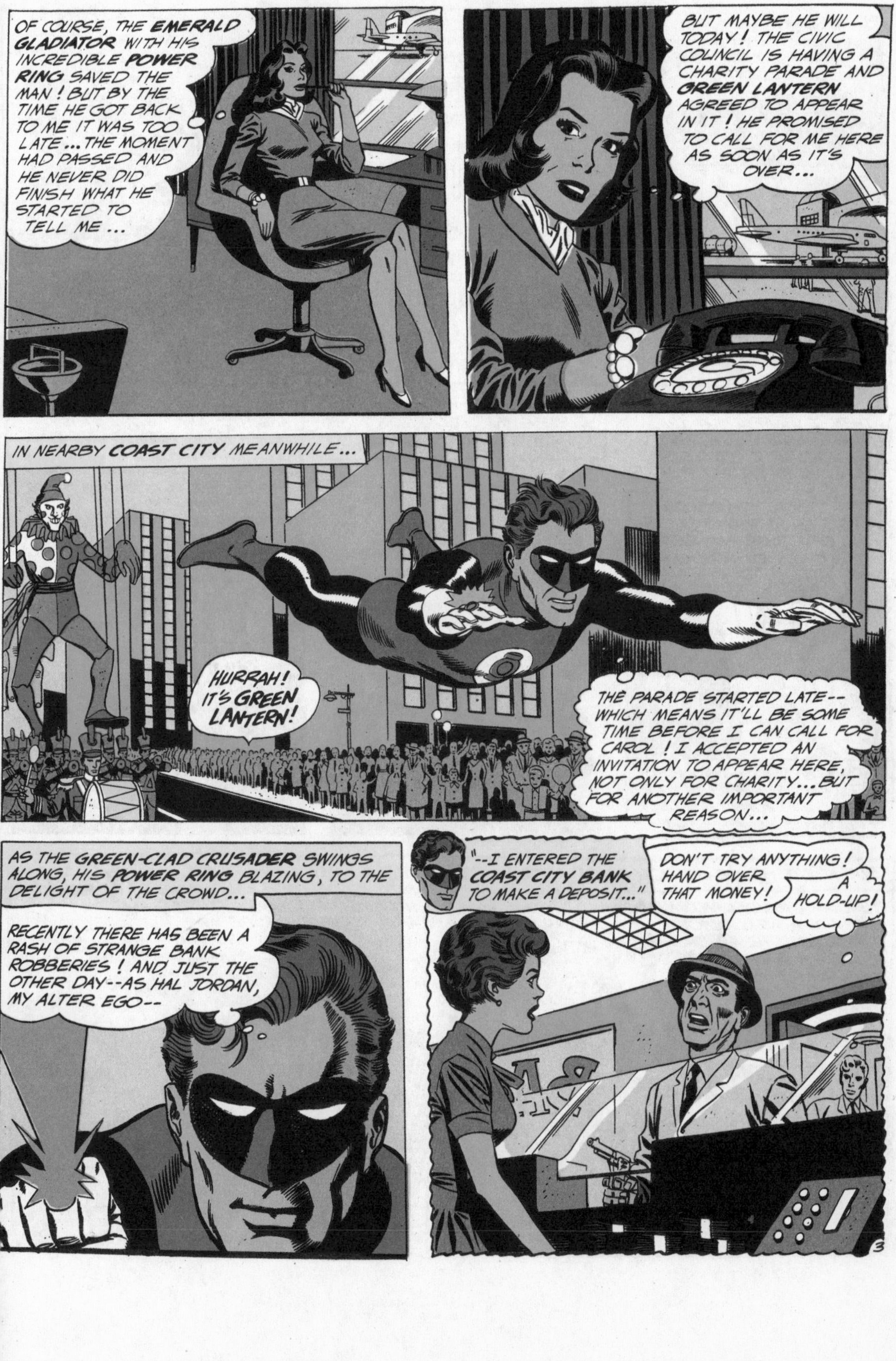
OF COURSE, THE EMERALD GLADIATOR WITH HIS INCREDIBLE POWER RING SAVED THE MAN! BUT BY THE TIME HE GOT BACK TO ME IT WAS TOO LATE... THE MOMENT HAD PASSED AND HE NEVER DID FINISH WHAT HE STARTED TO TELL ME...
BUT MAYBE HE WILL TODAY! THE CIVIC COUNCIL IS HAVING A CHARITY PARADE AND GREEN LANTERN AGREED TO APPEAR IN IT! HE PROMISED TO CALL FOR ME HERE AS SOON AS IT'S OVER...
IN NEARBY COAST CITY MEANWHILE...
HURRAH! IT'S GREEN LANTERN!
THE PARADE STARTED LATE-- WHICH MEANS IT'LL BE SOME TIME BEFORE I CAN CALL FOR CAROL! I ACCEPTED AN INVITATION TO APPEAR HERE, NOT ONLY FOR CHARITY... BUT FOR ANOTHER IMPORTANT REASON...
AS THE GREEN-CLAD CRUSADER SWINGS ALONG, HIS POWER RING BLAZING, TO THE DELIGHT OF THE CROWD...
RECENTLY THERE HAS BEEN A RASH OF STRANGE BANK ROBBERIES! AND JUST THE OTHER DAY--AS HAL JORDAN, MY ALTER EGO--
"--I ENTERED THE COAST CITY BANK TO MAKE A DEPOSIT..."
DON'T TRY ANYTHING! HAND OVER THAT MONEY!
A HOLD-UP!
3

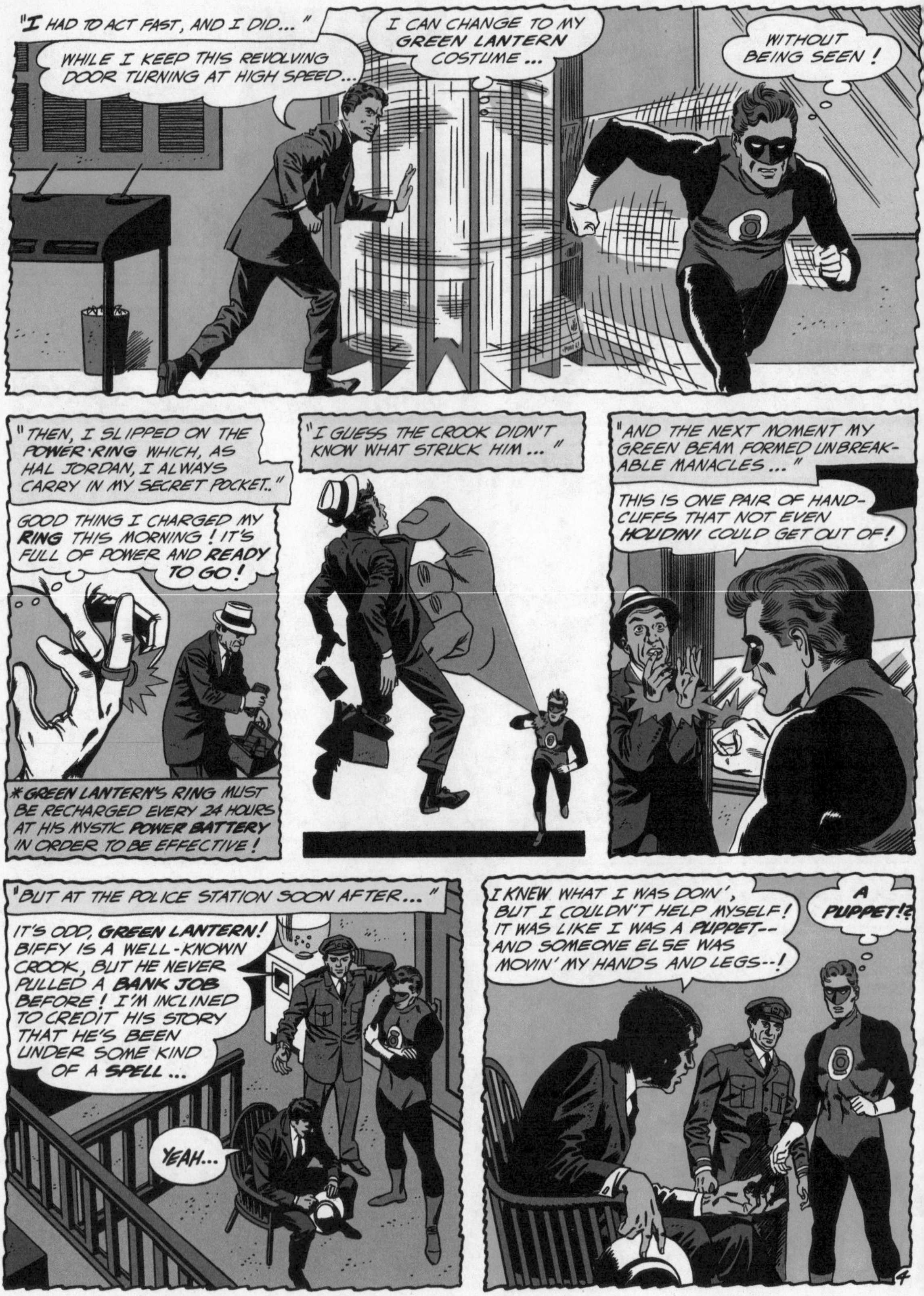
"I HAD TO ACT FAST, AND I DID..."
WHILE I KEEP THIS REVOLVING DOOR TURNING AT HIGH SPEED...
I CAN CHANGE TO MY GREEN LANTERN COSTUME...
WITHOUT BEING SEEN!
"THEN, I SLIPPED ON THE POWER-RING WHICH, AS HAL JORDAN, I ALWAYS CARRY IN MY SECRET POCKET."
GOOD THING I CHARGED MY RING THIS MORNING! IT'S FULL OF POWER AND READY TO GO!
*GREEN LANTERN'S RING MUST BE RECHARGED EVERY 24 HOURS AT HIS MYSTIC POWER BATTERY IN ORDER TO BE EFFECTIVE!
"I GUESS THE CROOK DIDN'T KNOW WHAT STRUCK HIM..."
"AND THE NEXT MOMENT MY GREEN BEAM FORMED UNBREAKABLE MANACLES..."
THIS IS ONE PAIR OF HANDCUFFS THAT NOT EVEN HOUDINI COULD GET OUT OF!
"BUT AT THE POLICE STATION SOON AFTER..."
IT'S ODD, GREEN LANTERN! BIFFY IS A WELL-KNOWN CROOK, BUT HE NEVER PULLED A BANK JOB BEFORE! I'M INCLINED TO CREDIT HIS STORY THAT HE'S BEEN UNDER SOME KIND OF A SPELL...
YEAH...
I KNEW WHAT I WAS DOIN', BUT I COULDN'T HELP MYSELF! IT WAS LIKE I WAS A PUPPET-- AND SOMEONE ELSE WAS MOVIN' MY HANDS AND LEGS--!
A PUPPET!?
4

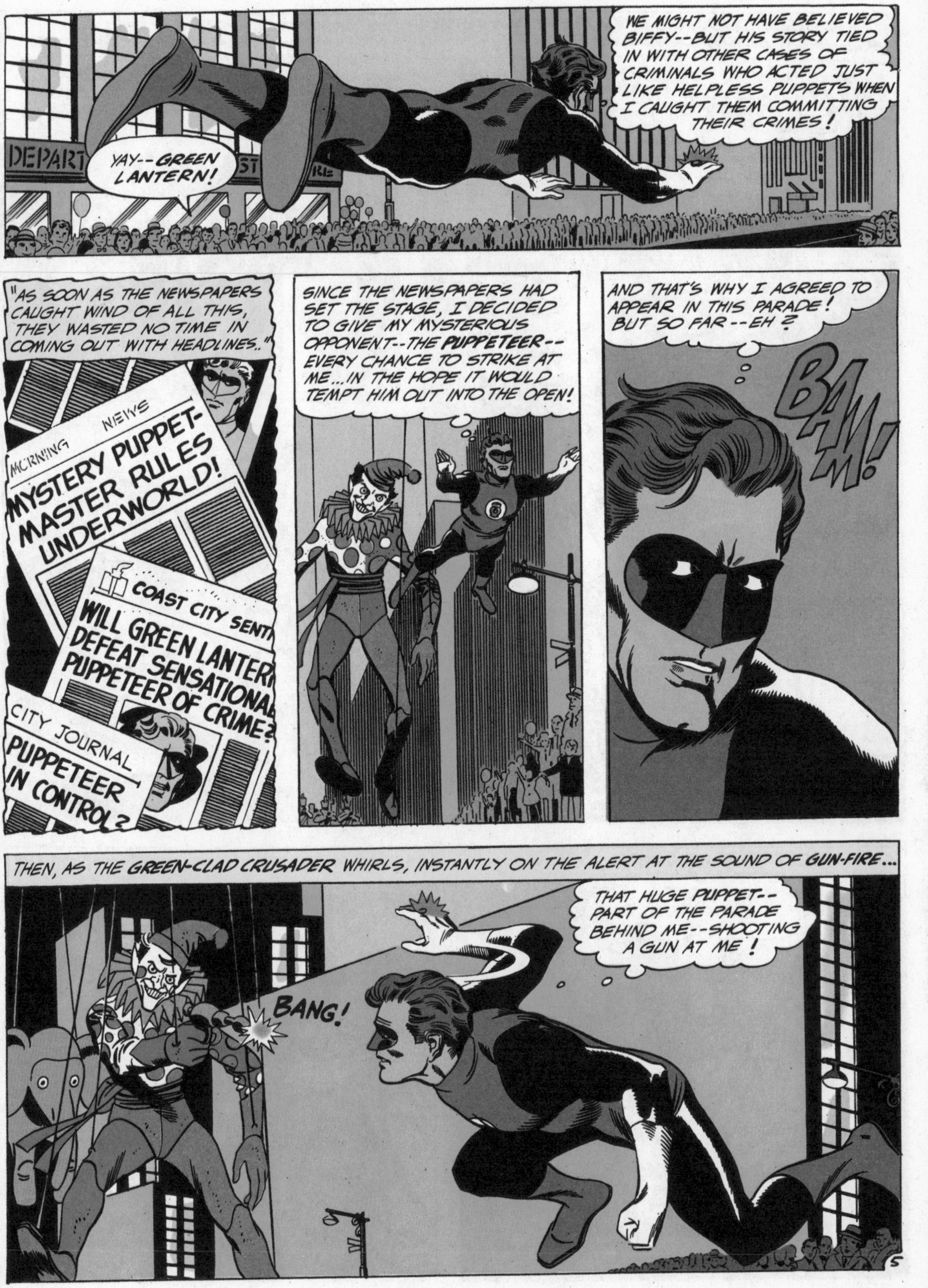

WE MIGHT NOT HAVE BELIEVED BIFFY--BUT HIS STORY TIED IN WITH OTHER CASES OF CRIMINALS WHO ACTED JUST LIKE HELPLESS PUPPETS WHEN I CAUGHT THEM COMMITTING THEIR CRIMES!
YAY--GREEN LANTERN!
DEPART
"AS SOON AS THE NEWSPAPERS CAUGHT WIND OF ALL THIS, THEY WASTED NO TIME IN COMING OUT WITH HEADLINES.."
MORNING NEWS
MYSTERY PUPPET-MASTER RULES UNDERWORLD!
COAST CITY SENT
WILL GREEN LANTER DEFEAT SENSATIONAL PUPPETEER OF CRIME?
CITY JOURNAL
PUPPETEER IN CONTROL?
SINCE THE NEWSPAPERS HAD SET THE STAGE, I DECIDED TO GIVE MY MYSTERIOUS OPPONENT--THE PUPPETEER--EVERY CHANCE TO STRIKE AT ME...IN THE HOPE IT WOULD TEMPT HIM OUT INTO THE OPEN!
AND THAT'S WHY I AGREED TO APPEAR IN THIS PARADE! BUT SO FAR--EH?
BAM!
THEN, AS THE GREEN-CLAD CRUSADER WHIRLS, INSTANTLY ON THE ALERT AT THE SOUND OF GUN-FIRE...
THAT HUGE PUPPET--PART OF THE PARADE BEHIND ME--SHOOTING A GUN AT ME!
BANG!
5

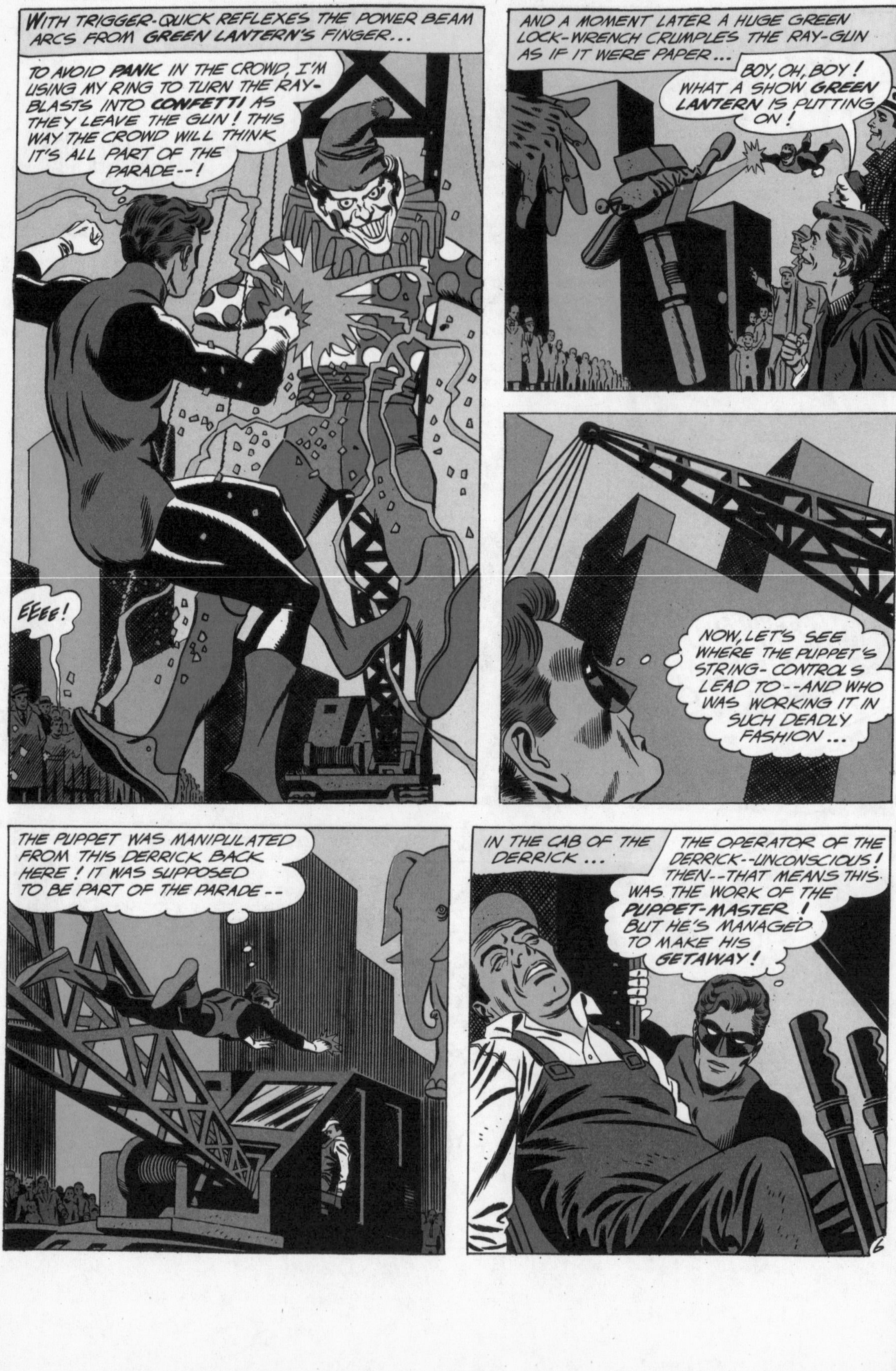
WITH TRIGGER-QUICK REFLEXES THE POWER BEAM ARCS FROM GREEN LANTERN'S FINGER...
TO AVOID PANIC IN THE CROWD, I'M USING MY RING TO TURN THE RAY-BLASTS INTO CONFETTI AS THEY LEAVE THE GUN! THIS WAY THE CROWD WILL THINK IT'S ALL PART OF THE PARADE--!
EEEE!
AND A MOMENT LATER A HUGE GREEN LOCK-WRENCH CRUMPLES THE RAY-GUN AS IF IT WERE PAPER...
BOY, OH, BOY! WHAT A SHOW GREEN LANTERN IS PUTTING ON!
NOW, LET'S SEE WHERE THE PUPPET'S STRING-CONTROLS LEAD TO--AND WHO WAS WORKING IT IN SUCH DEADLY FASHION...
THE PUPPET WAS MANIPULATED FROM THIS DERRICK BACK HERE! IT WAS SUPPOSED TO BE PART OF THE PARADE--
IN THE CAB OF THE DERRICK...
THE OPERATOR OF THE DERRICK--UNCONSCIOUS! THEN--THAT MEANS THIS WAS THE WORK OF THE PUPPET-MASTER! BUT HE'S MANAGED TO MAKE HIS GETAWAY!
6

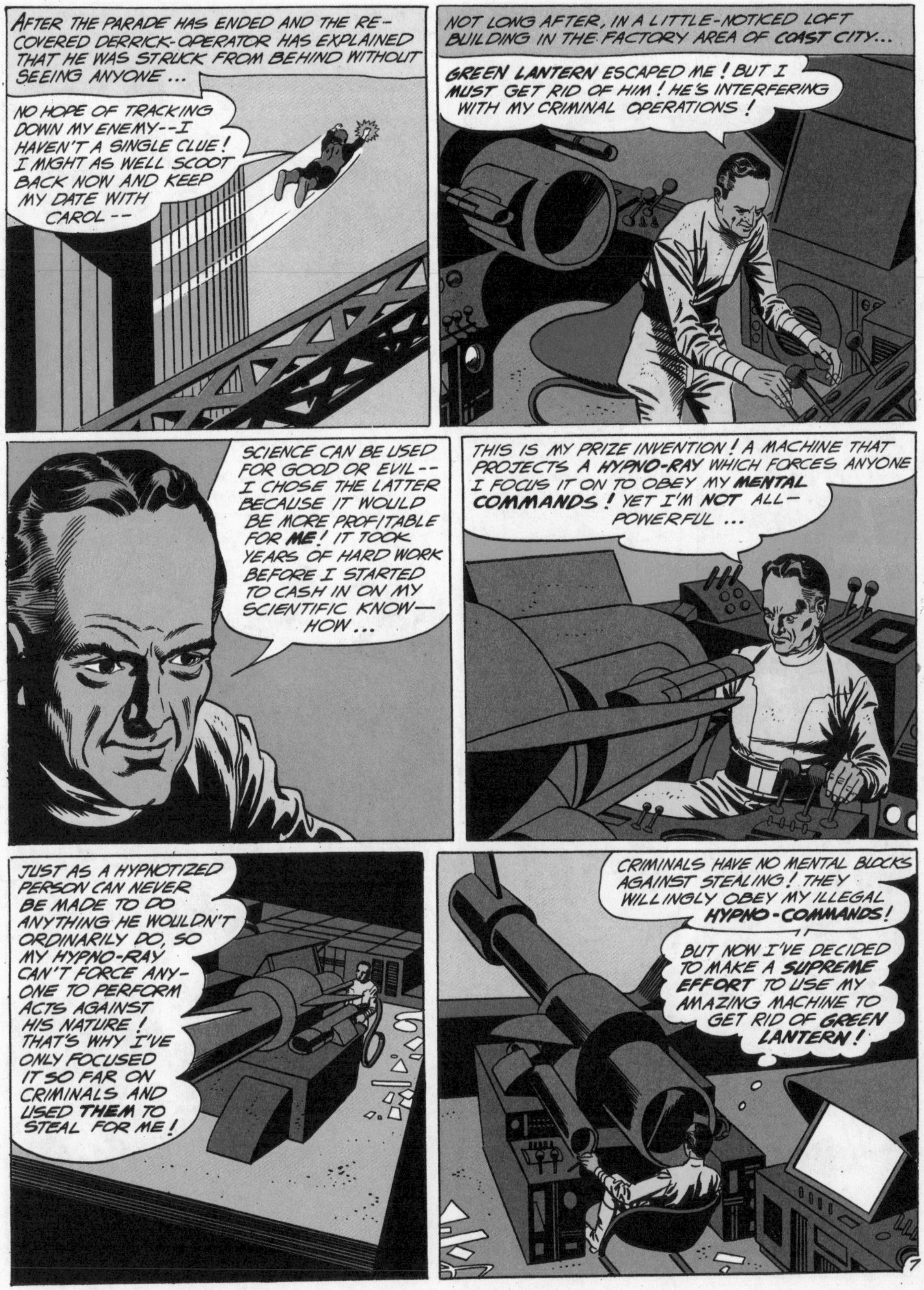
AFTER THE PARADE HAS ENDED AND THE RE-COVERED DERRICK-OPERATOR HAS EXPLAINED THAT HE WAS STRUCK FROM BEHIND WITHOUT SEEING ANYONE ...
NO HOPE OF TRACKING DOWN MY ENEMY--I HAVEN'T A SINGLE CLUE! I MIGHT AS WELL SCOOT BACK NOW AND KEEP MY DATE WITH CAROL--
NOT LONG AFTER, IN A LITTLE-NOTICED LOFT BUILDING IN THE FACTORY AREA OF COAST CITY...
GREEN LANTERN ESCAPED ME! BUT I MUST GET RID OF HIM! HE'S INTERFERING WITH MY CRIMINAL OPERATIONS!
SCIENCE CAN BE USED FOR GOOD OR EVIL-- I CHOSE THE LATTER BECAUSE IT WOULD BE MORE PROFITABLE FOR ME! IT TOOK YEARS OF HARD WORK BEFORE I STARTED TO CASH IN ON MY SCIENTIFIC KNOW-HOW...
THIS IS MY PRIZE INVENTION! A MACHINE THAT PROJECTS A HYPNO-RAY WHICH FORCES ANYONE I FOCUS IT ON TO OBEY MY MENTAL COMMANDS! YET I'M NOT ALL-POWERFUL ...
JUST AS A HYPNOTIZED PERSON CAN NEVER BE MADE TO DO ANYTHING HE WOULDN'T ORDINARILY DO, SO MY HYPNO-RAY CAN'T FORCE ANY-ONE TO PERFORM ACTS AGAINST HIS NATURE! THAT'S WHY I'VE ONLY FOCUSED IT SO FAR ON CRIMINALS AND USED THEM TO STEAL FOR ME!
CRIMINALS HAVE NO MENTAL BLOCKS AGAINST STEALING! THEY WILLINGLY OBEY MY ILLEGAL HYPNO-COMMANDS!
BUT NOW I'VE DECIDED TO MAKE A SUPREME EFFORT TO USE MY AMAZING MACHINE TO GET RID OF GREEN LANTERN!
7

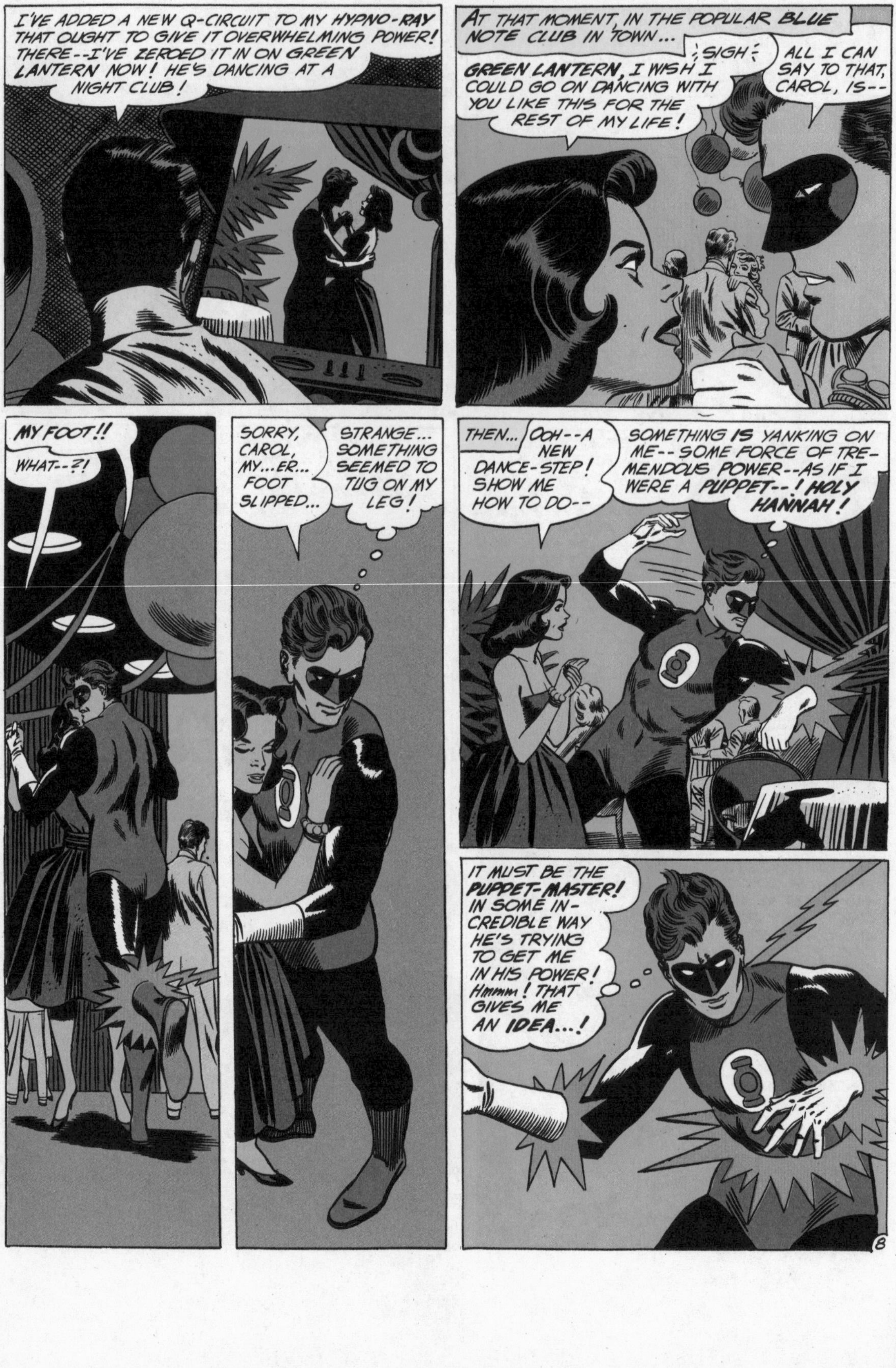

I'VE ADDED A NEW Q-CIRCUIT TO MY HYPNO-RAY THAT OUGHT TO GIVE IT OVERWHELMING POWER! THERE--I'VE ZEROED IT IN ON GREEN LANTERN NOW! HE'S DANCING AT A NIGHT CLUB!
AT THAT MOMENT, IN THE POPULAR BLUE NOTE CLUB IN TOWN...
SIGH
GREEN LANTERN, I WISH I COULD GO ON DANCING WITH YOU LIKE THIS FOR THE REST OF MY LIFE!
ALL I CAN SAY TO THAT, CAROL, IS--
MY FOOT!!
WHAT--?!
SORRY, CAROL, MY...ER... FOOT SLIPPED...
STRANGE... SOMETHING SEEMED TO TUG ON MY LEG!
THEN...
OOH--A NEW DANCE-STEP! SHOW ME HOW TO DO--
SOMETHING IS YANKING ON ME--SOME FORCE OF TREMENDOUS POWER--AS IF I WERE A PUPPET--! HOLY HANNAH!
IT MUST BE THE PUPPET-MASTER! IN SOME INCREDIBLE WAY HE'S TRYING TO GET ME IN HIS POWER! Hmmm! THAT GIVES ME AN IDEA...!
8

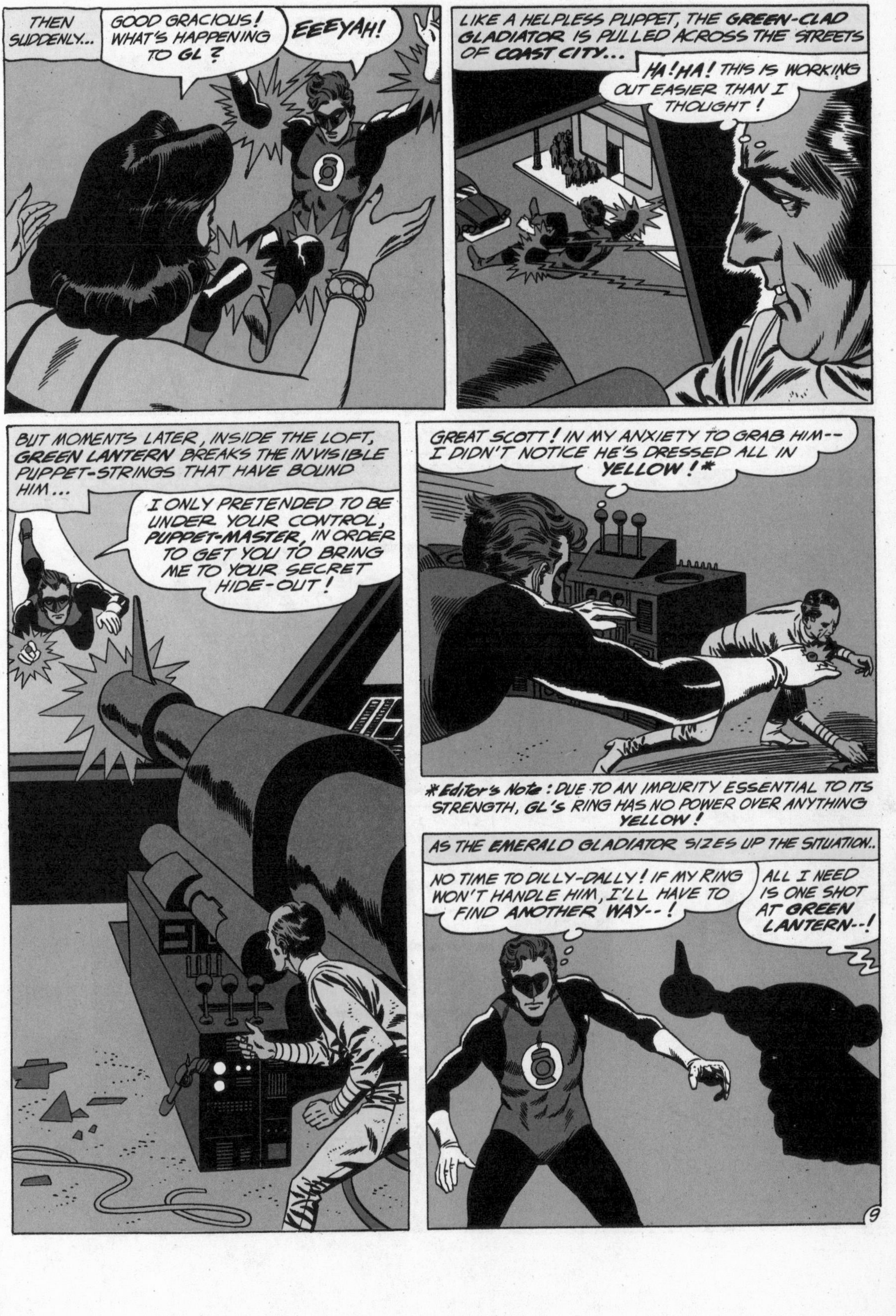

THEN SUDDENLY...
GOOD GRACIOUS! WHAT'S HAPPENING TO GL?
EEEYAH!
LIKE A HELPLESS PUPPET, THE GREEN-CLAD GLADIATOR IS PULLED ACROSS THE STREETS OF COAST CITY...
HA! HA! THIS IS WORKING OUT EASIER THAN I THOUGHT!
BUT MOMENTS LATER, INSIDE THE LOFT, GREEN LANTERN BREAKS THE INVISIBLE PUPPET-STRINGS THAT HAVE BOUND HIM...
I ONLY PRETENDED TO BE UNDER YOUR CONTROL, PUPPET-MASTER, IN ORDER TO GET YOU TO BRING ME TO YOUR SECRET HIDE-OUT!
GREAT SCOTT! IN MY ANXIETY TO GRAB HIM-- I DIDN'T NOTICE HE'S DRESSED ALL IN YELLOW!*
*Editor's Note: DUE TO AN IMPURITY ESSENTIAL TO ITS STRENGTH, GL'S RING HAS NO POWER OVER ANYTHING YELLOW!
AS THE EMERALD GLADIATOR SIZES UP THE SITUATION..
NO TIME TO DILLY-DALLY! IF MY RING WON'T HANDLE HIM, I'LL HAVE TO FIND ANOTHER WAY--!
ALL I NEED IS ONE SHOT AT GREEN LANTERN--!
9

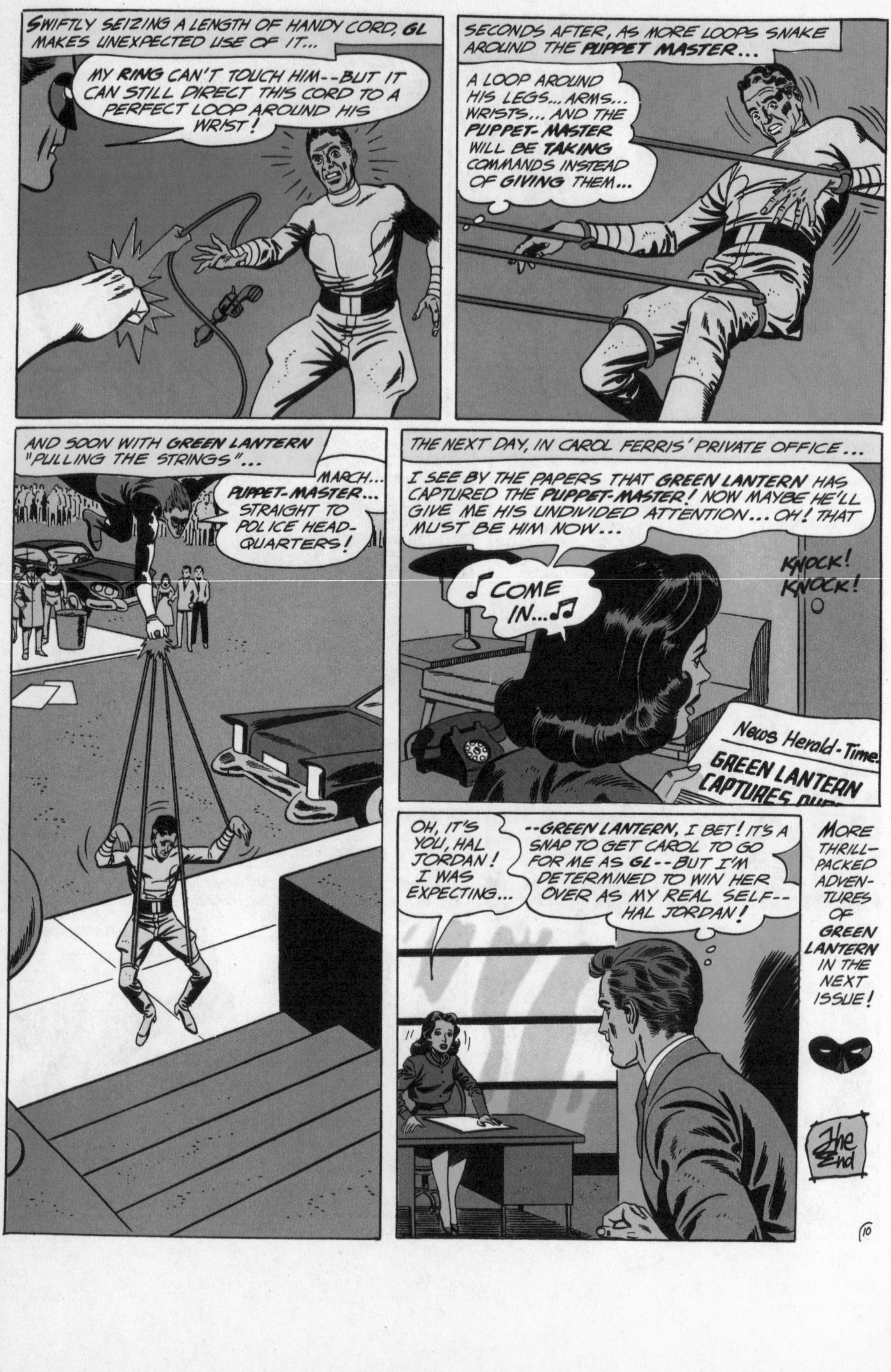
SWIFTLY SEIZING A LENGTH OF HANDY CORD, GL MAKES UNEXPECTED USE OF IT...
MY RING CAN'T TOUCH HIM--BUT IT CAN STILL DIRECT THIS CORD TO A PERFECT LOOP AROUND HIS WRIST!
SECONDS AFTER, AS MORE LOOPS SNAKE AROUND THE PUPPET MASTER...
A LOOP AROUND HIS LEGS... ARMS... WRISTS... AND THE PUPPET-MASTER WILL BE TAKING COMMANDS INSTEAD OF GIVING THEM...
AND SOON WITH GREEN LANTERN "PULLING THE STRINGS"...
MARCH... PUPPET-MASTER... STRAIGHT TO POLICE HEAD-QUARTERS!
THE NEXT DAY, IN CAROL FERRIS' PRIVATE OFFICE...
I SEE BY THE PAPERS THAT GREEN LANTERN HAS CAPTURED THE PUPPET-MASTER! NOW MAYBE HE'LL GIVE ME HIS UNDIVIDED ATTENTION... OH! THAT MUST BE HIM NOW...
KNOCK! KNOCK!
COME IN...
News Herald-Time
GREEN LANTERN CAPTURES
OH, IT'S YOU, HAL JORDAN! I WAS EXPECTING...
--GREEN LANTERN, I BET! IT'S A SNAP TO GET CAROL TO GO FOR ME AS GL--BUT I'M DETERMINED TO WIN HER OVER AS MY REAL SELF--HAL JORDAN!
MORE THRILL-PACKED ADVEN-TURES OF GREEN LANTERN IN THE NEXT ISSUE!
The End
10

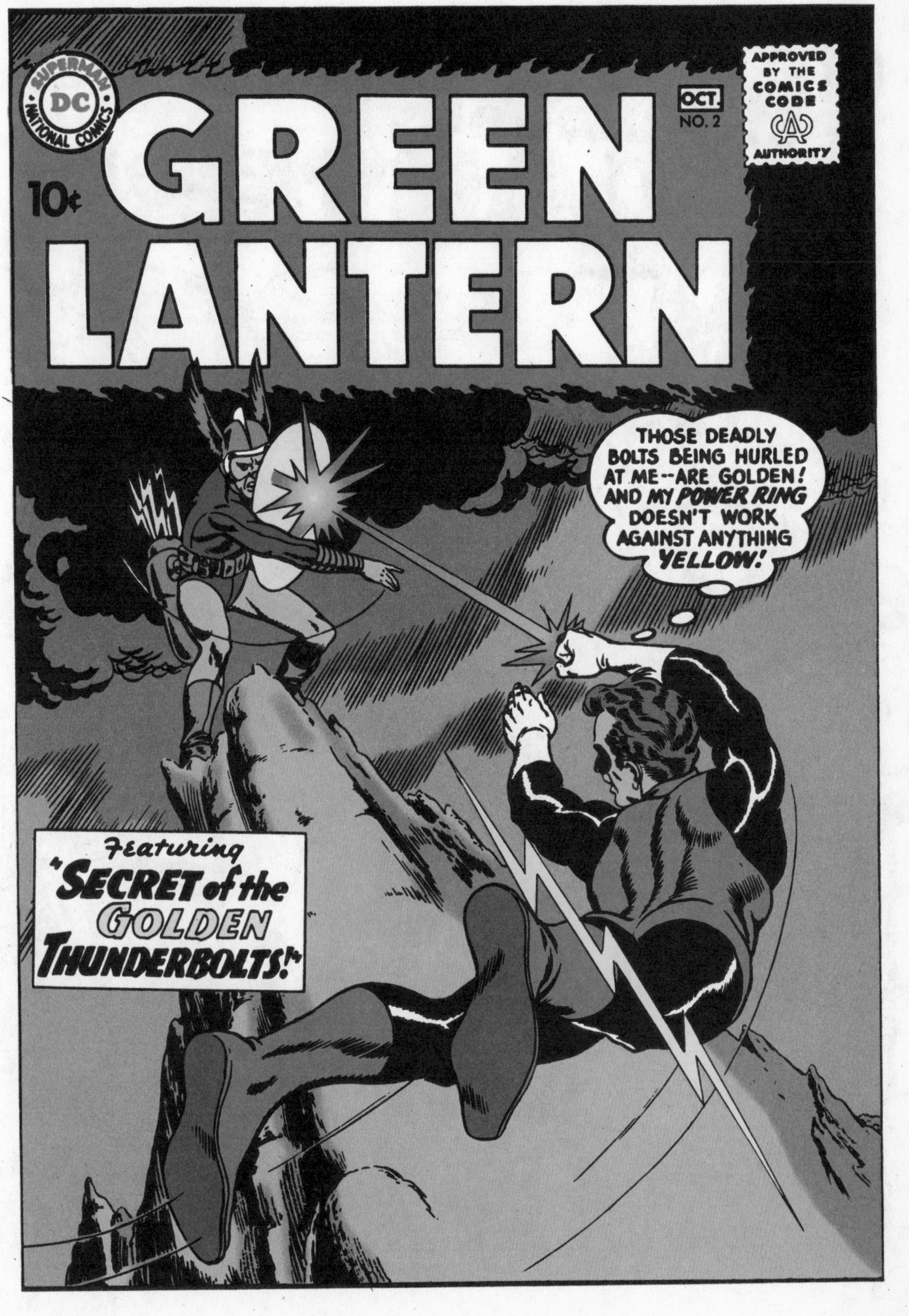
SUPERMAN DC NATIONAL COMICS
10¢
GREEN LANTERN
OCT. NO. 2
APPROVED BY THE COMICS CODE AUTHORITY
THOSE DEADLY BOLTS BEING HURLED AT ME--ARE GOLDEN! AND MY POWER RING DOESN'T WORK AGAINST ANYTHING YELLOW!
Featuring "SECRET of the GOLDEN THUNDERBOLTS!"

GREEN LANTERN

THIS FELLOW'S STORY IS INCREDIBLE! TRYING TO TELL ME HE'S FROM THE *ANTI-MATTER* UNIVERSE OF *QWARD*-- AND THAT HE'S BEEN FOLLOWED BY A SINISTER *DESTROYER* CAPABLE OF THROWING THUNDER-BOLTS OF FANTASTIC FORCE!

GREEN LANTERN, ONLY *YOU* CAN HELP ME!

GREEN LANTERN'S SKEPTICISM WAS NATURAL IN THE BEGINNING- BEFORE HE HAD SEEN A *DESTROYER* OR MET THE EVIL- LOVING *WEAPONERS OF QWARD*... OR LEARNED THE STARTLING TRUTH ABOUT THEIR SINISTER REASONS FOR COMING TO EARTH! REASONS THAT NO ONE COULD HAVE SUSPECTED, AND WHICH WERE LINKED UP WITH...

The SECRET OF THE GOLDEN THUNDERBOLTS!

KANE + GIELLA

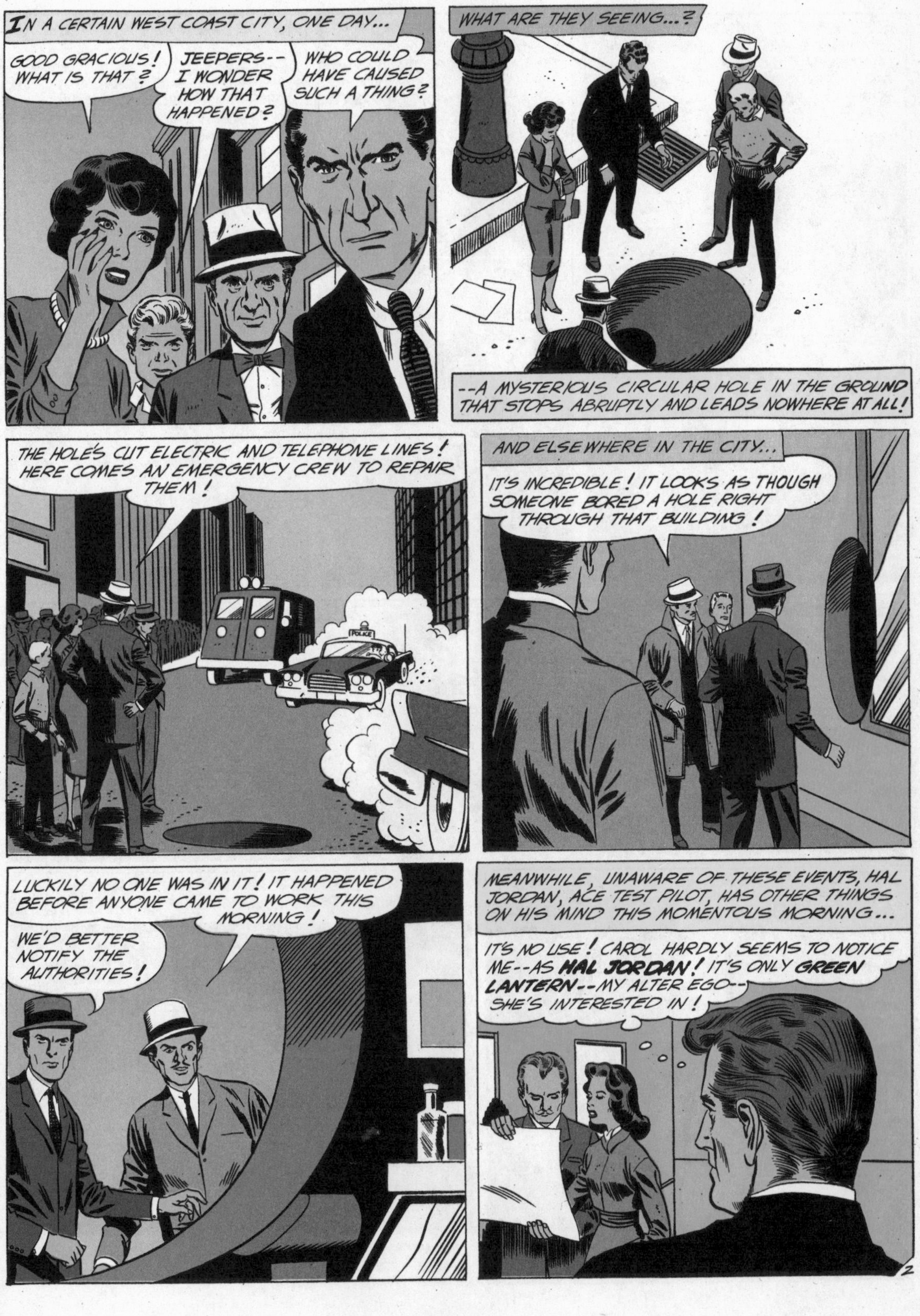
IN A CERTAIN WEST COAST CITY, ONE DAY...
GOOD GRACIOUS! WHAT IS THAT?
JEEPERS-- I WONDER HOW THAT HAPPENED?
WHO COULD HAVE CAUSED SUCH A THING?
WHAT ARE THEY SEEING...?
--A MYSTERIOUS CIRCULAR HOLE IN THE GROUND THAT STOPS ABRUPTLY AND LEADS NOWHERE AT ALL!
THE HOLE'S CUT ELECTRIC AND TELEPHONE LINES! HERE COMES AN EMERGENCY CREW TO REPAIR THEM!
POLICE
AND ELSEWHERE IN THE CITY...
IT'S INCREDIBLE! IT LOOKS AS THOUGH SOMEONE BORED A HOLE RIGHT THROUGH THAT BUILDING!
LUCKILY NO ONE WAS IN IT! IT HAPPENED BEFORE ANYONE CAME TO WORK THIS MORNING!
WE'D BETTER NOTIFY THE AUTHORITIES!
MEANWHILE, UNAWARE OF THESE EVENTS, HAL JORDAN, ACE TEST PILOT, HAS OTHER THINGS ON HIS MIND THIS MOMENTOUS MORNING...
IT'S NO USE! CAROL HARDLY SEEMS TO NOTICE ME--AS HAL JORDAN! IT'S ONLY GREEN LANTERN--MY ALTER EGO--SHE'S INTERESTED IN!
2

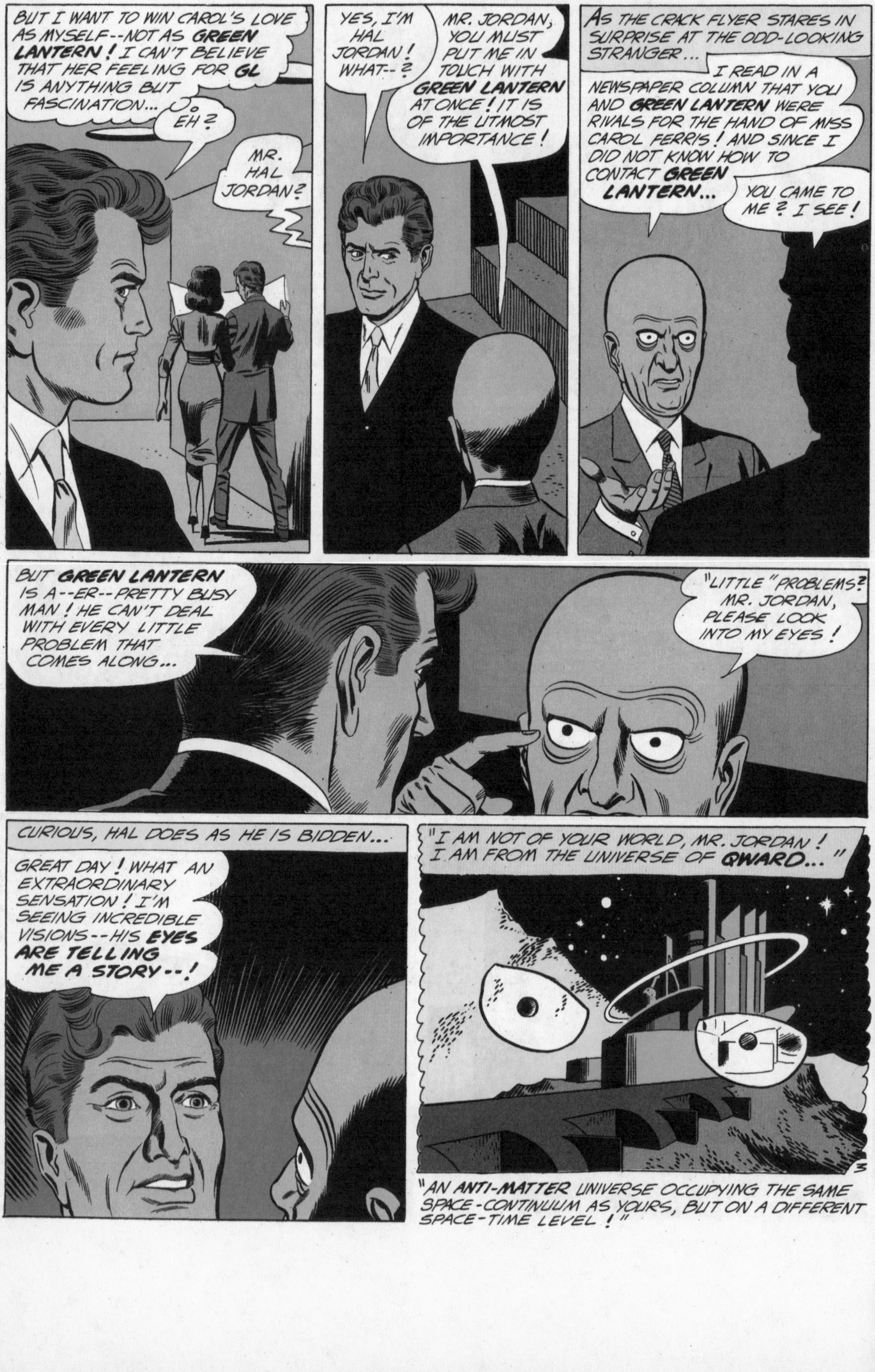

BUT I WANT TO WIN CAROL'S LOVE AS MYSELF--NOT AS GREEN LANTERN! I CAN'T BELIEVE THAT HER FEELING FOR GL IS ANYTHING BUT FASCINATION...
EH?
MR. HAL JORDAN?
YES, I'M HAL JORDAN! WHAT--?
MR. JORDAN, YOU MUST PUT ME IN TOUCH WITH GREEN LANTERN AT ONCE! IT IS OF THE UTMOST IMPORTANCE!
AS THE CRACK FLYER STARES IN SURPRISE AT THE ODD-LOOKING STRANGER...
I READ IN A NEWSPAPER COLUMN THAT YOU AND GREEN LANTERN WERE RIVALS FOR THE HAND OF MISS CAROL FERRIS! AND SINCE I DID NOT KNOW HOW TO CONTACT GREEN LANTERN...
YOU CAME TO ME? I SEE!
BUT GREEN LANTERN IS A--ER--PRETTY BUSY MAN! HE CAN'T DEAL WITH EVERY LITTLE PROBLEM THAT COMES ALONG...
"LITTLE" PROBLEMS? MR. JORDAN, PLEASE LOOK INTO MY EYES!
CURIOUS, HAL DOES AS HE IS BIDDEN...
GREAT DAY! WHAT AN EXTRAORDINARY SENSATION! I'M SEEING INCREDIBLE VISIONS--HIS EYES ARE TELLING ME A STORY--!
"I AM NOT OF YOUR WORLD, MR. JORDAN! I AM FROM THE UNIVERSE OF QWARD..."
3
"AN ANTI-MATTER UNIVERSE OCCUPYING THE SAME SPACE-CONTINUUM AS YOURS, BUT ON A DIFFERENT SPACE-TIME LEVEL!"

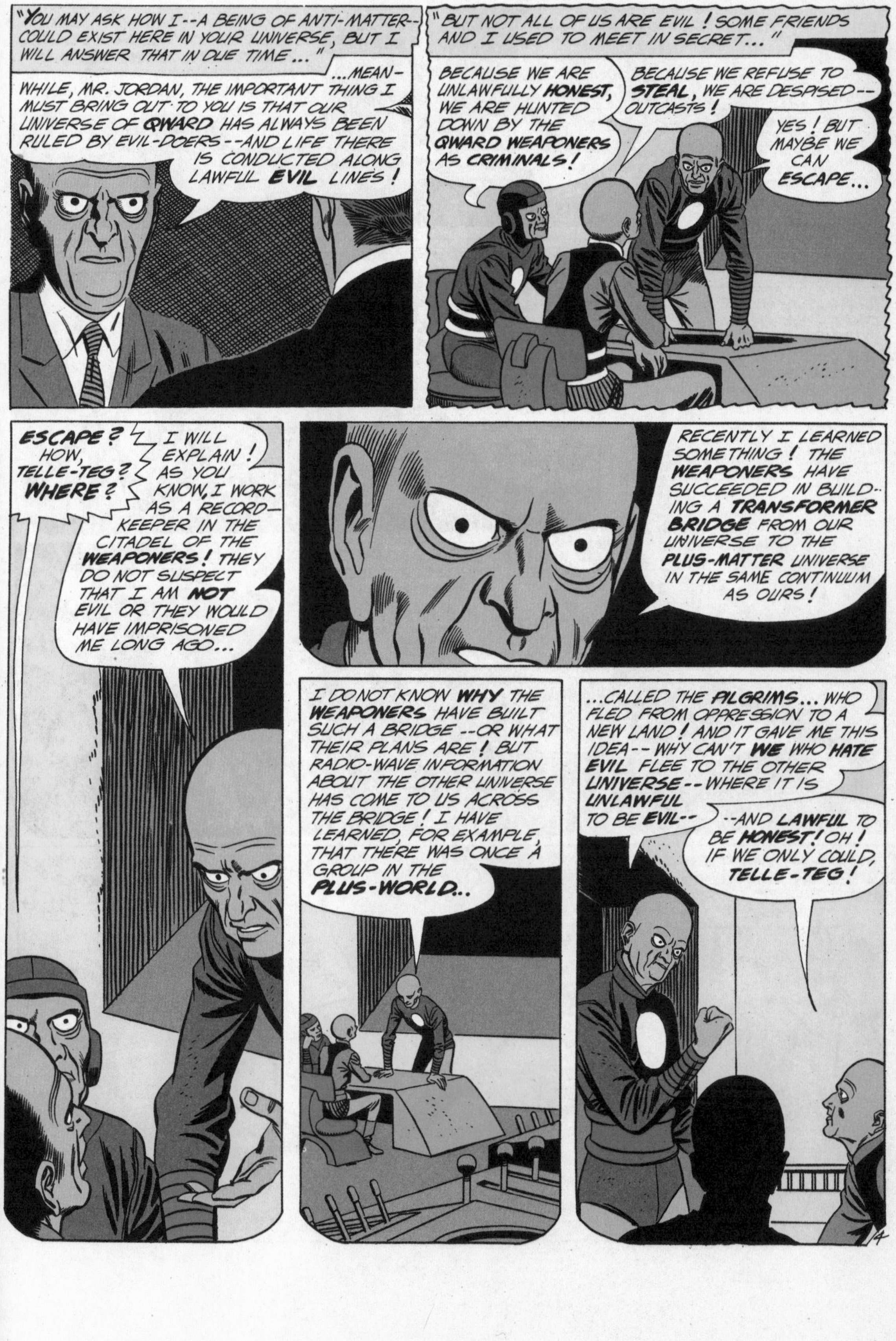
"YOU MAY ASK HOW I--A BEING OF ANTI-MATTER--COULD EXIST HERE IN YOUR UNIVERSE, BUT I WILL ANSWER THAT IN DUE TIME..."
...MEAN-WHILE, MR. JORDAN, THE IMPORTANT THING I MUST BRING OUT TO YOU IS THAT OUR UNIVERSE OF QWARD HAS ALWAYS BEEN RULED BY EVIL-DOERS--AND LIFE THERE IS CONDUCTED ALONG LAWFUL EVIL LINES!
"BUT NOT ALL OF US ARE EVIL! SOME FRIENDS AND I USED TO MEET IN SECRET..."
BECAUSE WE ARE UNLAWFULLY HONEST, WE ARE HUNTED DOWN BY THE QWARD WEAPONERS AS CRIMINALS!
BECAUSE WE REFUSE TO STEAL, WE ARE DESPISED--OUTCASTS!
YES! BUT MAYBE WE CAN ESCAPE...
ESCAPE? HOW, TELLE-TEG? WHERE?
I WILL EXPLAIN! AS YOU KNOW, I WORK AS A RECORD-KEEPER IN THE CITADEL OF THE WEAPONERS! THEY DO NOT SUSPECT THAT I AM NOT EVIL OR THEY WOULD HAVE IMPRISONED ME LONG AGO...
RECENTLY I LEARNED SOMETHING! THE WEAPONERS HAVE SUCCEEDED IN BUILDING A TRANSFORMER BRIDGE FROM OUR UNIVERSE TO THE PLUS-MATTER UNIVERSE IN THE SAME CONTINUUM AS OURS!
I DO NOT KNOW WHY THE WEAPONERS HAVE BUILT SUCH A BRIDGE--OR WHAT THEIR PLANS ARE! BUT RADIO-WAVE INFORMATION ABOUT THE OTHER UNIVERSE HAS COME TO US ACROSS THE BRIDGE! I HAVE LEARNED, FOR EXAMPLE, THAT THERE WAS ONCE A GROUP IN THE PLUS-WORLD...
...CALLED THE PILGRIMS... WHO FLED FROM OPPRESSION TO A NEW LAND! AND IT GAVE ME THIS IDEA--WHY CAN'T WE WHO HATE EVIL FLEE TO THE OTHER UNIVERSE--WHERE IT IS UNLAWFUL TO BE EVIL--
--AND LAWFUL TO BE HONEST! OH! IF WE ONLY COULD, TELLE-TEG!
4

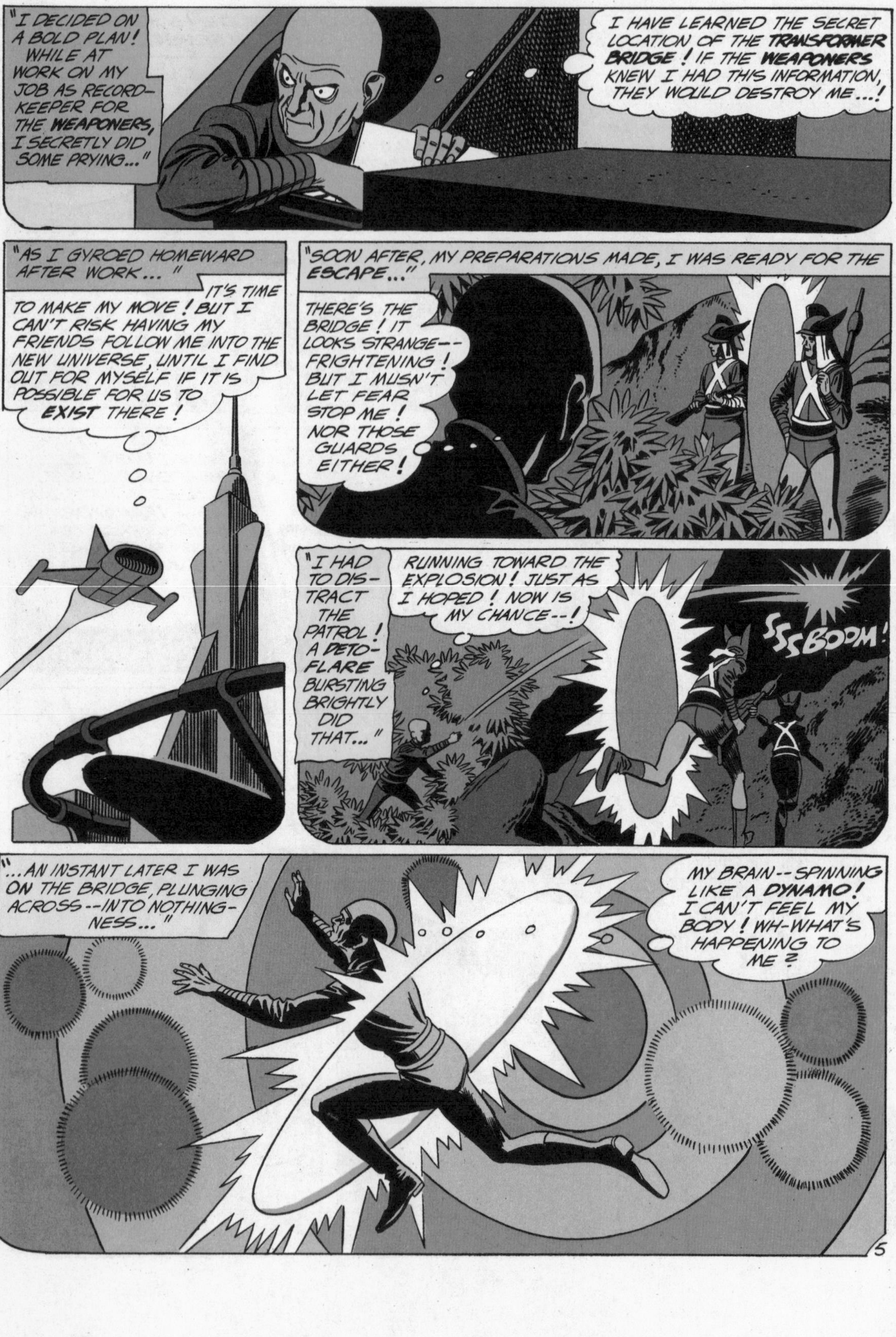
"I DECIDED ON A BOLD PLAN! WHILE AT WORK ON MY JOB AS RECORD-KEEPER FOR THE WEAPONERS, I SECRETLY DID SOME PRYING..."
I HAVE LEARNED THE SECRET LOCATION OF THE TRANSFORMER BRIDGE! IF THE WEAPONERS KNEW I HAD THIS INFORMATION, THEY WOULD DESTROY ME...!
"AS I GYROED HOMEWARD AFTER WORK..."
IT'S TIME TO MAKE MY MOVE! BUT I CAN'T RISK HAVING MY FRIENDS FOLLOW ME INTO THE NEW UNIVERSE, UNTIL I FIND OUT FOR MYSELF IF IT IS POSSIBLE FOR US TO EXIST THERE!
"SOON AFTER, MY PREPARATIONS MADE, I WAS READY FOR THE ESCAPE..."
THERE'S THE BRIDGE! IT LOOKS STRANGE--FRIGHTENING! BUT I MUSN'T LET FEAR STOP ME! NOR THOSE GUARDS EITHER!
"I HAD TO DISTRACT THE PATROL! A DETO-FLARE BURSTING BRIGHTLY DID THAT..."
RUNNING TOWARD THE EXPLOSION! JUST AS I HOPED! NOW IS MY CHANCE--!
SSSBOOM!
"...AN INSTANT LATER I WAS ON THE BRIDGE, PLUNGING ACROSS--INTO NOTHINGNESS..."
MY BRAIN--SPINNING LIKE A DYNAMO! I CAN'T FEEL MY BODY! WH-WHAT'S HAPPENING TO ME?
5

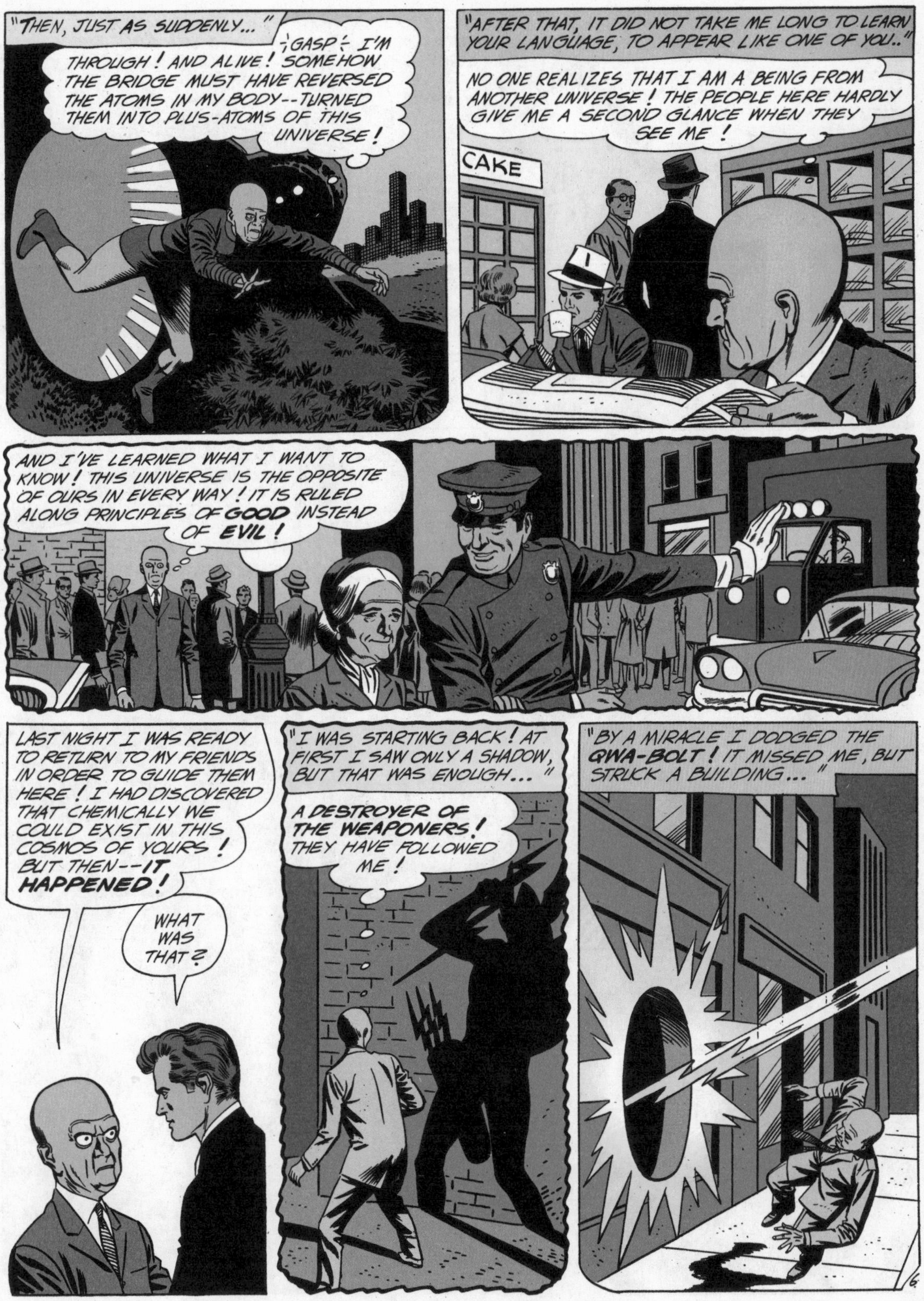
"THEN, JUST AS SUDDENLY..."
-GASP- I'M THROUGH! AND ALIVE! SOMEHOW THE BRIDGE MUST HAVE REVERSED THE ATOMS IN MY BODY--TURNED THEM INTO PLUS-ATOMS OF THIS UNIVERSE!
"AFTER THAT, IT DID NOT TAKE ME LONG TO LEARN YOUR LANGUAGE, TO APPEAR LIKE ONE OF YOU.."
NO ONE REALIZES THAT I AM A BEING FROM ANOTHER UNIVERSE! THE PEOPLE HERE HARDLY GIVE ME A SECOND GLANCE WHEN THEY SEE ME!
CAKE
AND I'VE LEARNED WHAT I WANT TO KNOW! THIS UNIVERSE IS THE OPPOSITE OF OURS IN EVERY WAY! IT IS RULED ALONG PRINCIPLES OF GOOD INSTEAD OF EVIL!
LAST NIGHT I WAS READY TO RETURN TO MY FRIENDS IN ORDER TO GUIDE THEM HERE! I HAD DISCOVERED THAT CHEMICALLY WE COULD EXIST IN THIS COSMOS OF YOURS! BUT THEN--IT HAPPENED!
WHAT WAS THAT?
"I WAS STARTING BACK! AT FIRST I SAW ONLY A SHADOW, BUT THAT WAS ENOUGH..."
A DESTROYER OF THE WEAPONERS! THEY HAVE FOLLOWED ME!
"BY A MIRACLE I DODGED THE QWA-BOLT! IT MISSED ME, BUT STRUCK A BUILDING..."
6

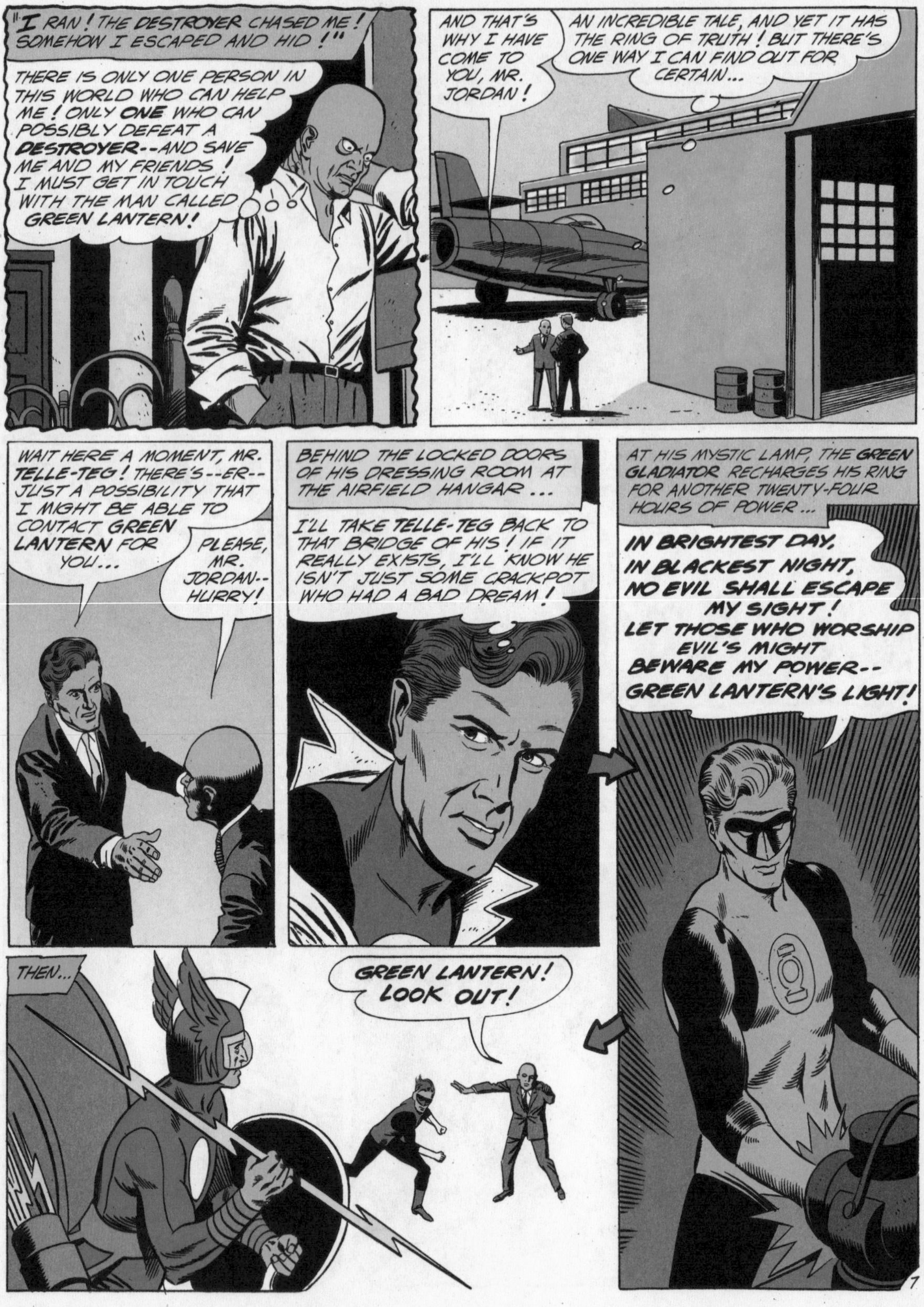
"I RAN! THE DESTROYER CHASED ME! SOMEHOW I ESCAPED AND HID!"
THERE IS ONLY ONE PERSON IN THIS WORLD WHO CAN HELP ME! ONLY ONE WHO CAN POSSIBLY DEFEAT A DESTROYER--AND SAVE ME AND MY FRIENDS! I MUST GET IN TOUCH WITH THE MAN CALLED GREEN LANTERN!
AND THAT'S WHY I HAVE COME TO YOU, MR. JORDAN!
AN INCREDIBLE TALE, AND YET IT HAS THE RING OF TRUTH! BUT THERE'S ONE WAY I CAN FIND OUT FOR CERTAIN...
WAIT HERE A MOMENT, MR. TELLE-TEG! THERE'S--ER--JUST A POSSIBILITY THAT I MIGHT BE ABLE TO CONTACT GREEN LANTERN FOR YOU...
PLEASE, MR. JORDAN--HURRY!
BEHIND THE LOCKED DOORS OF HIS DRESSING ROOM AT THE AIRFIELD HANGAR...
I'LL TAKE TELLE-TEG BACK TO THAT BRIDGE OF HIS! IF IT REALLY EXISTS, I'LL KNOW HE ISN'T JUST SOME CRACKPOT WHO HAD A BAD DREAM!
AT HIS MYSTIC LAMP, THE GREEN GLADIATOR RECHARGES HIS RING FOR ANOTHER TWENTY-FOUR HOURS OF POWER...
IN BRIGHTEST DAY, IN BLACKEST NIGHT, NO EVIL SHALL ESCAPE MY SIGHT! LET THOSE WHO WORSHIP EVIL'S MIGHT BEWARE MY POWER-- GREEN LANTERN'S LIGHT!
THEN...
GREEN LANTERN! LOOK OUT!
7

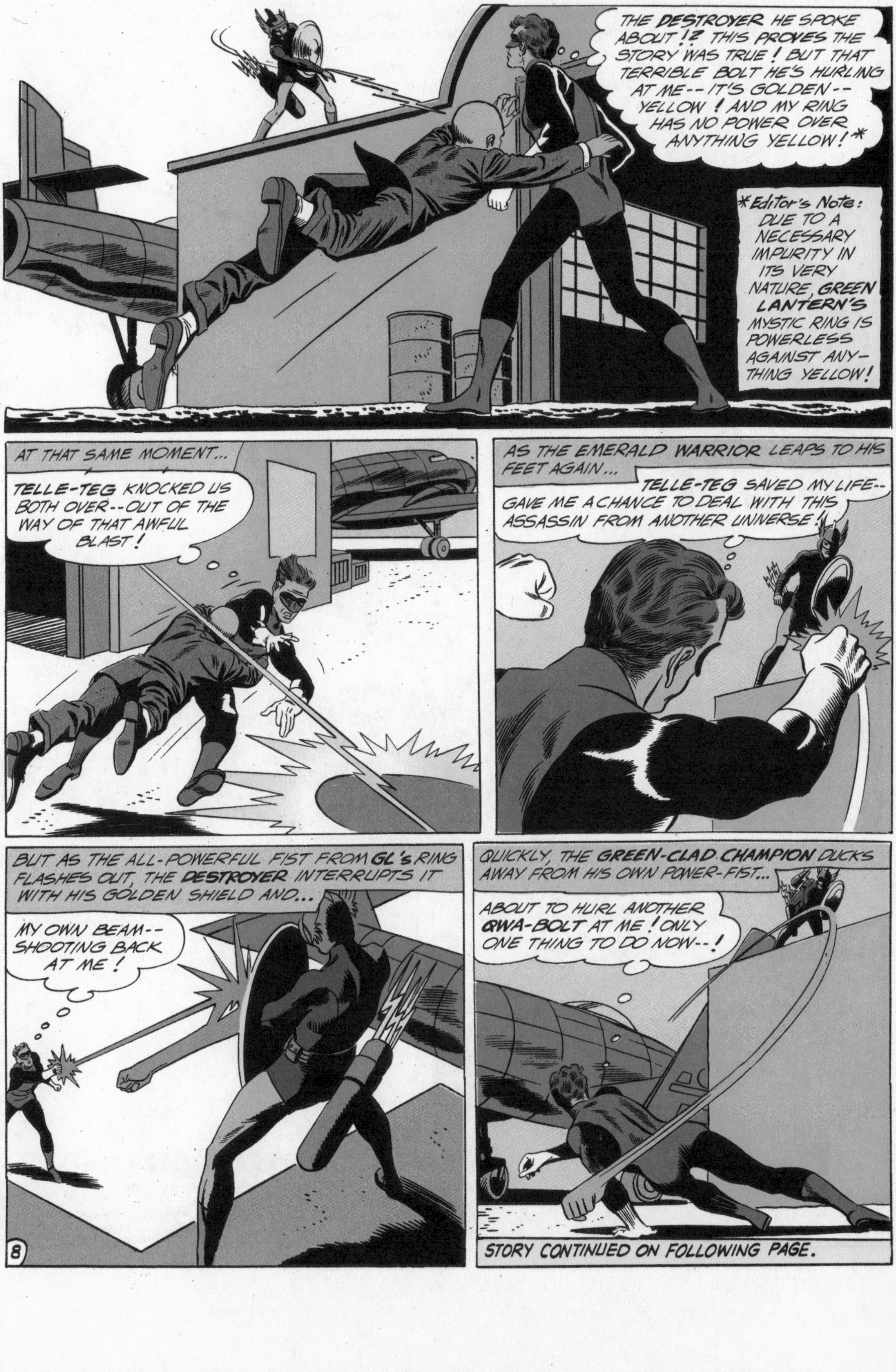

THE DESTROYER HE SPOKE ABOUT!? THIS PROVES THE STORY WAS TRUE! BUT THAT TERRIBLE BOLT HE'S HURLING AT ME--IT'S GOLDEN--YELLOW! AND MY RING HAS NO POWER OVER ANYTHING YELLOW!*
*Editor's Note: DUE TO A NECESSARY IMPURITY IN ITS VERY NATURE, GREEN LANTERN'S MYSTIC RING IS POWERLESS AGAINST ANYTHING YELLOW!
AT THAT SAME MOMENT...
TELLE-TEG KNOCKED US BOTH OVER--OUT OF THE WAY OF THAT AWFUL BLAST!
AS THE EMERALD WARRIOR LEAPS TO HIS FEET AGAIN...
TELLE-TEG SAVED MY LIFE--GAVE ME A CHANCE TO DEAL WITH THIS ASSASSIN FROM ANOTHER UNIVERSE!
BUT AS THE ALL-POWERFUL FIST FROM GL's RING FLASHES OUT, THE DESTROYER INTERRUPTS IT WITH HIS GOLDEN SHIELD AND...
MY OWN BEAM--SHOOTING BACK AT ME!
8
QUICKLY, THE GREEN-CLAD CHAMPION DUCKS AWAY FROM HIS OWN POWER-FIST...
ABOUT TO HURL ANOTHER QWA-BOLT AT ME! ONLY ONE THING TO DO NOW--!
STORY CONTINUED ON FOLLOWING PAGE.

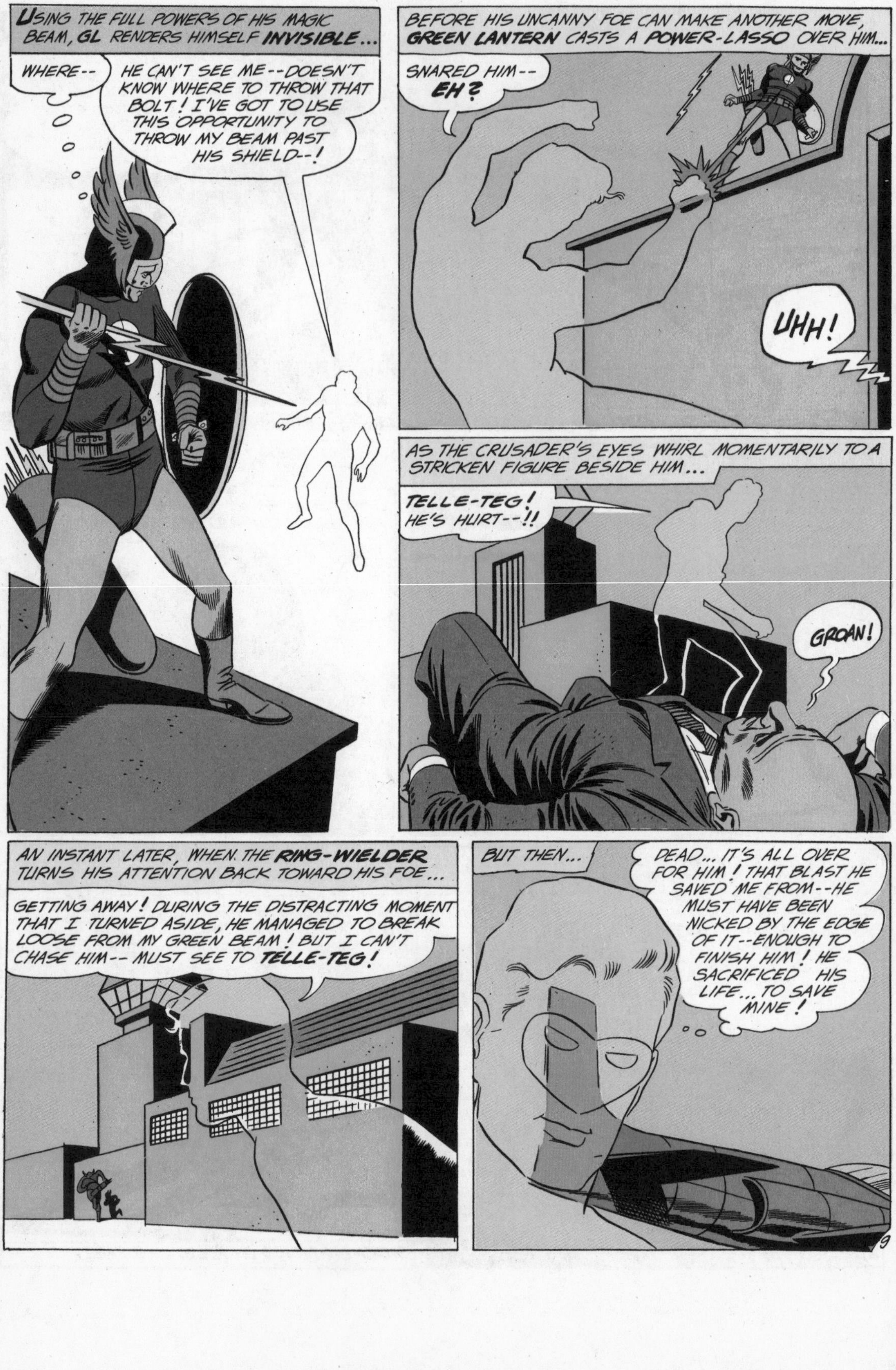
USING THE FULL POWERS OF HIS MAGIC BEAM, GL RENDERS HIMSELF INVISIBLE...
WHERE--
HE CAN'T SEE ME--DOESN'T KNOW WHERE TO THROW THAT BOLT! I'VE GOT TO USE THIS OPPORTUNITY TO THROW MY BEAM PAST HIS SHIELD--!
BEFORE HIS UNCANNY FOE CAN MAKE ANOTHER MOVE, GREEN LANTERN CASTS A POWER-LASSO OVER HIM...
SNARED HIM-- EH?
UHH!
AS THE CRUSADER'S EYES WHIRL MOMENTARILY TO A STRICKEN FIGURE BESIDE HIM...
TELLE-TEG! HE'S HURT--!!
GROAN!
AN INSTANT LATER, WHEN THE RING-WIELDER TURNS HIS ATTENTION BACK TOWARD HIS FOE...
GETTING AWAY! DURING THE DISTRACTING MOMENT THAT I TURNED ASIDE, HE MANAGED TO BREAK LOOSE FROM MY GREEN BEAM! BUT I CAN'T CHASE HIM-- MUST SEE TO TELLE-TEG!
BUT THEN...
DEAD... IT'S ALL OVER FOR HIM! THAT BLAST HE SAVED ME FROM--HE MUST HAVE BEEN NICKED BY THE EDGE OF IT--ENOUGH TO FINISH HIM! HE SACRIFICED HIS LIFE... TO SAVE MINE!
9

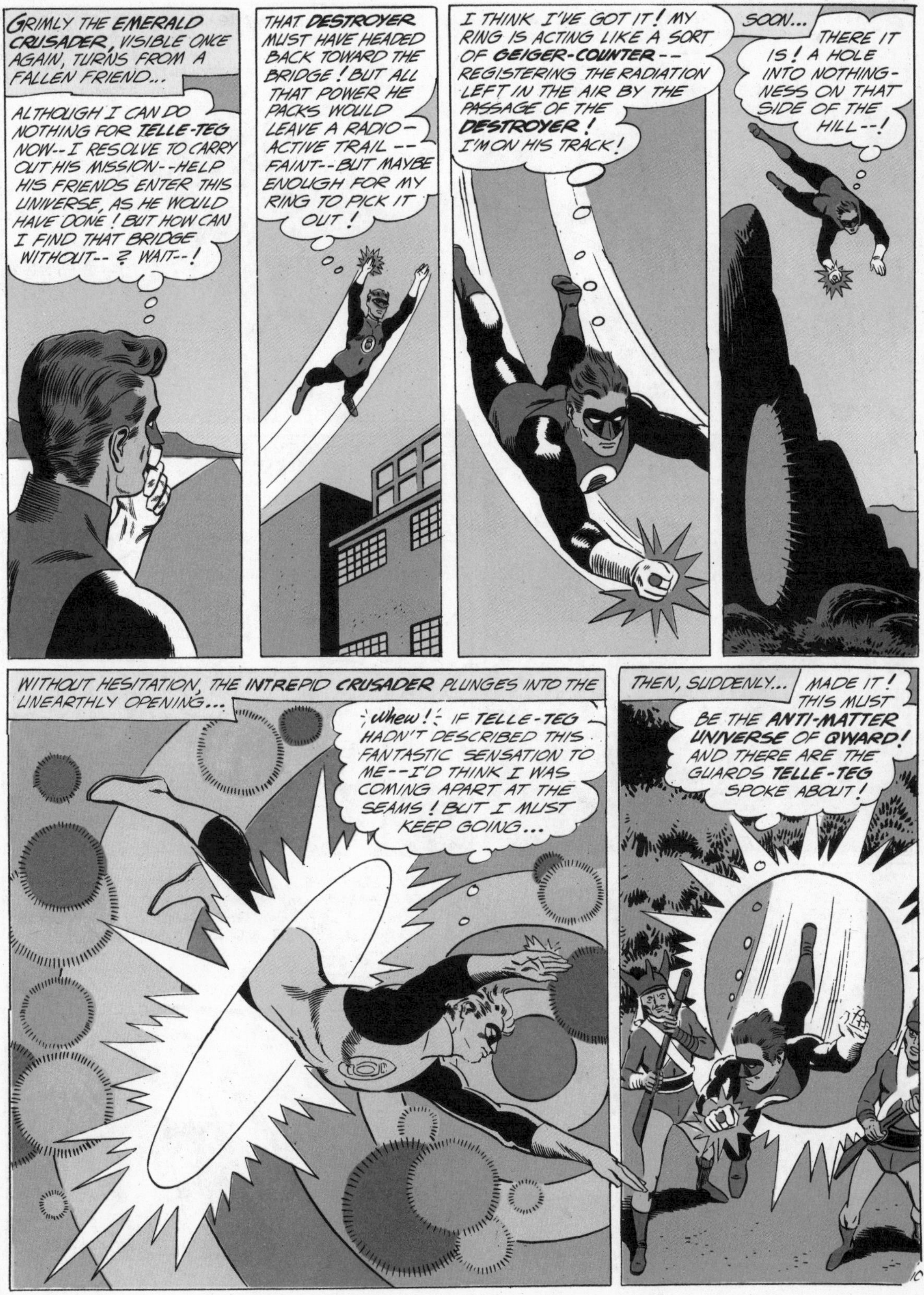
GRIMLY THE EMERALD CRUSADER, VISIBLE ONCE AGAIN, TURNS FROM A FALLEN FRIEND...
ALTHOUGH I CAN DO NOTHING FOR TELLE-TEG NOW--I RESOLVE TO CARRY OUT HIS MISSION--HELP HIS FRIENDS ENTER THIS UNIVERSE, AS HE WOULD HAVE DONE! BUT HOW CAN I FIND THAT BRIDGE WITHOUT--? WAIT--!
THAT DESTROYER MUST HAVE HEADED BACK TOWARD THE BRIDGE! BUT ALL THAT POWER HE PACKS WOULD LEAVE A RADIO-ACTIVE TRAIL--FAINT--BUT MAYBE ENOUGH FOR MY RING TO PICK IT OUT!
I THINK I'VE GOT IT! MY RING IS ACTING LIKE A SORT OF GEIGER-COUNTER--REGISTERING THE RADIATION LEFT IN THE AIR BY THE PASSAGE OF THE DESTROYER! I'M ON HIS TRACK!
SOON...
THERE IT IS! A HOLE INTO NOTHINGNESS ON THAT SIDE OF THE HILL--!
WITHOUT HESITATION, THE INTREPID CRUSADER PLUNGES INTO THE UNEARTHLY OPENING...
Whew! IF TELLE-TEG HADN'T DESCRIBED THIS FANTASTIC SENSATION TO ME--I'D THINK I WAS COMING APART AT THE SEAMS! BUT I MUST KEEP GOING...
THEN, SUDDENLY...
MADE IT! THIS MUST BE THE ANTI-MATTER UNIVERSE OF QWARD! AND THERE ARE THE GUARDS TELLE-TEG SPOKE ABOUT!
10

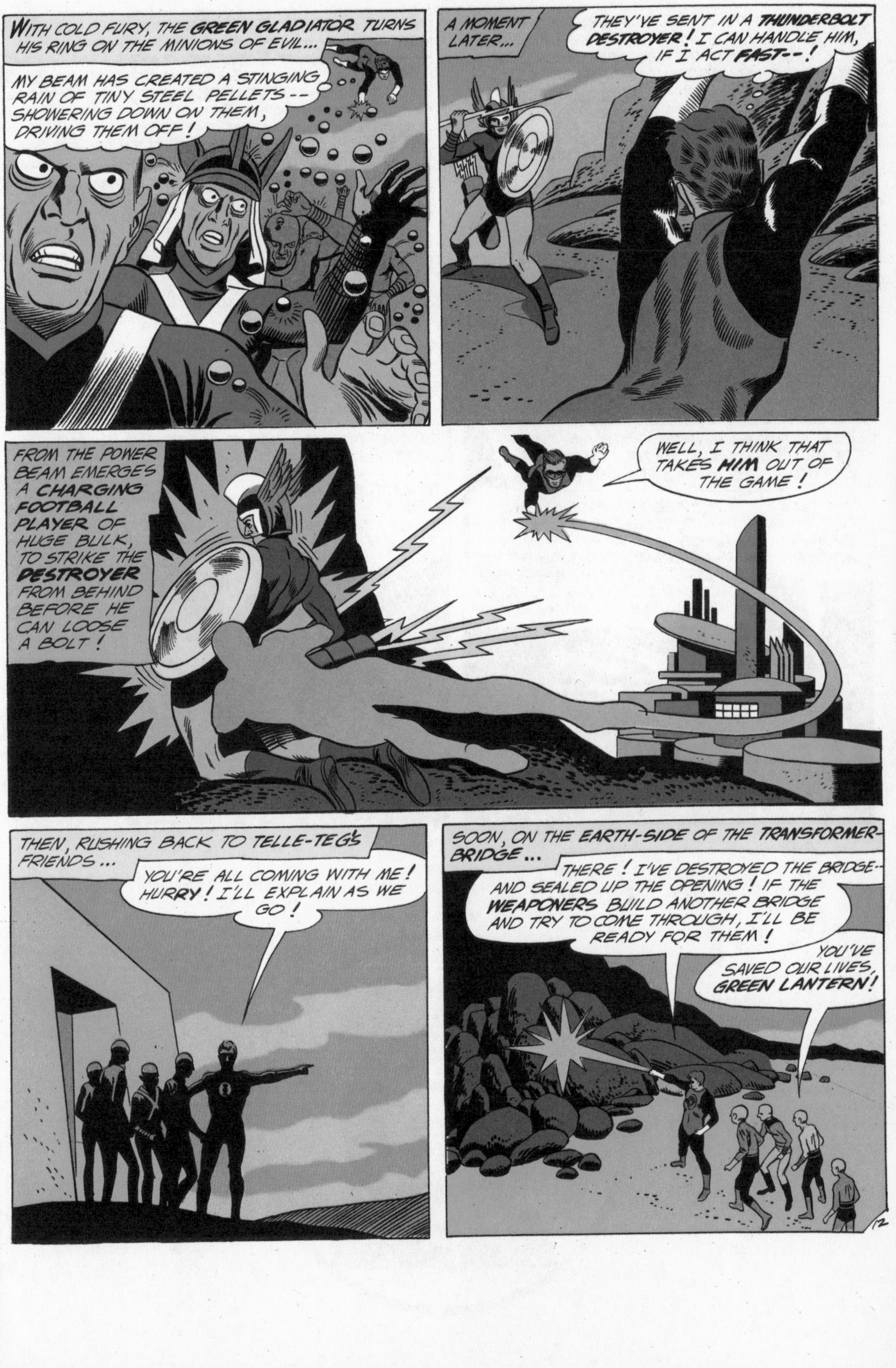
WITH COLD FURY, THE GREEN GLADIATOR TURNS HIS RING ON THE MINIONS OF EVIL...
MY BEAM HAS CREATED A STINGING RAIN OF TINY STEEL PELLETS -- SHOWERING DOWN ON THEM, DRIVING THEM OFF!
A MOMENT LATER...
THEY'VE SENT IN A THUNDERBOLT DESTROYER! I CAN HANDLE HIM, IF I ACT FAST--!
FROM THE POWER BEAM EMERGES A CHARGING FOOTBALL PLAYER OF HUGE BULK, TO STRIKE THE DESTROYER FROM BEHIND BEFORE HE CAN LOOSE A BOLT!
WELL, I THINK THAT TAKES HIM OUT OF THE GAME!
THEN, RUSHING BACK TO TELLE-TEG'S FRIENDS...
YOU'RE ALL COMING WITH ME! HURRY! I'LL EXPLAIN AS WE GO!
SOON, ON THE EARTH-SIDE OF THE TRANSFORMER-BRIDGE...
THERE! I'VE DESTROYED THE BRIDGE-- AND SEALED UP THE OPENING! IF THE WEAPONERS BUILD ANOTHER BRIDGE AND TRY TO COME THROUGH, I'LL BE READY FOR THEM!
YOU'VE SAVED OUR LIVES, GREEN LANTERN!
12

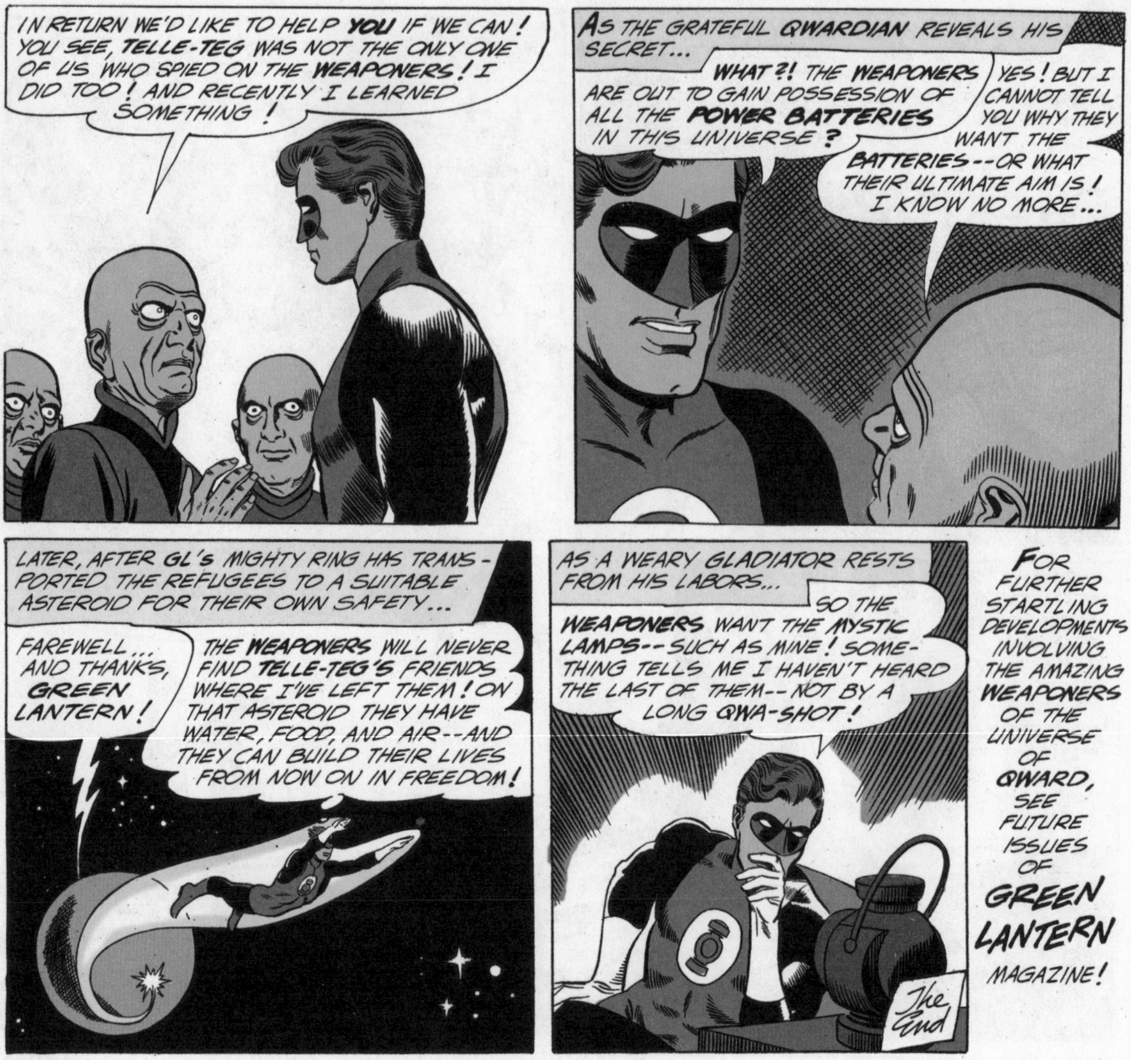
IN RETURN WE'D LIKE TO HELP YOU IF WE CAN! YOU SEE, TELLE-TEG WAS NOT THE ONLY ONE OF US WHO SPIED ON THE WEAPONERS! I DID TOO! AND RECENTLY I LEARNED SOMETHING!
AS THE GRATEFUL QWARDIAN REVEALS HIS SECRET...
WHAT ?! THE WEAPONERS ARE OUT TO GAIN POSSESSION OF ALL THE POWER BATTERIES IN THIS UNIVERSE?
YES! BUT I CANNOT TELL YOU WHY THEY WANT THE BATTERIES--OR WHAT THEIR ULTIMATE AIM IS! I KNOW NO MORE...
LATER, AFTER GL'S MIGHTY RING HAS TRANS-PORTED THE REFUGEES TO A SUITABLE ASTEROID FOR THEIR OWN SAFETY...
FAREWELL... AND THANKS, GREEN LANTERN!
THE WEAPONERS WILL NEVER FIND TELLE-TEG'S FRIENDS WHERE I'VE LEFT THEM! ON THAT ASTEROID THEY HAVE WATER, FOOD, AND AIR--AND THEY CAN BUILD THEIR LIVES FROM NOW ON IN FREEDOM!
AS A WEARY GLADIATOR RESTS FROM HIS LABORS...
SO THE WEAPONERS WANT THE MYSTIC LAMPS--SUCH AS MINE! SOME-THING TELLS ME I HAVEN'T HEARD THE LAST OF THEM--NOT BY A LONG QWA-SHOT!
The End
FOR FURTHER STARTLING DEVELOPMENTS INVOLVING THE AMAZING WEAPONERS OF THE UNIVERSE OF QWARD, SEE FUTURE ISSUES OF GREEN LANTERN MAGAZINE!

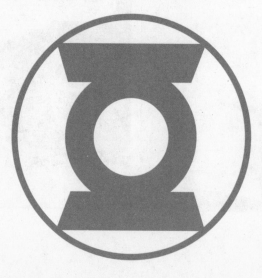

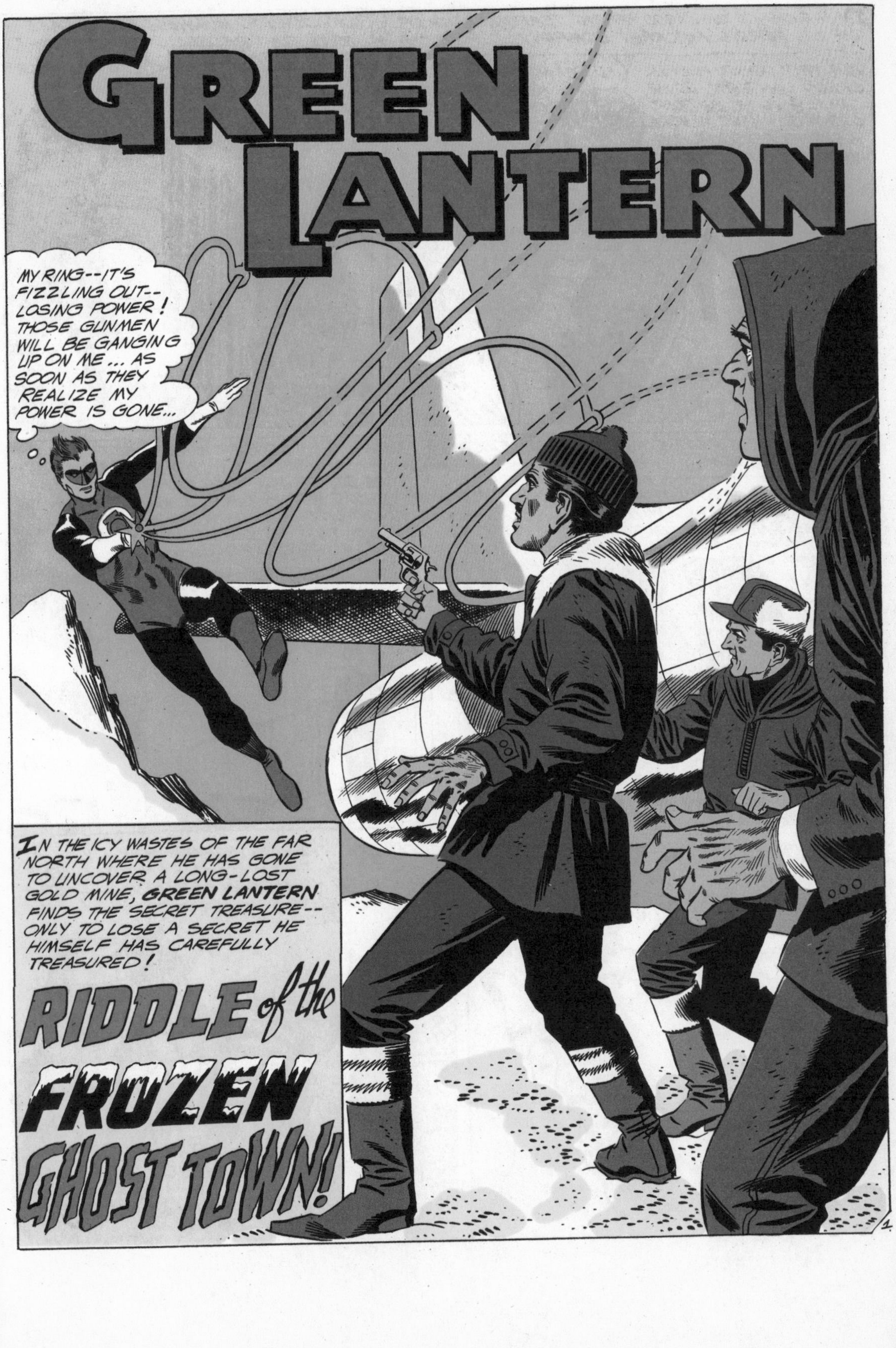
GREEN LANTERN
MY RING--IT'S FIZZLING OUT--LOSING POWER! THOSE GUNMEN WILL BE GANGING UP ON ME... AS SOON AS THEY REALIZE MY POWER IS GONE...
IN THE ICY WASTES OF THE FAR NORTH WHERE HE HAS GONE TO UNCOVER A LONG-LOST GOLD MINE, GREEN LANTERN FINDS THE SECRET TREASURE--ONLY TO LOSE A SECRET HE HIMSELF HAS CAREFULLY TREASURED!
RIDDLE of the FROZEN GHOST TOWN!
1

IN THE OFFICE OF CAROL FERRIS, TEMPORARY CHIEF OF THE FERRIS AIRCRAFT COMPANY...

BUT WHY DO YOU PREFER GREEN LANTERN TO ME, CAROL? IS HE BETTER LOOKING--HAVE A MORE PLEASING PERSONALITY-- MORE STERLING CHARACTER--*

MR. JORDAN, I DID NOT SUMMON YOU HERE TO QUIZ ME ON MY SOCIAL LIFE!

*Editor's Note:

THERE'S NO DOUBT ABOUT THE ANSWERS AS FAR AS HAL JORDAN IS CON- CERNED--FOR IN HIS SECRET IDENTITY, HE IS GREEN LANTERN!

NOW--DOWN TO BUSINESS! WE'VE JUST RECEIVED NOTICE--THOMAS KALMAKU, YOUR MECHANIC, IS LEAVING AT THE END OF THE WEEK! WE'LL HAVE TO HIRE SOMEONE ELSE!

PIEFACE-- QUITTING?!

AS THE ACE TEST PILOT EXHIBITS EXTREME CON- CERN AT THE NEWS...

LET HIM GO, CAROL! THAT ESKIMO IS A WIZARD WITH JET ENGINES AND I COULDN'T DO WITHOUT HIM! GIVE HIM A RAISE! HE'S GOT TO STAY!

WE CAN'T! HE SAID IT WASN'T MONEY! BUT IF YOU WANT TO TALK TO HIM, HAL, GO AHEAD...

SHORTLY... I WONDER WHAT'S GOT INTO PIEFACE? LAST TIME I SAW HIM, HE DIDN'T ACT LIKE THERE WAS ANY- THING WRONG! BUT I REALIZE NOW HOW LITTLE I KNOW ABOUT HIM-- ONLY THAT HE SERVED WITH OUR ARMED FORCES IN ALASKA...

...WHERE HE GOT TO BE AN EXPERT ON SERVICING JETS! AND THAT AFTERWARDS HE CAME DOWN HERE TO THE STATES AND GOT A JOB WITH THE FERRIS COMPANY--AS MY MECHANIC! HE AND I ALWAYS WORKED TOGETHER PERFECTLY--

EH?

GREAT DAY! THERE'S PIEFACE NOW--IN A TUSSLE WITH TWO BIG LUGS! NO TIME TO CHANGE TO MY GREEN LANTERN COSTUME!

2

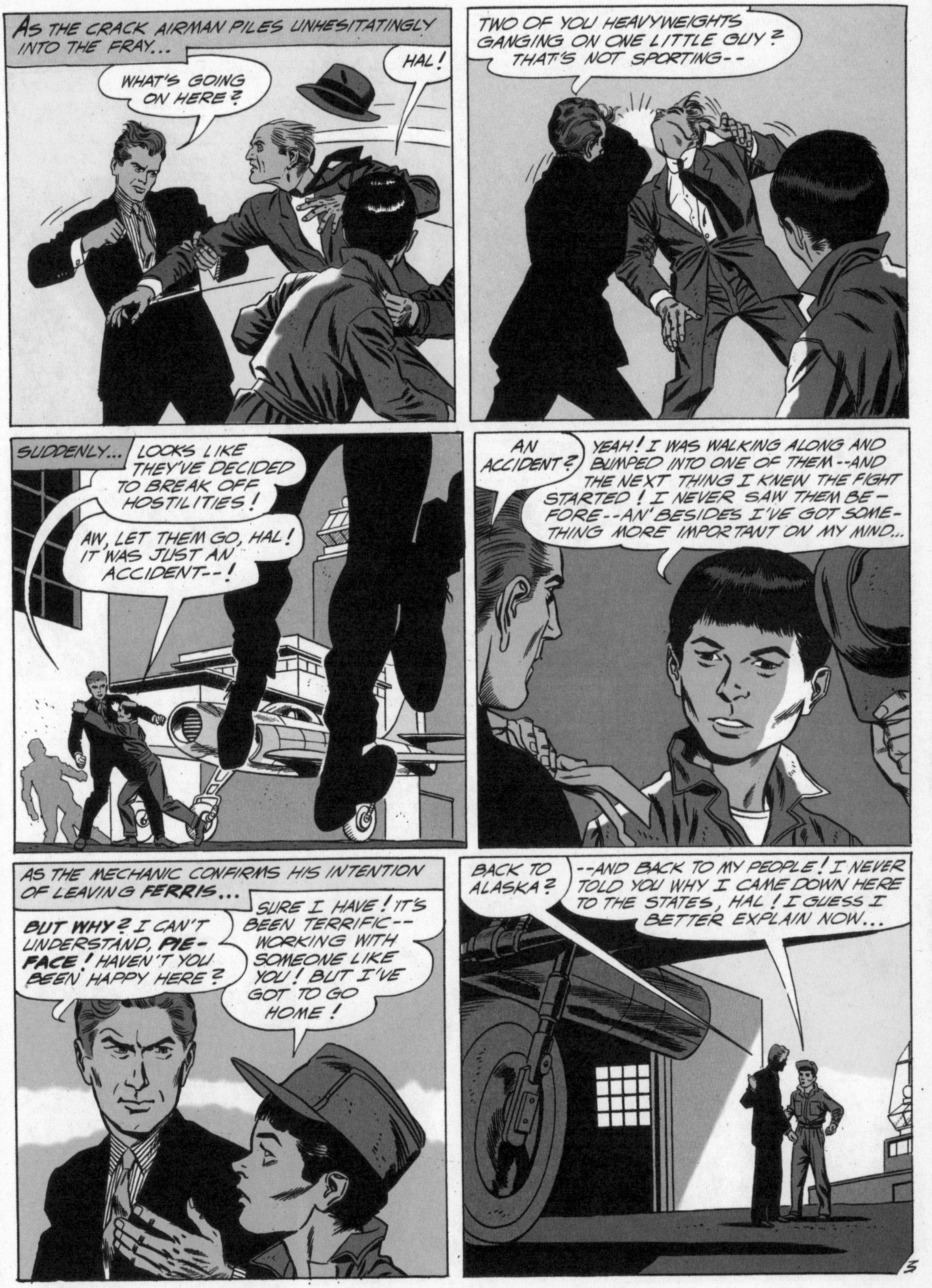

AS THE CRACK AIRMAN PILES UNHESITATINGLY INTO THE FRAY...
WHAT'S GOING ON HERE?
HAL!
TWO OF YOU HEAVYWEIGHTS GANGING ON ONE LITTLE GUY? THAT'S NOT SPORTING--
SUDDENLY...
LOOKS LIKE THEY'VE DECIDED TO BREAK OFF HOSTILITIES!
AW, LET THEM GO, HAL! IT WAS JUST AN ACCIDENT--!
AN ACCIDENT?
YEAH! I WAS WALKING ALONG AND BUMPED INTO ONE OF THEM--AND THE NEXT THING I KNEW THE FIGHT STARTED! I NEVER SAW THEM BE-FORE--AN' BESIDES I'VE GOT SOME-THING MORE IMPORTANT ON MY MIND...
AS THE MECHANIC CONFIRMS HIS INTENTION OF LEAVING FERRIS...
BUT WHY? I CAN'T UNDERSTAND, PIE-FACE! HAVEN'T YOU BEEN HAPPY HERE?
SURE I HAVE! IT'S BEEN TERRIFIC--WORKING WITH SOMEONE LIKE YOU! BUT I'VE GOT TO GO HOME!
BACK TO ALASKA?
--AND BACK TO MY PEOPLE! I NEVER TOLD YOU WHY I CAME DOWN HERE TO THE STATES, HAL! I GUESS I BETTER EXPLAIN NOW...
3

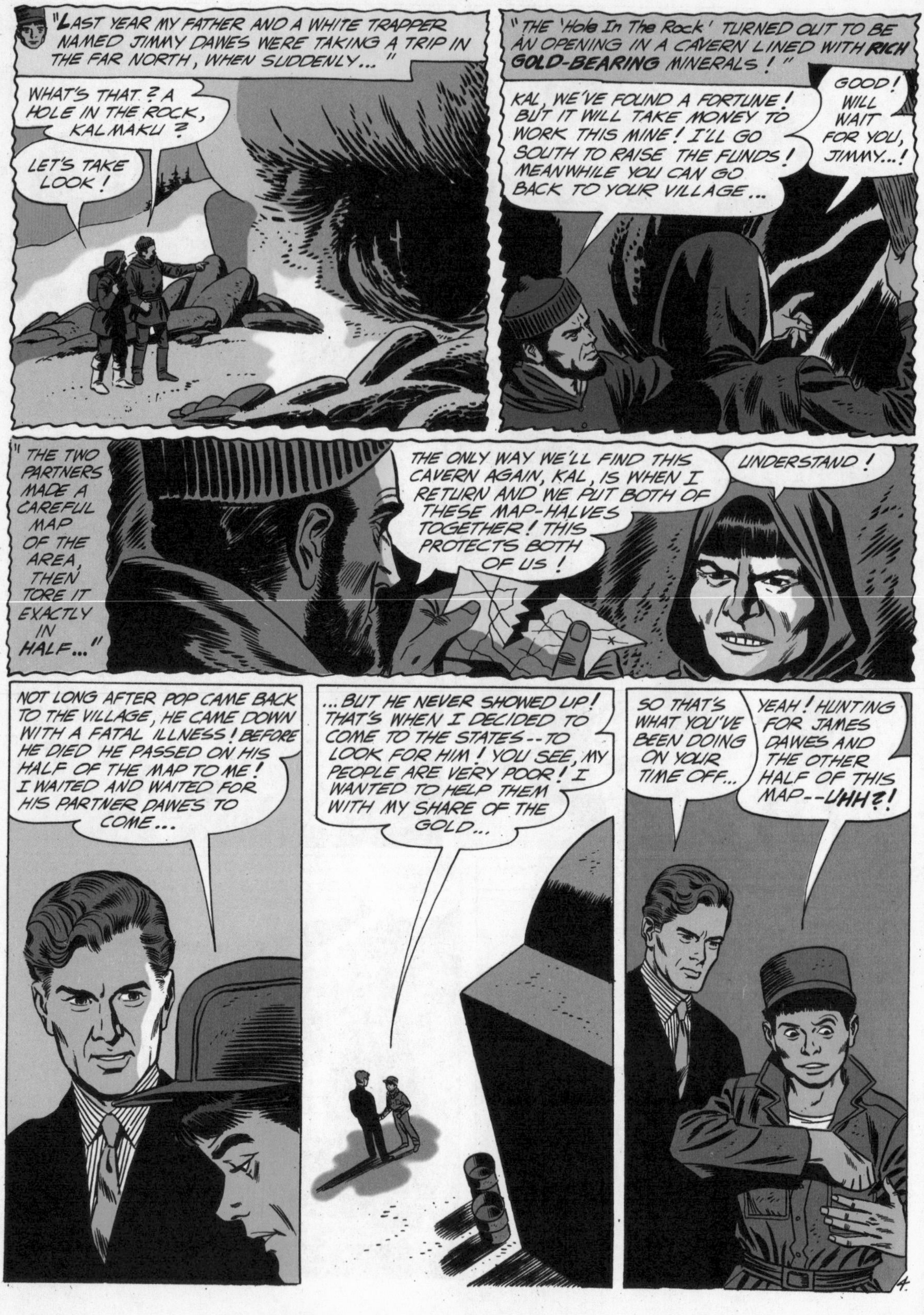
"LAST YEAR MY FATHER AND A WHITE TRAPPER NAMED JIMMY DAWES WERE TAKING A TRIP IN THE FAR NORTH, WHEN SUDDENLY..."
WHAT'S THAT ? A HOLE IN THE ROCK, KALMAKU ?
LET'S TAKE LOOK !
"THE 'Hole In The Rock' TURNED OUT TO BE AN OPENING IN A CAVERN LINED WITH RICH GOLD-BEARING MINERALS !"
KAL, WE'VE FOUND A FORTUNE ! BUT IT WILL TAKE MONEY TO WORK THIS MINE ! I'LL GO SOUTH TO RAISE THE FUNDS ! MEANWHILE YOU CAN GO BACK TO YOUR VILLAGE...
GOOD ! WILL WAIT FOR YOU, JIMMY...!
"THE TWO PARTNERS MADE A CAREFUL MAP OF THE AREA, THEN TORE IT EXACTLY IN HALF..."
THE ONLY WAY WE'LL FIND THIS CAVERN AGAIN, KAL, IS WHEN I RETURN AND WE PUT BOTH OF THESE MAP-HALVES TOGETHER ! THIS PROTECTS BOTH OF US !
UNDERSTAND !
NOT LONG AFTER POP CAME BACK TO THE VILLAGE, HE CAME DOWN WITH A FATAL ILLNESS ! BEFORE HE DIED HE PASSED ON HIS HALF OF THE MAP TO ME ! I WAITED AND WAITED FOR HIS PARTNER DAWES TO COME...
...BUT HE NEVER SHOWED UP ! THAT'S WHEN I DECIDED TO COME TO THE STATES--TO LOOK FOR HIM ! YOU SEE, MY PEOPLE ARE VERY POOR ! I WANTED TO HELP THEM WITH MY SHARE OF THE GOLD...
SO THAT'S WHAT YOU'VE BEEN DOING ON YOUR TIME OFF...
YEAH ! HUNTING FOR JAMES DAWES AND THE OTHER HALF OF THIS MAP--UHH?!
4.

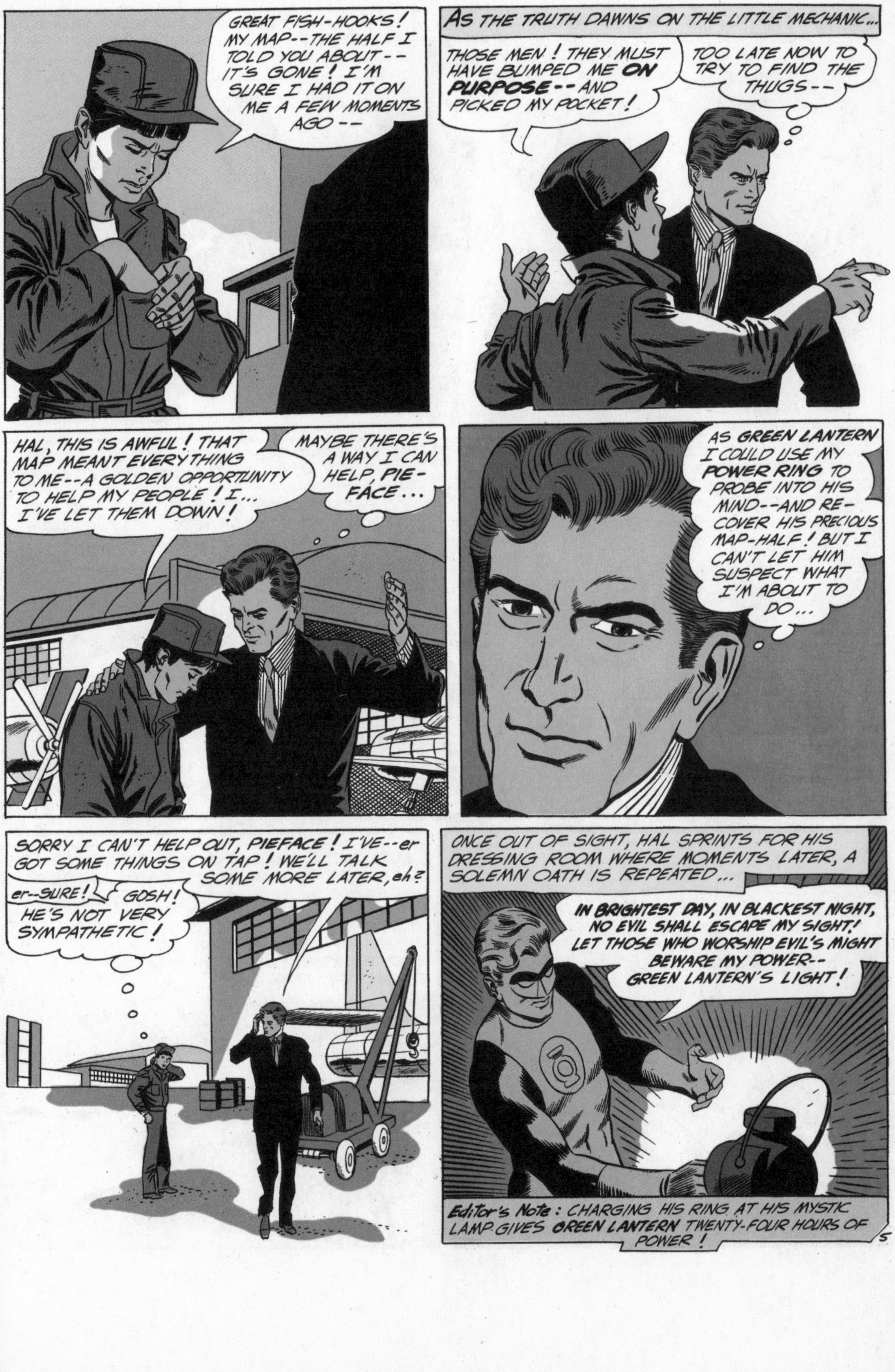
GREAT FISH-HOOKS! MY MAP--THE HALF I TOLD YOU ABOUT-- IT'S GONE! I'M SURE I HAD IT ON ME A FEW MOMENTS AGO--
AS THE TRUTH DAWNS ON THE LITTLE MECHANIC...
THOSE MEN! THEY MUST HAVE BUMPED ME ON PURPOSE--AND PICKED MY POCKET!
TOO LATE NOW TO TRY TO FIND THE THUGS--
HAL, THIS IS AWFUL! THAT MAP MEANT EVERYTHING TO ME--A GOLDEN OPPORTUNITY TO HELP MY PEOPLE! I... I'VE LET THEM DOWN!
MAYBE THERE'S A WAY I CAN HELP, PIE-FACE...
AS GREEN LANTERN I COULD USE MY POWER RING TO PROBE INTO HIS MIND--AND RE-COVER HIS PRECIOUS MAP-HALF! BUT I CAN'T LET HIM SUSPECT WHAT I'M ABOUT TO DO...
SORRY I CAN'T HELP OUT, PIEFACE! I'VE--er GOT SOME THINGS ON TAP! WE'LL TALK SOME MORE LATER, eh?
er--SURE!
GOSH! HE'S NOT VERY SYMPATHETIC!
ONCE OUT OF SIGHT, HAL SPRINTS FOR HIS DRESSING ROOM WHERE MOMENTS LATER, A SOLEMN OATH IS REPEATED...
IN BRIGHTEST DAY, IN BLACKEST NIGHT, NO EVIL SHALL ESCAPE MY SIGHT! LET THOSE WHO WORSHIP EVIL'S MIGHT BEWARE MY POWER-- GREEN LANTERN'S LIGHT!
Editor's Note: CHARGING HIS RING AT HIS MYSTIC LAMP GIVES GREEN LANTERN TWENTY-FOUR HOURS OF POWER!
5

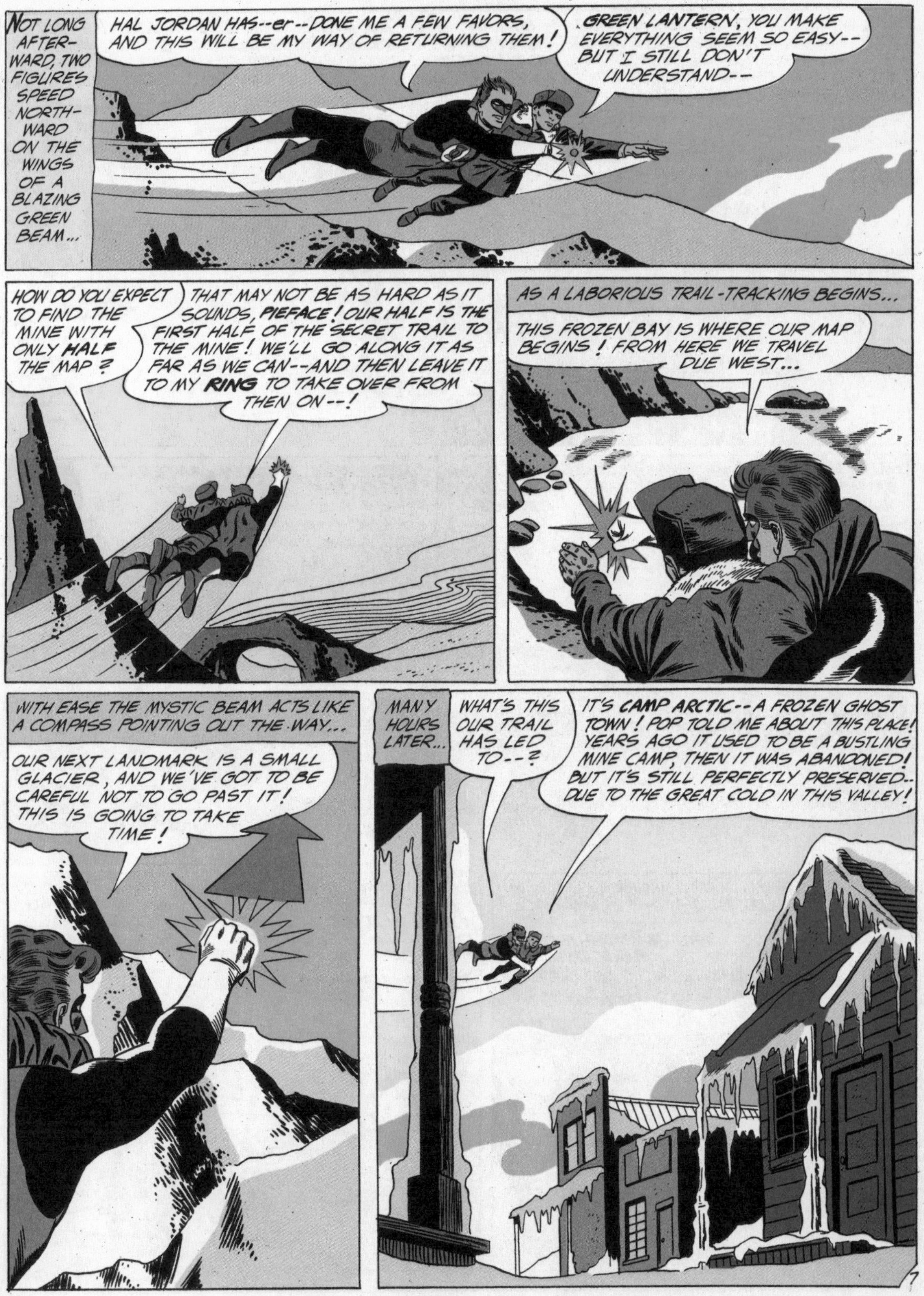
NOT LONG AFTERWARD, TWO FIGURES SPEED NORTHWARD ON THE WINGS OF A BLAZING GREEN BEAM...
HAL JORDAN HAS--er--DONE ME A FEW FAVORS, AND THIS WILL BE MY WAY OF RETURNING THEM!
GREEN LANTERN, YOU MAKE EVERYTHING SEEM SO EASY-- BUT I STILL DON'T UNDERSTAND--
HOW DO YOU EXPECT TO FIND THE MINE WITH ONLY HALF THE MAP?
THAT MAY NOT BE AS HARD AS IT SOUNDS, PIEFACE! OUR HALF IS THE FIRST HALF OF THE SECRET TRAIL TO THE MINE! WE'LL GO ALONG IT AS FAR AS WE CAN--AND THEN LEAVE IT TO MY RING TO TAKE OVER FROM THEN ON--!
AS A LABORIOUS TRAIL-TRACKING BEGINS...
THIS FROZEN BAY IS WHERE OUR MAP BEGINS! FROM HERE WE TRAVEL DUE WEST...
WITH EASE THE MYSTIC BEAM ACTS LIKE A COMPASS POINTING OUT THE WAY...
OUR NEXT LANDMARK IS A SMALL GLACIER, AND WE'VE GOT TO BE CAREFUL NOT TO GO PAST IT! THIS IS GOING TO TAKE TIME!
MANY HOURS LATER...
WHAT'S THIS OUR TRAIL HAS LED TO--?
IT'S CAMP ARCTIC--A FROZEN GHOST TOWN! POP TOLD ME ABOUT THIS PLACE! YEARS AGO IT USED TO BE A BUSTLING MINE CAMP, THEN IT WAS ABANDONED! BUT IT'S STILL PERFECTLY PRESERVED.. DUE TO THE GREAT COLD IN THIS VALLEY!
7

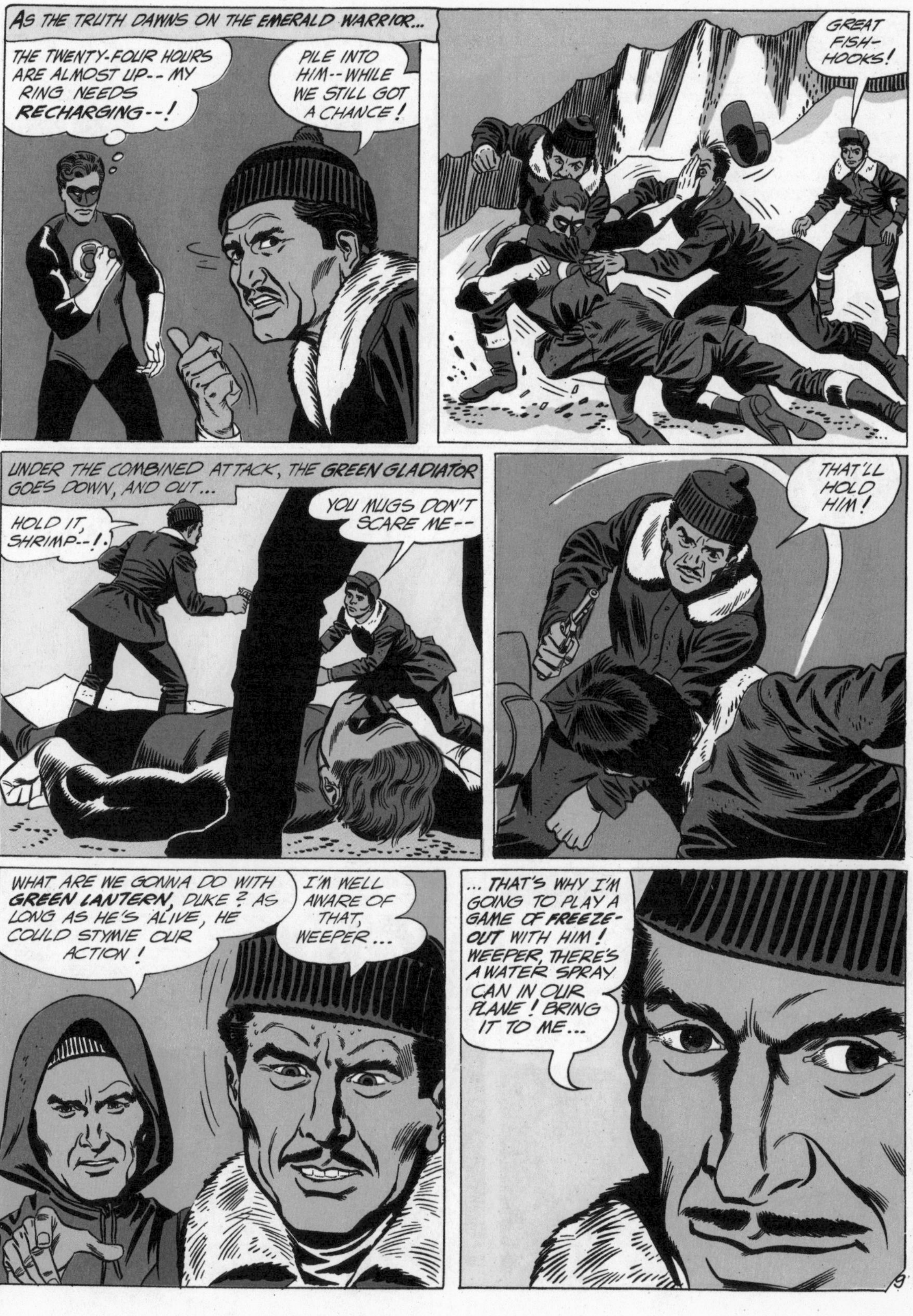
AS THE TRUTH DAWNS ON THE EMERALD WARRIOR...
THE TWENTY-FOUR HOURS ARE ALMOST UP-- MY RING NEEDS RECHARGING--!
PILE INTO HIM--WHILE WE STILL GOT A CHANCE!
GREAT FISH-HOOKS!
UNDER THE COMBINED ATTACK, THE GREEN GLADIATOR GOES DOWN, AND OUT...
HOLD IT, SHRIMP--!
YOU MUGS DON'T SCARE ME--
THAT'LL HOLD HIM!
WHAT ARE WE GONNA DO WITH GREEN LANTERN, DUKE? AS LONG AS HE'S ALIVE, HE COULD STYMIE OUR ACTION!
I'M WELL AWARE OF THAT, WEEPER...
...THAT'S WHY I'M GOING TO PLAY A GAME OF FREEZE-OUT WITH HIM! WEEPER, THERE'S A WATER SPRAY CAN IN OUR PLANE! BRING IT TO ME...
9

SOON, BACK AT THE DANCE PALACE IN THE FROZEN GHOST TOWN...

YOU'RE SPRAYING GREEN LANTERN WITH WATER, DUKE? WHAT'S THE IDEA?

THIS VALLEY NEVER GETS ABOVE FREEZING, WEEPER! WE'RE TURNING GL INTO A PERMANENT STATUE!

SINCE NO ONE EVER COMES HERE, GREEN LANTERN WILL BE A PART OF THIS FROZEN GHOST TOWN-- FOREVER!

HA! HA! WE'VE IM- PROVED THIS PLACE 100 PERCENT!

AS THE TRIO DEPARTS...

UH-H-- WHERE... AM I...?

CAN'T MOVE...! ICE COVERING ME... LIKE STEEL! AND MY RING IS WITH- OUT POWER....! HOW CAN I GET OUT OF THIS?

IN THE EMERGENCY, GREEN LANTERN'S INDOMITABLE WILL SOARS TO THE FORE...

EVEN THOUGH MY RING IS PRACTICALLY EXHAUSTED, THERE MAY BE JUST A TINY BIT OF POWER LEFT IN IT! GOT TO TRY...

10.

AS THE CHAMPION OF JUSTICE CONCENTRATES HIS WILL POWER, POURING IT ON...

THERE'S JUST BARELY ENOUGH LEFT! USING MY RING, I'VE CAUSED THE GREEN BEAM TO FORM A **MINIATURE SUN**, BATHING ME WITH WARM RAYS! BUT WILL IT MELT THIS TERRIBLY COLD ICE?

AGONIZING MOMENTS LATER...

IT WORKED! BUT NOW MY RING **IS** ABSOLUTELY DEAD! YET I CAN'T THINK OF GETTING HOME TO CHARGE IT--GOT TO FIND **PIEFACE** AND THOSE MEN!

MEANWHILE, IN A NEARBY BUILDING...

YOU'RE COMING WITH US, KALMAKU! WE CAN USE YOU TO DIG WHEN WE FIND THE GOLD MINE! WE'RE GOING TO TAKE A BIG LOAD OUT IN THE JET--AS MUCH AS WE CAN!

YOU CROOKS-- YOU MUST HAVE STOLEN THAT OTHER MAP-HALF TOO--FROM JIM DAWES!

WRONG! HE LOST IT TO ME GAMBLING--PLUS EVERY- THING ELSE HE OWNED! THEN, AFTER I WON IT, I DECIDED TO GET THE OTHER HALF YOU SEE, DUKE DANFIELD **ALWAYS** GETS WHAT HE GOES AFTER...

YOU MEAN **ALMOST** ALWAYS-- DON'T YOU, DUKE?

GREEN LANTERN AGAIN! HE'S LOOSE!

LOOK OUT FOR HIS RING!

HIS RING ISN'T WORK- ING!

YES--BUT PRETENDING THAT IT WAS GAVE ME JUST THE MOMENT I NEEDED TO TAKE CARE OF THESE GUNMEN!

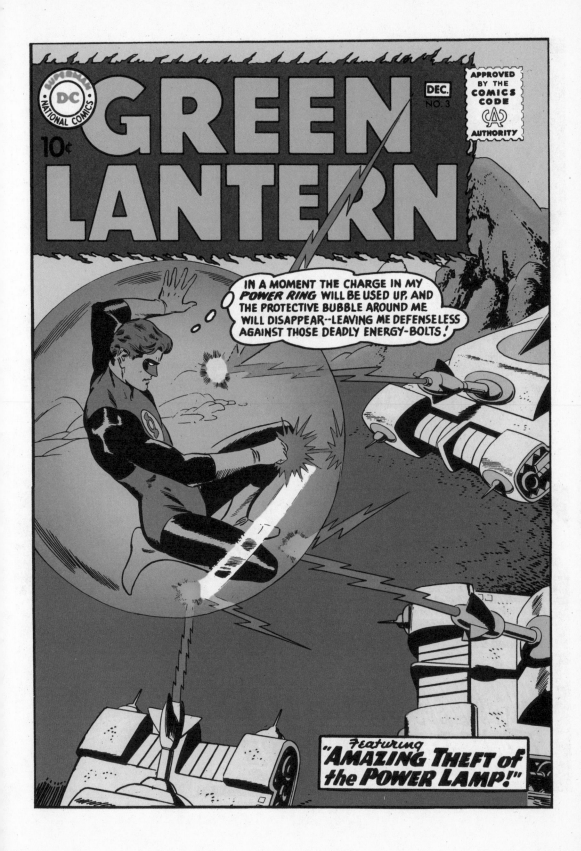

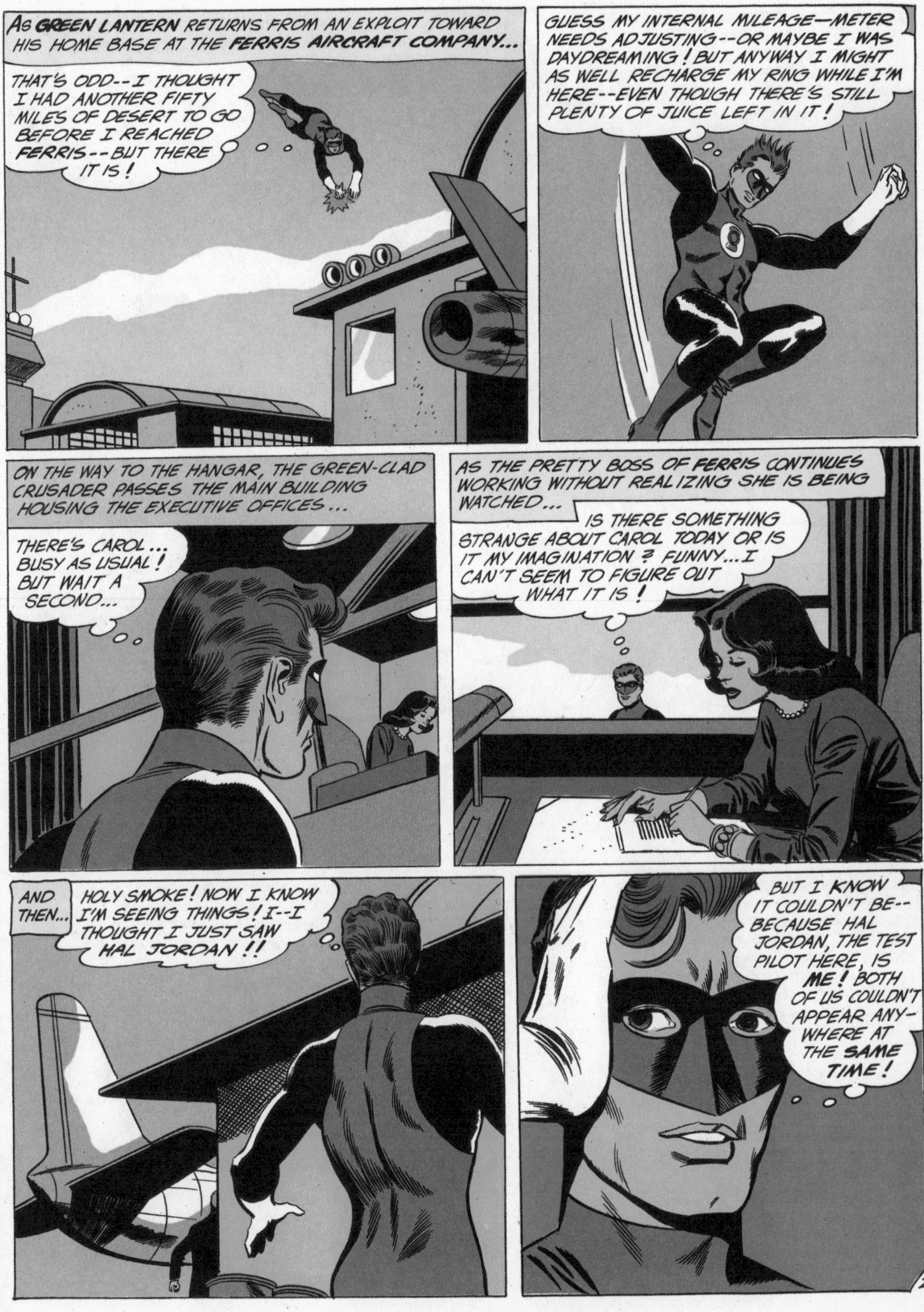

AS GREEN LANTERN RETURNS FROM AN EXPLOIT TOWARD HIS HOME BASE AT THE FERRIS AIRCRAFT COMPANY...
THAT'S ODD--I THOUGHT I HAD ANOTHER FIFTY MILES OF DESERT TO GO BEFORE I REACHED FERRIS--BUT THERE IT IS!
GUESS MY INTERNAL MILEAGE-METER NEEDS ADJUSTING--OR MAYBE I WAS DAYDREAMING! BUT ANYWAY I MIGHT AS WELL RECHARGE MY RING WHILE I'M HERE--EVEN THOUGH THERE'S STILL PLENTY OF JUICE LEFT IN IT!
ON THE WAY TO THE HANGAR, THE GREEN-CLAD CRUSADER PASSES THE MAIN BUILDING HOUSING THE EXECUTIVE OFFICES...
THERE'S CAROL... BUSY AS USUAL! BUT WAIT A SECOND...
AS THE PRETTY BOSS OF FERRIS CONTINUES WORKING WITHOUT REALIZING SHE IS BEING WATCHED...
IS THERE SOMETHING STRANGE ABOUT CAROL TODAY OR IS IT MY IMAGINATION? FUNNY...I CAN'T SEEM TO FIGURE OUT WHAT IT IS!
AND THEN...
HOLY SMOKE! NOW I KNOW I'M SEEING THINGS! I--I THOUGHT I JUST SAW HAL JORDAN!!
BUT I KNOW IT COULDN'T BE--BECAUSE HAL JORDAN, THE TEST PILOT HERE, IS ME! BOTH OF US COULDN'T APPEAR ANYWHERE AT THE SAME TIME!
2

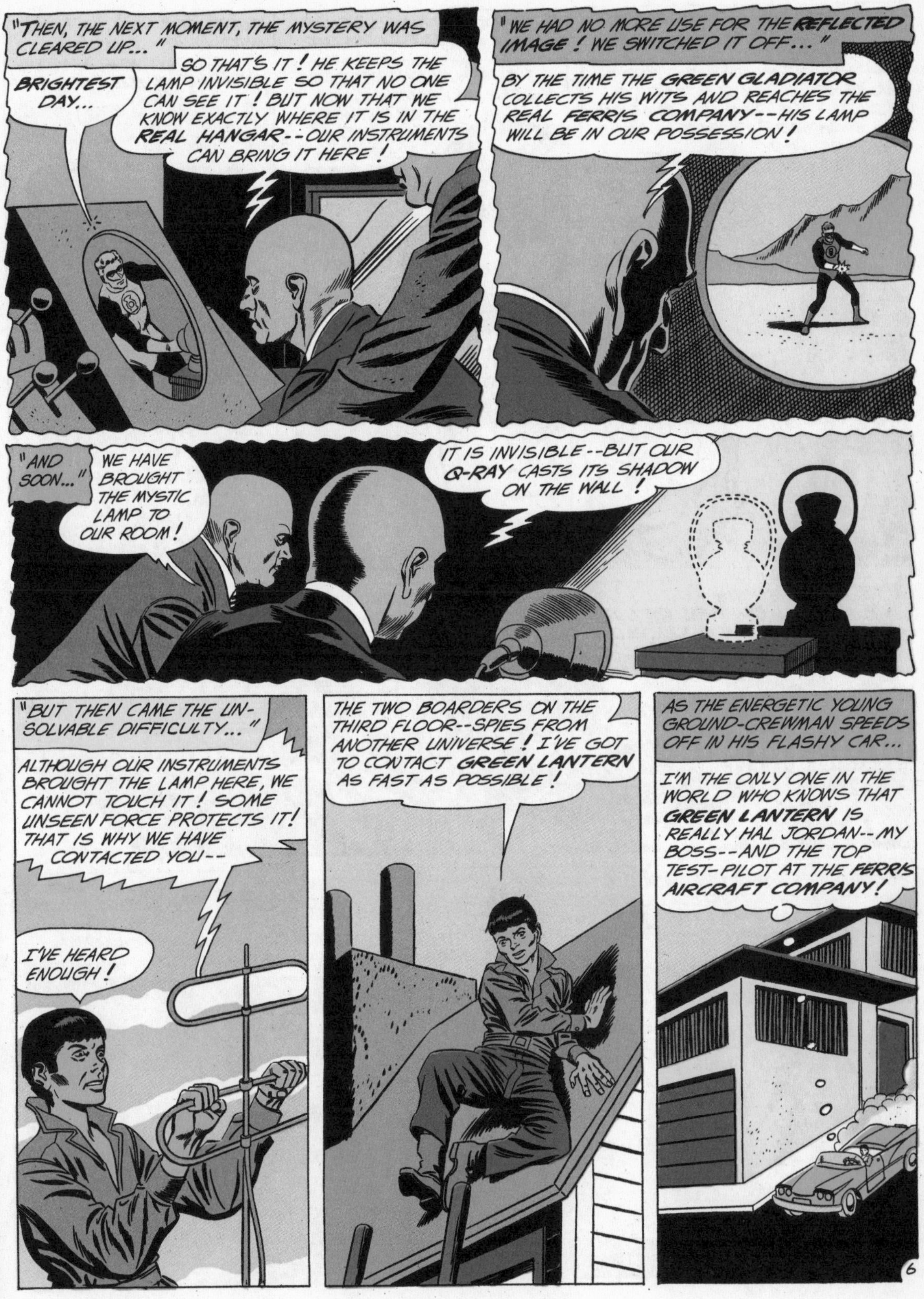
"THEN, THE NEXT MOMENT, THE MYSTERY WAS CLEARED UP..."
BRIGHTEST DAY...
SO THAT'S IT! HE KEEPS THE LAMP INVISIBLE SO THAT NO ONE CAN SEE IT! BUT NOW THAT WE KNOW EXACTLY WHERE IT IS IN THE REAL HANGAR--OUR INSTRUMENTS CAN BRING IT HERE!
"WE HAD NO MORE USE FOR THE REFLECTED IMAGE! WE SWITCHED IT OFF..."
BY THE TIME THE GREEN GLADIATOR COLLECTS HIS WITS AND REACHES THE REAL FERRIS COMPANY--HIS LAMP WILL BE IN OUR POSSESSION!
"AND SOON..."
WE HAVE BROUGHT THE MYSTIC LAMP TO OUR ROOM!
IT IS INVISIBLE--BUT OUR Q-RAY CASTS ITS SHADOW ON THE WALL!
"BUT THEN CAME THE UNSOLVABLE DIFFICULTY..."
ALTHOUGH OUR INSTRUMENTS BROUGHT THE LAMP HERE, WE CANNOT TOUCH IT! SOME UNSEEN FORCE PROTECTS IT! THAT IS WHY WE HAVE CONTACTED YOU--
I'VE HEARD ENOUGH!
THE TWO BOARDERS ON THE THIRD FLOOR--SPIES FROM ANOTHER UNIVERSE! I'VE GOT TO CONTACT GREEN LANTERN AS FAST AS POSSIBLE!
AS THE ENERGETIC YOUNG GROUND-CREWMAN SPEEDS OFF IN HIS FLASHY CAR...
I'M THE ONLY ONE IN THE WORLD WHO KNOWS THAT GREEN LANTERN IS REALLY HAL JORDAN--MY BOSS--AND THE TOP TEST-PILOT AT THE FERRIS AIRCRAFT COMPANY!
6

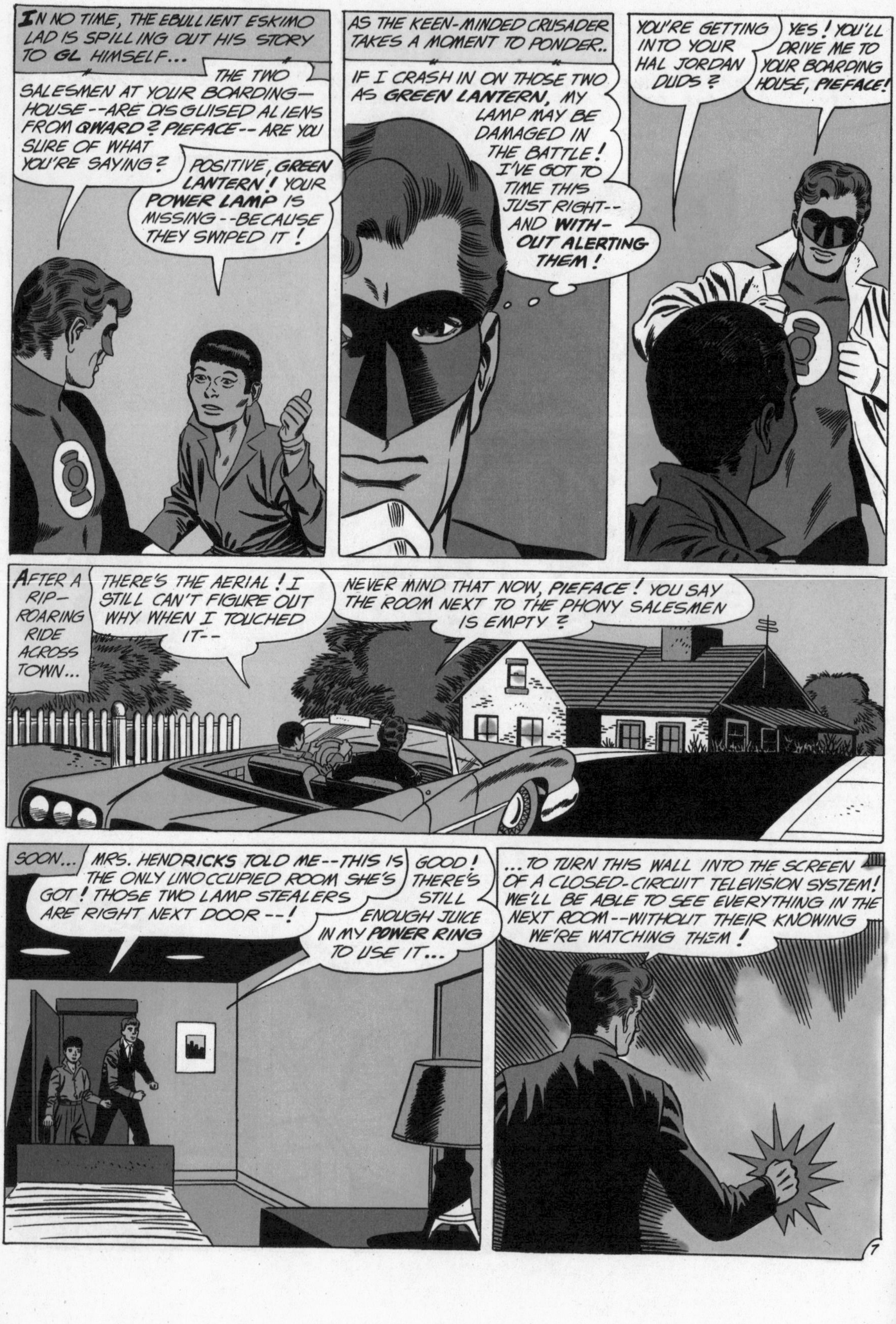
IN NO TIME, THE EBULLIENT ESKIMO LAD IS SPILLING OUT HIS STORY TO GL HIMSELF...
THE TWO SALESMEN AT YOUR BOARDING-HOUSE--ARE DISGUISED ALIENS FROM QWARD? PIEFACE--ARE YOU SURE OF WHAT YOU'RE SAYING?
POSITIVE, GREEN LANTERN! YOUR POWER LAMP IS MISSING--BECAUSE THEY SWIPED IT!
AS THE KEEN-MINDED CRUSADER TAKES A MOMENT TO PONDER..
IF I CRASH IN ON THOSE TWO AS GREEN LANTERN, MY LAMP MAY BE DAMAGED IN THE BATTLE! I'VE GOT TO TIME THIS JUST RIGHT--AND WITHOUT ALERTING THEM!
YOU'RE GETTING INTO YOUR HAL JORDAN DUDS?
YES! YOU'LL DRIVE ME TO YOUR BOARDING HOUSE, PIEFACE!
AFTER A RIP-ROARING RIDE ACROSS TOWN...
THERE'S THE AERIAL! I STILL CAN'T FIGURE OUT WHY WHEN I TOUCHED IT--
NEVER MIND THAT NOW, PIEFACE! YOU SAY THE ROOM NEXT TO THE PHONY SALESMEN IS EMPTY?
SOON...
MRS. HENDRICKS TOLD ME--THIS IS THE ONLY UNOCCUPIED ROOM SHE'S GOT! THOSE TWO LAMP STEALERS ARE RIGHT NEXT DOOR--!
GOOD! THERE'S STILL ENOUGH JUICE IN MY POWER RING TO USE IT...
...TO TURN THIS WALL INTO THE SCREEN OF A CLOSED-CIRCUIT TELEVISION SYSTEM! WE'LL BE ABLE TO SEE EVERYTHING IN THE NEXT ROOM--WITHOUT THEIR KNOWING WE'RE WATCHING THEM!
7

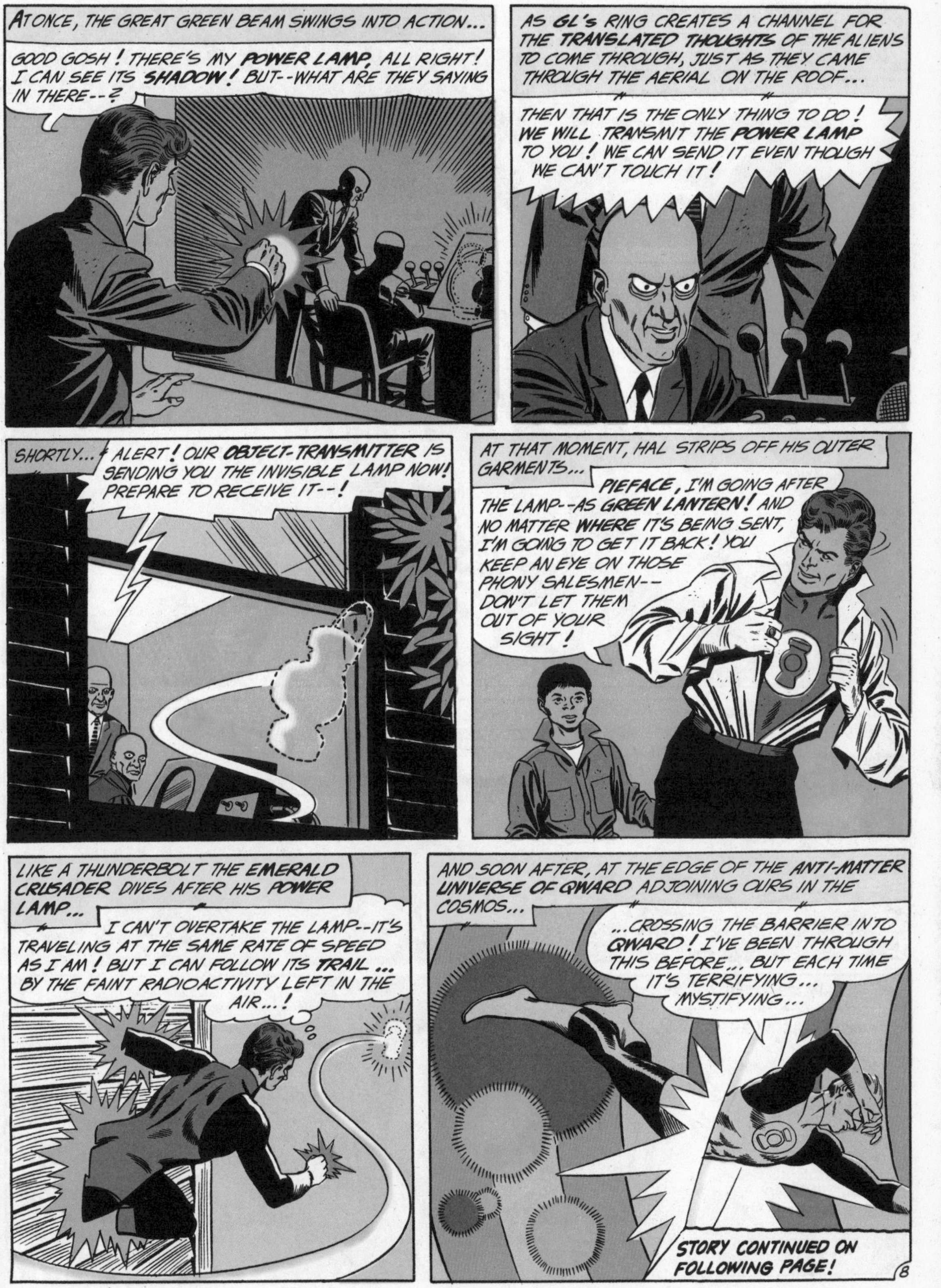
AT ONCE, THE GREAT GREEN BEAM SWINGS INTO ACTION...
GOOD GOSH! THERE'S MY POWER LAMP, ALL RIGHT! I CAN SEE ITS SHADOW! BUT--WHAT ARE THEY SAYING IN THERE--?
AS GL's RING CREATES A CHANNEL FOR THE TRANSLATED THOUGHTS OF THE ALIENS TO COME THROUGH, JUST AS THEY CAME THROUGH THE AERIAL ON THE ROOF...
THEN THAT IS THE ONLY THING TO DO! WE WILL TRANSMIT THE POWER LAMP TO YOU! WE CAN SEND IT EVEN THOUGH WE CAN'T TOUCH IT!
SHORTLY...
ALERT! OUR OBJECT-TRANSMITTER IS SENDING YOU THE INVISIBLE LAMP NOW! PREPARE TO RECEIVE IT--!
AT THAT MOMENT, HAL STRIPS OFF HIS OUTER GARMENTS...
PIEFACE, I'M GOING AFTER THE LAMP--AS GREEN LANTERN! AND NO MATTER WHERE IT'S BEING SENT, I'M GOING TO GET IT BACK! YOU KEEP AN EYE ON THOSE PHONY SALESMEN--DON'T LET THEM OUT OF YOUR SIGHT!
LIKE A THUNDERBOLT THE EMERALD CRUSADER DIVES AFTER HIS POWER LAMP...
I CAN'T OVERTAKE THE LAMP--IT'S TRAVELING AT THE SAME RATE OF SPEED AS I AM! BUT I CAN FOLLOW ITS TRAIL... BY THE FAINT RADIOACTIVITY LEFT IN THE AIR...!
AND SOON AFTER, AT THE EDGE OF THE ANTI-MATTER UNIVERSE OF QWARD ADJOINING OURS IN THE COSMOS...
...CROSSING THE BARRIER INTO QWARD! I'VE BEEN THROUGH THIS BEFORE... BUT EACH TIME IT'S TERRIFYING... MYSTIFYING...
STORY CONTINUED ON FOLLOWING PAGE!
8

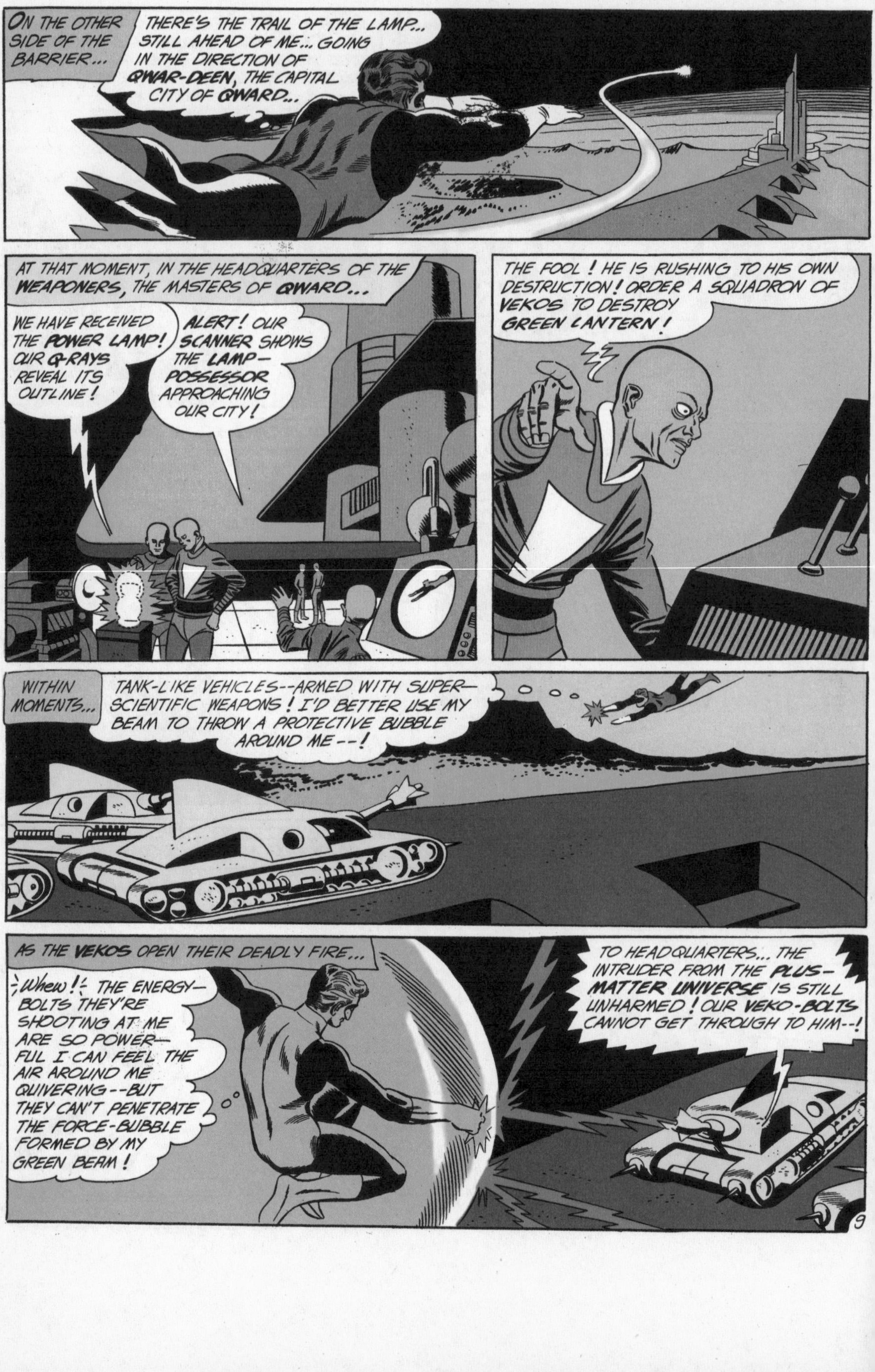
ON THE OTHER SIDE OF THE BARRIER...
THERE'S THE TRAIL OF THE LAMP... STILL AHEAD OF ME... GOING IN THE DIRECTION OF QWAR-DEEN, THE CAPITAL CITY OF QWARD...
AT THAT MOMENT, IN THE HEADQUARTERS OF THE WEAPONERS, THE MASTERS OF QWARD...
WE HAVE RECEIVED THE POWER LAMP! OUR Q-RAYS REVEAL ITS OUTLINE!
ALERT! OUR SCANNER SHOWS THE LAMP-POSSESSOR APPROACHING OUR CITY!
THE FOOL! HE IS RUSHING TO HIS OWN DESTRUCTION! ORDER A SQUADRON OF VEKOS TO DESTROY GREEN LANTERN!
WITHIN MOMENTS...
TANK-LIKE VEHICLES--ARMED WITH SUPER-SCIENTIFIC WEAPONS! I'D BETTER USE MY BEAM TO THROW A PROTECTIVE BUBBLE AROUND ME--!
AS THE VEKOS OPEN THEIR DEADLY FIRE...
Whew! THE ENERGY-BOLTS THEY'RE SHOOTING AT ME ARE SO POWER-FUL I CAN FEEL THE AIR AROUND ME QUIVERING--BUT THEY CAN'T PENETRATE THE FORCE-BUBBLE FORMED BY MY GREEN BEAM!
TO HEADQUARTERS... THE INTRUDER FROM THE PLUS-MATTER UNIVERSE IS STILL UNHARMED! OUR VEKO-BOLTS CANNOT GET THROUGH TO HIM--!
9

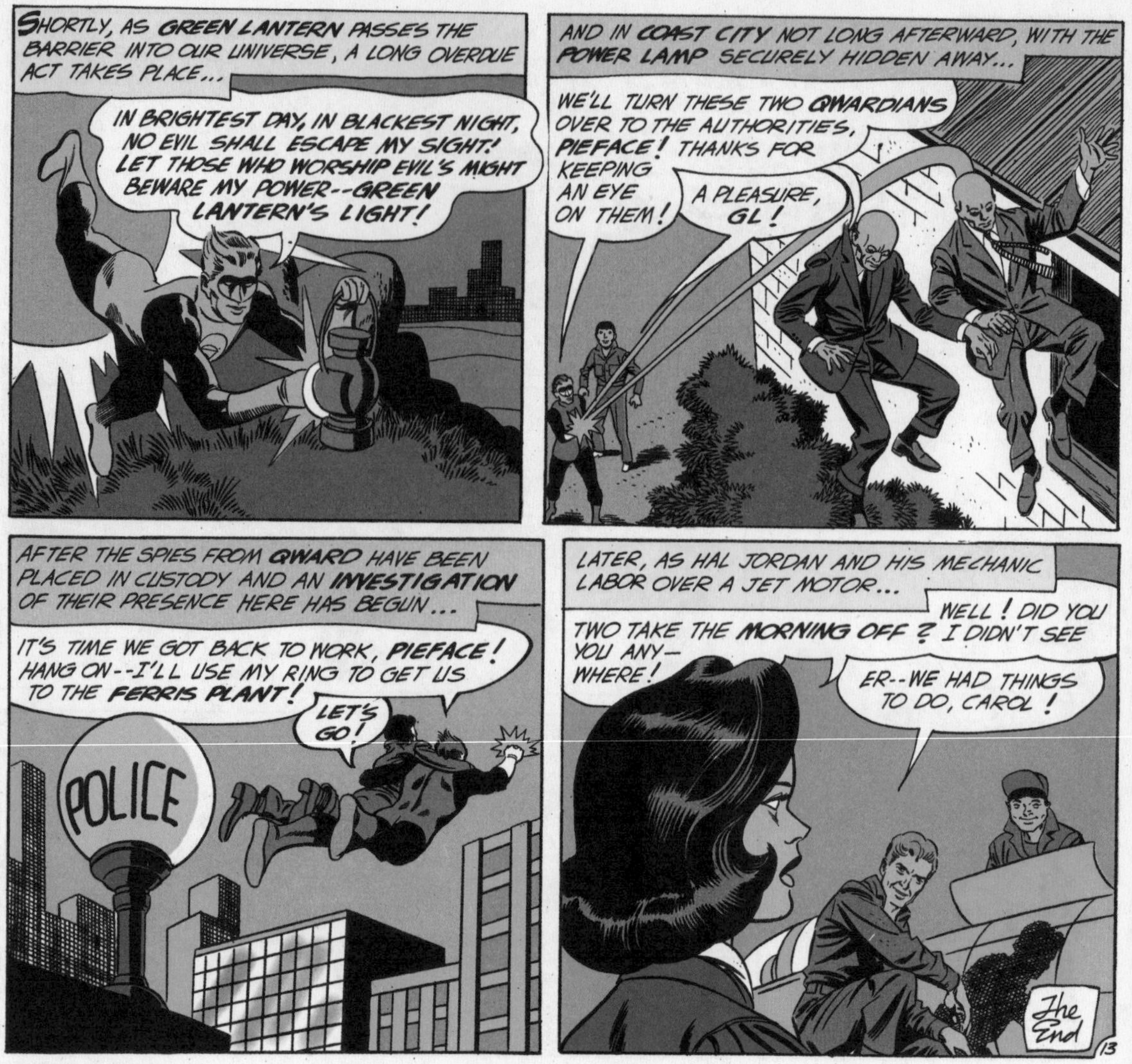
SHORTLY, AS GREEN LANTERN PASSES THE BARRIER INTO OUR UNIVERSE, A LONG OVERDUE ACT TAKES PLACE...
IN BRIGHTEST DAY, IN BLACKEST NIGHT, NO EVIL SHALL ESCAPE MY SIGHT! LET THOSE WHO WORSHIP EVIL'S MIGHT BEWARE MY POWER--GREEN LANTERN'S LIGHT!
AND IN COAST CITY NOT LONG AFTERWARD, WITH THE POWER LAMP SECURELY HIDDEN AWAY...
WE'LL TURN THESE TWO QWARDIANS OVER TO THE AUTHORITIES, PIEFACE! THANKS FOR KEEPING AN EYE ON THEM!
A PLEASURE, GL!
AFTER THE SPIES FROM QWARD HAVE BEEN PLACED IN CUSTODY AND AN INVESTIGATION OF THEIR PRESENCE HERE HAS BEGUN...
IT'S TIME WE GOT BACK TO WORK, PIEFACE! HANG ON--I'LL USE MY RING TO GET US TO THE FERRIS PLANT!
LET'S GO!
POLICE
LATER, AS HAL JORDAN AND HIS MECHANIC LABOR OVER A JET MOTOR...
WELL! DID YOU TWO TAKE THE MORNING OFF? I DIDN'T SEE YOU ANY-WHERE!
ER--WE HAD THINGS TO DO, CAROL!
The End
13

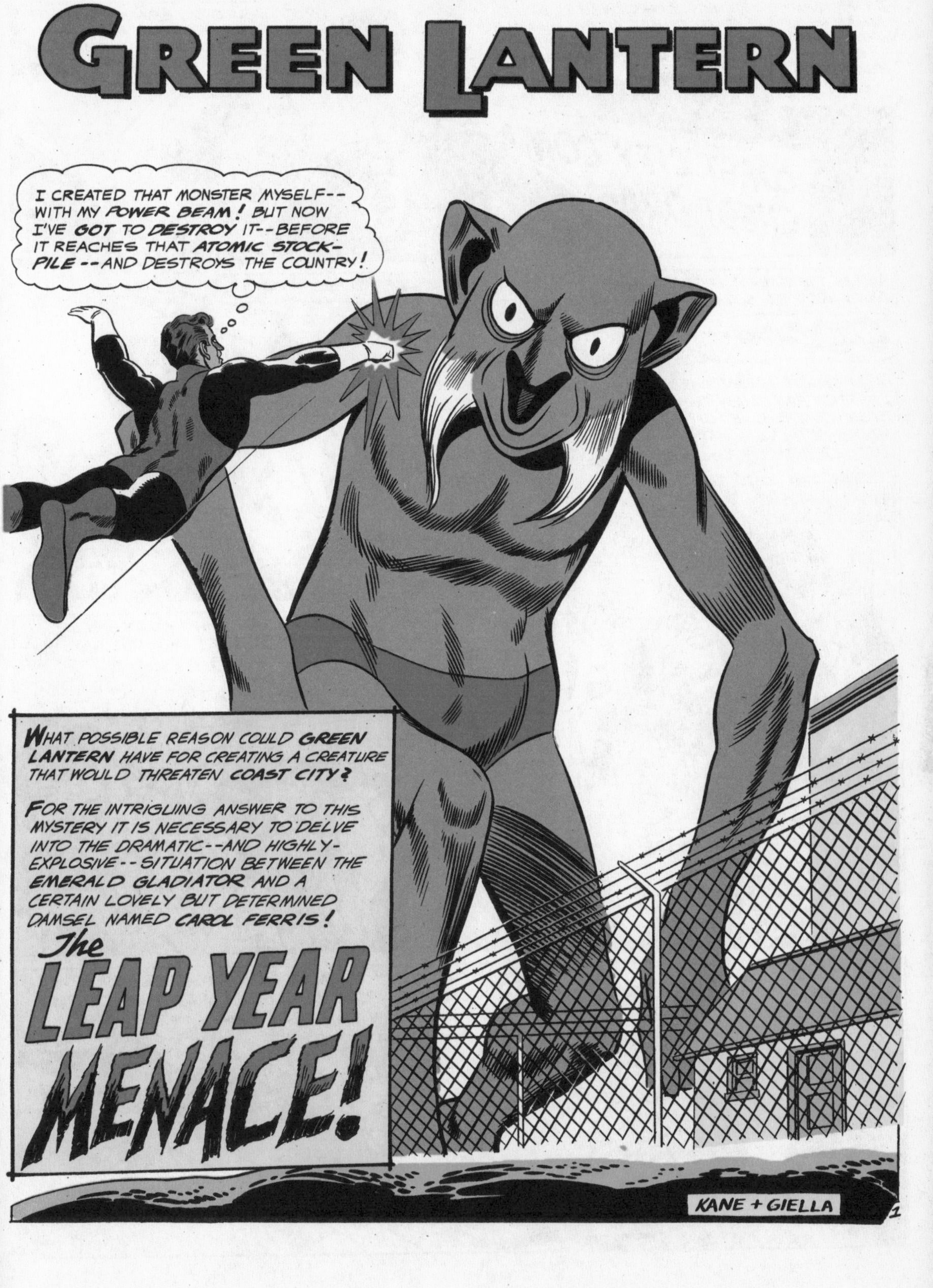
GREEN LANTERN
I CREATED THAT MONSTER MYSELF-- WITH MY POWER BEAM! BUT NOW I'VE GOT TO DESTROY IT--BEFORE IT REACHES THAT ATOMIC STOCK-PILE--AND DESTROYS THE COUNTRY!
WHAT POSSIBLE REASON COULD GREEN LANTERN HAVE FOR CREATING A CREATURE THAT WOULD THREATEN COAST CITY?
FOR THE INTRIGUING ANSWER TO THIS MYSTERY IT IS NECESSARY TO DELVE INTO THE DRAMATIC--AND HIGHLY-EXPLOSIVE--SITUATION BETWEEN THE EMERALD GLADIATOR AND A CERTAIN LOVELY BUT DETERMINED DAMSEL NAMED CAROL FERRIS!
The LEAP YEAR MENACE!
KANE + GIELLA
1

149

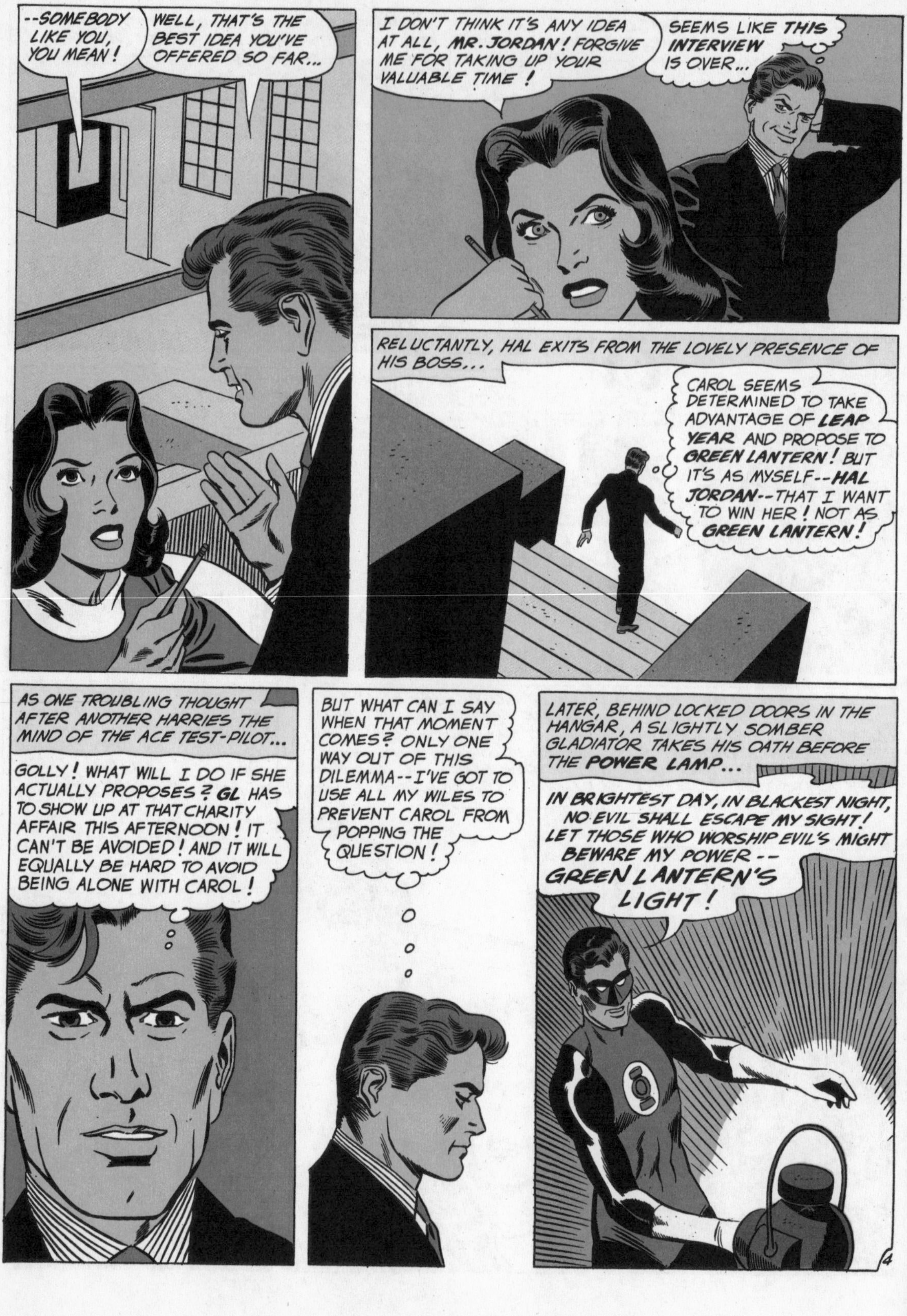

--SOMEBODY LIKE YOU, YOU MEAN!
WELL, THAT'S THE BEST IDEA YOU'VE OFFERED SO FAR...
I DON'T THINK IT'S ANY IDEA AT ALL, MR. JORDAN! FORGIVE ME FOR TAKING UP YOUR VALUABLE TIME!
SEEMS LIKE THIS INTERVIEW IS OVER...
RELUCTANTLY, HAL EXITS FROM THE LOVELY PRESENCE OF HIS BOSS...
CAROL SEEMS DETERMINED TO TAKE ADVANTAGE OF LEAP YEAR AND PROPOSE TO GREEN LANTERN! BUT IT'S AS MYSELF--HAL JORDAN--THAT I WANT TO WIN HER! NOT AS GREEN LANTERN!
AS ONE TROUBLING THOUGHT AFTER ANOTHER HARRIES THE MIND OF THE ACE TEST-PILOT...
GOLLY! WHAT WILL I DO IF SHE ACTUALLY PROPOSES? GL HAS TO SHOW UP AT THAT CHARITY AFFAIR THIS AFTERNOON! IT CAN'T BE AVOIDED! AND IT WILL EQUALLY BE HARD TO AVOID BEING ALONE WITH CAROL!
BUT WHAT CAN I SAY WHEN THAT MOMENT COMES? ONLY ONE WAY OUT OF THIS DILEMMA--I'VE GOT TO USE ALL MY WILES TO PREVENT CAROL FROM POPPING THE QUESTION!
LATER, BEHIND LOCKED DOORS IN THE HANGAR, A SLIGHTLY SOMBER GLADIATOR TAKES HIS OATH BEFORE THE POWER LAMP...
IN BRIGHTEST DAY, IN BLACKEST NIGHT, NO EVIL SHALL ESCAPE MY SIGHT! LET THOSE WHO WORSHIP EVIL'S MIGHT BEWARE MY POWER -- GREEN LANTERN'S LIGHT!
4

Panel 1: I'VE NEVER *SEEN* YOU CARRY ON LIKE THIS, *GREEN LANTERN!* YOU'RE USUALLY SO... QUIET! ARE YOU SURE YOU'RE ALL RIGHT?

GOOD! I'VE GOT HER TO SWITCH THE CONVERSATION TO SOMETHING ELSE...

Panel 2: AS A MATTER OF FACT, I HAVEN'T BEEN FEELING TOO WELL... PROBABLY SOMETHING I ATE--! MAYBE I OUGHT TO--

--OUGHT TO GET *MARRIED! THAT'S* YOUR TROUBLE, DARLING...

Panel 3: LIVING BY YOURSELF--EATING GOODNESS KNOWS WHAT FOR MEALS! HOW CAN YOU FEEL GOOD? IT STANDS TO REASON...

EXCUSE ME, CAROL, I...CAN HARDLY HEAR YOU! THOSE NOISY MODEL AIRPLANES...

BZZZZ!

Panel 4: I'VE GAINED A MOMENT'S TIME! BUT I'VE GOT TO DO SOMETHING DRASTIC OR SHE'LL COME OUT WITH IT AGAIN! WAIT A SECOND-- I HAVE AN IDEA...

BZZZ!

Panel 5: SECRETLY, THE *GREEN GLADIATOR* PREPARES HIS RING FOR ACTION...

I'VE NEVER *USED* MY RING TO *CREATE* A MENACE! BUT THAT'S WHAT I NEED NOW-- A CHILLER-DILLER MENACE THAT I'LL HAVE TO COMBAT-- AND GIVE ME A LEGITIMATE EXCUSE TO GET AWAY FROM HERE --AND CAROL--

BZZZZZZZ!

Panel 6: OUT FROM GL'S SIDE THE BEAM SHOOTS, UNSEEN BY HIS FAIR COMPANION...

I'LL TALK LOUDER-- YELL WHAT I HAVE TO SAY, IF NECESSARY! THIS IS LEAP YEAR-- AND *IT'S A WOMAN'S PRIVILEGE TO--*

CAROL! LOOK--!!

BZZZ!

7

153

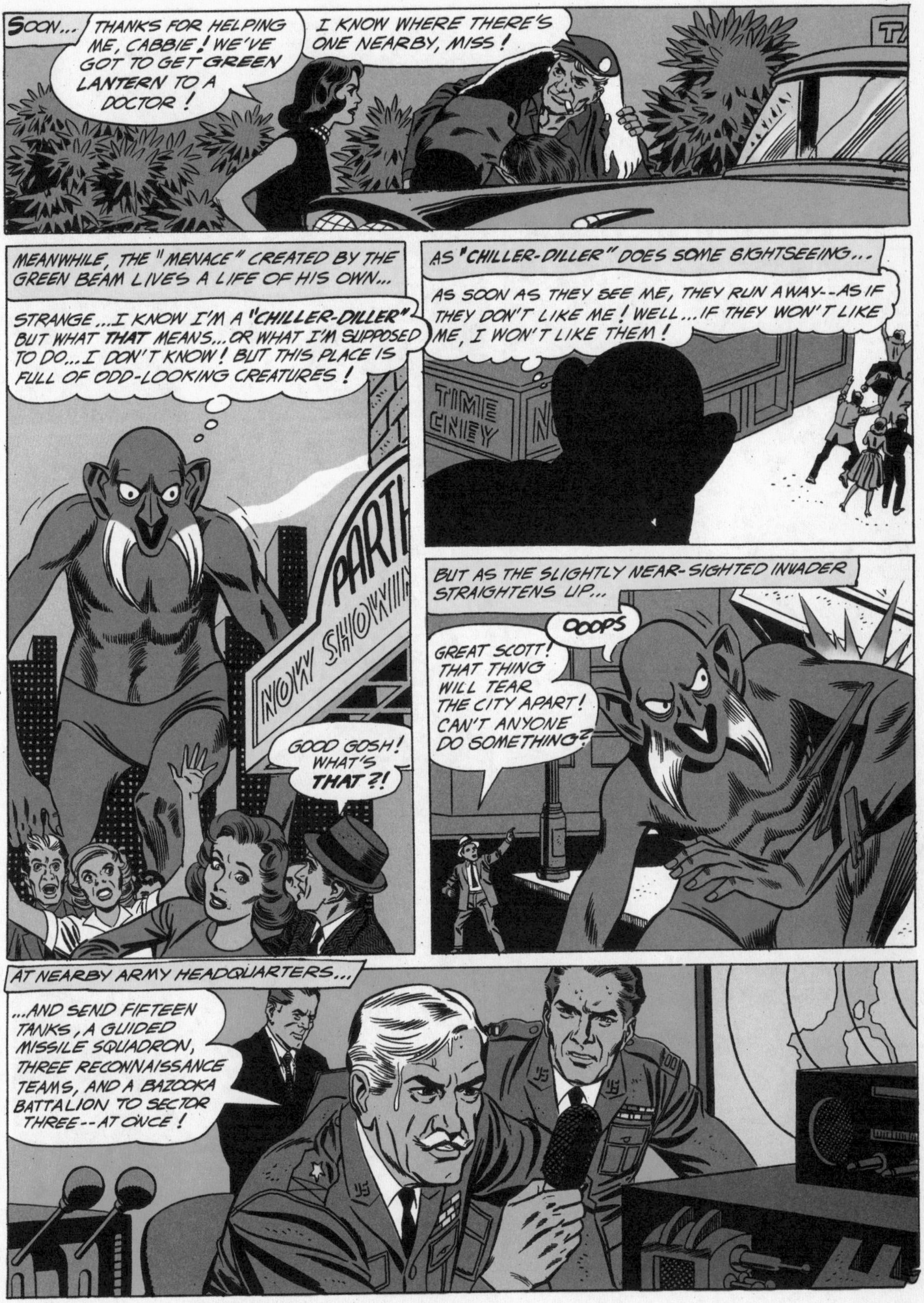
SOON...
THANKS FOR HELPING ME, CABBIE! WE'VE GOT TO GET GREEN LANTERN TO A DOCTOR!
I KNOW WHERE THERE'S ONE NEARBY, MISS!
MEANWHILE, THE "MENACE" CREATED BY THE GREEN BEAM LIVES A LIFE OF HIS OWN...
STRANGE...I KNOW I'M A "CHILLER-DILLER" BUT WHAT THAT MEANS...OR WHAT I'M SUPPOSED TO DO...I DON'T KNOW! BUT THIS PLACE IS FULL OF ODD-LOOKING CREATURES!
NOW SHOWIN
GOOD GOSH! WHAT'S THAT?!
AS "CHILLER-DILLER" DOES SOME SIGHTSEEING...
AS SOON AS THEY SEE ME, THEY RUN AWAY--AS IF THEY DON'T LIKE ME! WELL...IF THEY WON'T LIKE ME, I WON'T LIKE THEM!
BUT AS THE SLIGHTLY NEAR-SIGHTED INVADER STRAIGHTENS UP...
OOOPS
GREAT SCOTT! THAT THING WILL TEAR THE CITY APART! CAN'T ANYONE DO SOMETHING?
AT NEARBY ARMY HEADQUARTERS...
...AND SEND FIFTEEN TANKS, A GUIDED MISSILE SQUADRON, THREE RECONNAISSANCE TEAMS, AND A BAZOOKA BATTALION TO SECTOR THREE--AT ONCE!

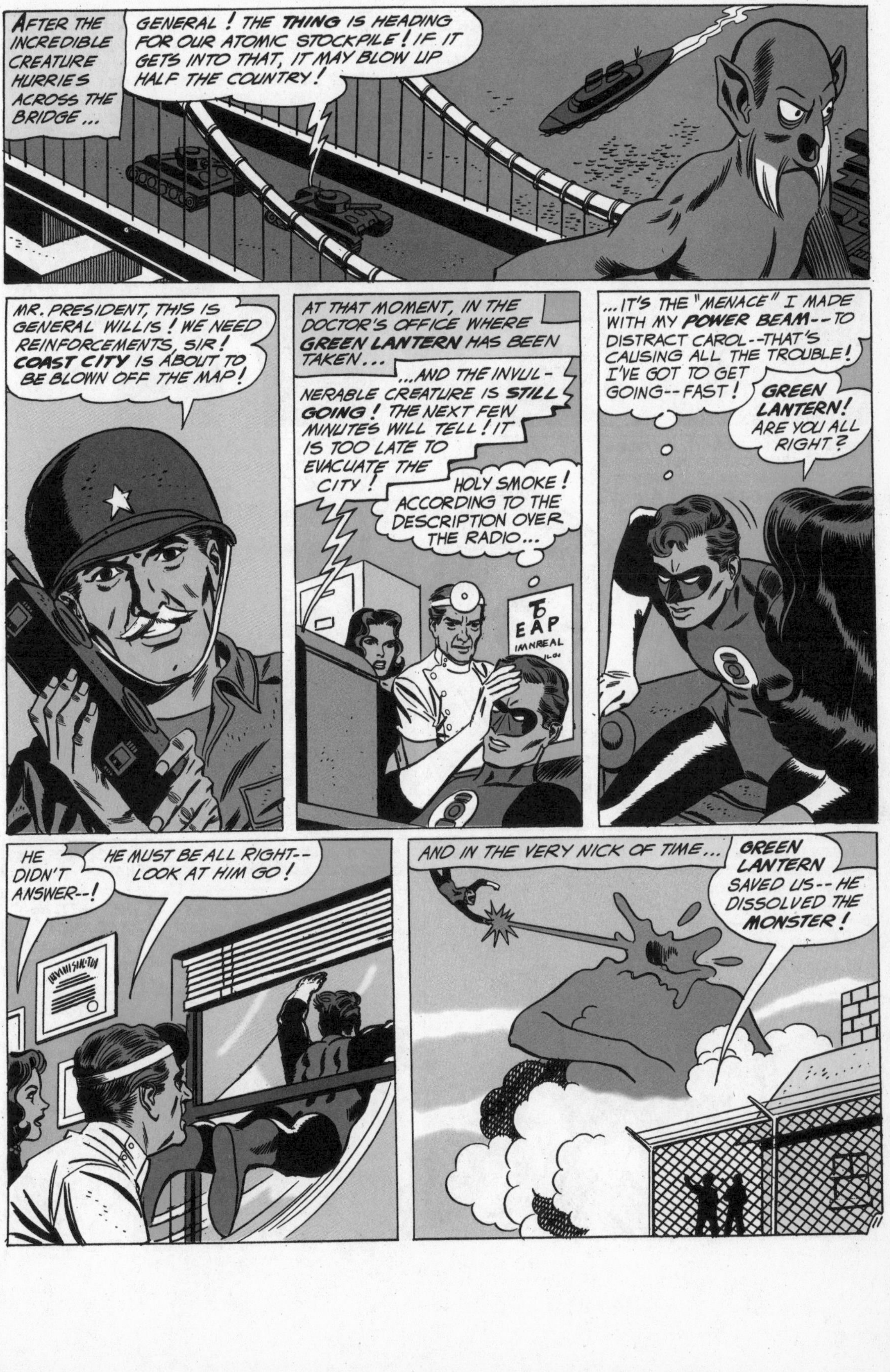
AFTER THE INCREDIBLE CREATURE HURRIES ACROSS THE BRIDGE ...
GENERAL ! THE THING IS HEADING FOR OUR ATOMIC STOCKPILE ! IF IT GETS INTO THAT, IT MAY BLOW UP HALF THE COUNTRY !
MR. PRESIDENT, THIS IS GENERAL WILLIS ! WE NEED REINFORCEMENTS, SIR! COAST CITY IS ABOUT TO BE BLOWN OFF THE MAP !
AT THAT MOMENT, IN THE DOCTOR'S OFFICE WHERE GREEN LANTERN HAS BEEN TAKEN ...
...AND THE INVULNERABLE CREATURE IS STILL GOING ! THE NEXT FEW MINUTES WILL TELL ! IT IS TOO LATE TO EVACUATE THE CITY !
HOLY SMOKE ! ACCORDING TO THE DESCRIPTION OVER THE RADIO...
...IT'S THE "MENACE" I MADE WITH MY POWER BEAM--TO DISTRACT CAROL--THAT'S CAUSING ALL THE TROUBLE ! I'VE GOT TO GET GOING--FAST !
GREEN LANTERN! ARE YOU ALL RIGHT ?
HE DIDN'T ANSWER--!
HE MUST BE ALL RIGHT-- LOOK AT HIM GO !
AND IN THE VERY NICK OF TIME...
GREEN LANTERN SAVED US-- HE DISSOLVED THE MONSTER !
11